Albert Ross

Thou shalt not

Albert Ross

Thou shalt not

ISBN/EAN: 9783337818326

Printed in Europe, USA, Canada, Australia, Japan

Cover: Foto ©ninafisch / pixelio.de

More available books at **www.hansebooks.com**

THOU SHALT NOT

(NEW SERIES.)

By Albert Ross.

AUTHOR OF

" His Private Character, " Speaking of Ellen,"
" In Stella's Shadow," " Why I'm Single,"
" Her Husband's Friend," Etc.

" Of course it's unpleasant when these things come into one's own family ; but you know they do happen, and happen every day. 'Pon my soul, we're not the ones who should cry baby."—Page 303.

ILLUSTRATED BY G. S. SNELL.

NEW YORK:
G. W. Dillingham Co., Publishers.
MDCCCXCVI.

Thou Shalt Not.

PHOTOGRAPHS

OF

ALBERT ROSS.

(Cabinet Size,)

Sent to any address on receipt of 25 cents
each.

G. W. DILLINGHAM CO.,
33 *West 23d Street, New York.*

THE ORIGINAL PREFACE.

I AM not a moralist, solely. I am a painter of scenes.

Given, a man : A man steeped in Pleasure, which is also called Vice ; breathing in Sin as other men breathe air and not finding it disagreeable ; a man to whom the word Conscience conveys no meaning. Unveil to that man, at one flash, his Soul. Take him to a mountain top. Let his gaze rest for a moment on the barren moor whence he came ; then turn his startled eyes to the Elysian Fields that lie beyond. See him tremblingly begin the journey. Paint his former and his latter self—and use all bright colors, if you can.

That man will have struggles ; he will have backward slips ; he will resolve again and again and break his resolutions. If he succeeds in wholly freeing himself from his entanglements he will accomplish a miracle. But suffer he must. And I have painted a sufferer.

If Prudery places her skinny hands before her face and screams ; if roués swear the drawing is incorrect and the shading too severe ; if people who admit that the world has pitfalls, but have a constitutional horror of warning signs, say, " It is so dreadful, you know," I cannot help it.

My scene is painted. It may have demerits, but I know the portraits are accurate.

ALBERT ROSS.

[v]

PREFACE FOR NEW EDITION.

————

THIS book was published eight years ago; two hundred thousand copies have been sold; the original plates are worn out; and now we begin again.

Prudery *did* "place her skinny hands before her face and scream." She even took my work to a grand jury and tried to suppress it. But the jury refused to listen, and the sale still goes on.

I have no apologies to make. As my purpose becomes better understood I shall be asked for none.

For your kindness to me, my million readers, I give you a million thanks.

ALBERT ROSS.

Cambridge, Mass., Sept., 1896.

[vi]

THOU SHALT NOT.

CHAPTER I.

THE day was dark and gloomy. Across the afternoon sky the clouds hung like spectral emblems of mourning. Occasionally, through the heavy air, raindrops fell. In the old forge, the sturdy blacksmith hammered his iron and drove his nails, carrying on meanwhile a conversation with the handsome, boyish-looking young man at his side. The latter was dressed in the latest style, even to kid gloves and patent leathers. His fashionable garb contrasted strongly with the rough clothing of the farrier, and not less so his velvety countenance with the grimy visage and sooty arms of his companion. That they should be on such evidently familiar terms seemed strange, as two men more dissimilar it would be difficult to imagine.

"So yer doin' mi'ty well down in York?" said the blacksmith, as he paused a moment to put his hand to the bellows. "Well, Walter, I'm glad on't, an' I know ye'll believe me when I say it. When ye left Springdale two years ago, I was awful set agin yer goin', I won't deny it. I've seen so many of our boys start off fer the city that didn't come to no good, that I was afraid fer yer. Some on 'em, who left here jest as pure as you, drifted back arterwards mere wrecks an' drunkards. Some I could name are doin' time in the State's prison. It's an allurin' place, is York, an' I've allus trembled when any one I cared about went thar. I do care fer you, Walter, an' ye know how I allus did from the time when I carried ye down here, a little bit of a baby, an' showed ye the fire thar, burnin' an' shinin,' jest as it does to-day. It's a great comfort to see ye back agin, lookin' jest like ye did when ye left here—only a little older, an' a good deal better dressed."

The blacksmith surveyed the young man with an expression of mingled affection and admiration. Then he took the red-hot shoe from the glowing embers, and struck it several times upon the anvil with his heavy hammer.

"Why, how did you expect me to look?" laughed Walter. "You know I never doubted that I should succeed. My expectations were reasonable. I didn't think I should become a millionaire, but I determined not to come back without something to hold to. All I wanted was a good situation, with a tip-top salary, and a chance to see a little of life, and that I've got. I enjoy every second of it. I wouldn't exchange two years of New York City for a century in this humdrum old town. Why, John Dinsmore, it's really all I can endure to stay out my week's vacation here, even with Clara and you, it all seems so still and deathlike."

The blacksmith placed the crescent upon one of the hoofs of the pony which he was shoeing, and drove the nails home carefully, clinching each as he proceeded. He had surveyed Walter's eager face with an uneasy expression as the young man talked. There was something in Dinsmore's calm blue eyes which seemed to go far away beyond the object upon which they rested. When his work was finished he came and sat down near his companion and resumed the conversation.

"Yer sister has read me a good deal out o' yer letters, Walter, and I noticed that they seemed to be full of a man named Greyburn. Ye've devoted pages to praisin' him, an' tellin' what a friend he's been to ye. An' yet I don't quite understand it. Tell it all over agin, jest as it happened."

"You may well say friend," cried Walter, with enthusiasm. "All my success is due to his kindness. If I hadn't met Hector Greyburn the day I entered New York, my whole life would have been entirely changed. Who else would have exerted themselves for a penniless stranger? Who else would have bade me make his house my home, and introduced me to his circle of acquaintances as though I was the richest young man in America? John Dinsmore, you should know Mr. Greyburn. He is one man in a million!"

"It was on the train that you met him, wa'n't it?" asked Dinsmore, not seeming wholly to share his young friend's enthusiasm.

"On my way to the city—yes. The merest chance in the world. He happened to get aboard at a way station, and took a seat with me. In five minutes he knew that I was going to New York, a perfect stranger, to seek my fortune. He was *so* frank with me. 'Have you any money?' 'Very little,' said I. 'Any friends in town?' 'Not one.' 'Any situation in view?' 'Not a situation.' 'Your age?' 'Seventeen.' That settled it. I must go to his house till I could find a suitable place. Of course I didn't refuse. Wasn't that a chance for a boy to meet with just on the threshold of the city?"

It was pleasant to witness the sparkle in the lad's eyes, and the glow which came into his face as he re-

called this story for the benefit of his friend. The
blacksmith warmed a little toward him as he proceeded.

"But didn't ye think he might be a confidence man,
or suthin' o' that sort ?" he asked, gazing with affec-
tionate regard at the beaming face of the other.

"Ridiculous !" laughed Walter. "I had only fifteen dollars in the world, and all my clothes and baggage wouldn't have brought as much more. Confidence men look for better game than I was then, let
me tell you. You would only have looked at him once to
throw away all doubt. Let me describe him. He
was about thirty years of age, and the handsomest
man I ever saw. His eyes were darkish gray, and
when he smiled, it was as if the first touch of the
morning sun lit up his face. His hair was of a beautiful shade of brown. His skin was as fair as a girl's,
and in his cheeks the warm, red blood of health showed
freely. In height he was a little above the average. Proportioned like a statue, he carried himself
with a grace which seemed entirely natural. He was
well dressed. His jewelry was rich but not flashy.
Everything about him seemed to say, ' Here you will
find true metal.' Suspect him ? It would have been
impossible !"

Walter paused a minute, and looked out of the
great door, to note that the clouds were clearing
away and that the shower was evidently ended.

"When we reached the station," he pursued, "Mr.
Greyburn took a carriage and we drove to his house
on Madison Avenue. He said nothing as we rode
through the streets, seeing probably that my eyes
were riveted on the unaccustomed sights we passed.
Everything seemed wonderful. The great buildings,
the immense number of people in the streets, the
noise and jar of business. I was in perfect amaze-

ment before I entered his house. And once inside, I was carried away completely."

" Carried away ?" echoed the listener.

" Yes, carried away. Not spirited off through the air, but simply dazed with wonder. As we went up the high steps the door was opened for us without any knock or ring, and when we reached the hall—oh ! I can't describe it ! I am seeing it now as I saw it then. It seemed to me a veritable palace of Aladdin ! There were the most elegant carpets, furniture, chandeliers, statuary and pictures, and by no means the least of all, one of the prettiest girls I had ever seen, closing the door after us. In all this splendor Mr. Greyburn was as much at ease as we are in this old shop. He turned to the girl and said, ' Annie, this is Mr. Walter Campbell. Consider him a guest of the house as long as he desires to remain.' I was overpowered and stammered something, I don't know what. It's a mercy I didn't swoon away."

The troubled expression had come back to the blacksmith's blue eyes.

" Was this young lady his—his daughter?" he asked, simply.

" Daughter? Certainly not," laughed Walter. " He's not a married man. She was only his dooropener ; one of the servants. He told me afterwards he got her to match the tints in the frescoing. Such a man, John ! Nothing too good for him ! But up in the second story we encountered another vision of beauty. ' Nettie,' said he, ' this is Mr. Walter,' and all the rest of it over again. Up another flight we went, and there was another, more and more attractive, and over the introduction he went again. Then he showed me into my room, which was the finest chamber I had ever seen. My trunk was brought up by a colored porter, after which Mr. Greyburn said he would leave me to myself for an hour, when he would call me for dinner. It took me most of that hour to collect my scattered senses, but I finally changed my dress and got ready. Punctual to the time he called me, and we went down to the dining-room. Oh ! that dining-room ! John Dinsmore, I shall never live long enough to forget how its splendors burst upon my vision. Nor can I ever forget the dinner, nor the beautiful lady who came in and sat with us at table —a lady, John, who threw all the others into the shade as the full moon does the smallest star of the evening. I can't describe it, I can't describe her, I can't describe anything. It all seemed more like a dream than reality."

"This last lady," said the blacksmith, very slowly, and looking on the ground as he spoke, "who was she ?"

"Why, just his housekeeper," cried Walter, bursting into spasmodic laughter. "Was there ever such a man ? An houri at the door, seraphs on each landing, and an angel to preside over them all. The dinner was perfect, everything you could think of, but my appetite was gone. One can eat any day, but to go at one step from earth to paradise is not a thing that happens any too often to a poor fellow like me."

A breath, which was almost a sigh, escaped John Dinsmore's lips.

"This Mr. Greyburn must be very wealthy," he said, more as if to hide what else he had in mind than for any value in the thought itself.

"Of course," assented the other. "A man couldn't maintain a place like that on a dollar a day. How did he get it ? I don't know. Inherited it, probably. Most of these rich men do ; or else they make a lucky speculation and blunder into a fortune at once. All I know is that he is in no business, and his hands are as soft and white as a child's. Everybody speaks of his hands, Why, mine aren't very ugly, but his are to mine like light to darkness. I could look at his hands by the hour, John. You can wager they never did much work, or they wouldn't look like that."

The blacksmith's blue eyes rested for a second on his own coarse and grimy members, and the mental comparison with the picture which young Campbell had drawn was not pleasing. Then he steadied himself a little for the question he had been for some minutes trying to propound.

" Does your—sister—know all about this ?"

"Clara ? Why, certainly. That is, she knows all the main parts of it. Of course I didn't expatiate on the beauty of the pretty women. You know what strict ideas she has of propriety, and she mightn't think it looked just right to have so many of them there in a sort of Bachelor's Hall, you know. For my part I can't see why a handsome girl is any worse than a homely one. If Mr. Greyburn fancies filling his handsome house with handsome servants, and can afford to do it, it's not my business. Clara is the dearest creature in the world, and I love her as much as a brother could, but she's a little old-fashioned in some things. Now, isn't she, John ?"

It was curious to watch the apologetic tone which ran through the young man's defense of his New York friend. His final appeal to the blacksmith went unanswered for some moments.

"Walter," said Dinsmore, at last, "ye've got the best little woman in this world for a sister, an' her ideas of right an' wrong are safe fer ye to foller. Old-fashioned they may be, but so is the earth we live in. That sky up thar is old-fashioned. The God who made it and the heavens beyond it are gittin' old-fashioned, too ; but we'll try and believe in 'em a while longer fer all that."

" Why, how sober you are !" said the younger man,

rising from where he sat, with some uneasiness in his demeanor. "I didn't mean to offend you, John. You know there's nothing in the world would make me do that intentionally. I love Clara better than any one else loves her or ever will, and that's why I didn't write her anything that I thought she would dislike to hear. If I had supposed you would take it in this way I wouldn't have told you, either. Come! You don't hold it against me, John, do you?"

The far-away look had come into Dinsmore's eyes again. He hardly heard what Walter was saying. The young man repeated his last words:

"You don't lay it up against me, John?"

"No, no! my boy," replied the blacksmith, heartily. "I lay up nothin' agin ye, an' I hope agin no man. But, Walter, yer father was as good a man as ever lived; yer mother was a good woman; an' now that you an' Miss Clara are all that's left, ye owe something to the memories of them who gave ye birth. She is jest what her mother was, pure an' sweet as the air of the brightest summer mornin'. Be careful, Walter, be very careful that nothin' comes over ye to make ye else than like her."

"Why, John, you are eloquent! I never heard you speak like that before."

The unlettered man had indeed found expressions such as had never before passed his lips. It was as if he had uttered a prayer and a benediction.

There were fifteen years difference in their ages, and Walter could not recall the time when Dinsmore's forge was not there, and Dinsmore himself striking the iron and pulling the handle of the old bellows. When big enough to go to his first school he used to stop at the old forge door, to see with a child's delight the sparks flying from the anvil and hear the merry cling-clang of the horseshoes. As a boy the blacksmith's shop had always been his resort whenever he had any trouble on his mind, and it had never failed to be lifted there. Who knew so well as John how to set the snares, to fix the traps, to find the first wild berries? Who could make better whistles out of willow or rig such a cross-bow?

The sky was now entirely clear again, and the evening sun sent his radiance like burnished gold over the little forge and in at the open doorway. As Walter ceased speaking a presence entered the shop which brought hardly less brightness with it. Clara Campbell had guessed that her brother would go straight to his old friend, and was not surprised when she found them together. The little maiden was indeed "as pure and sweet as the air of the brightest summer morning." Two years younger than Walter, she had that womanly way about her which comes so often to girls thrown at an early age upon their own resources. Looking not a day older than her seventeen years, she had the air of a woman of twenty. It was easy to tell the relation which she and Walter bore to each other. Had it not been, the radiant smile with which she met his glance, would have shown to any observer that he was very dear to her indeed.

"Good evening, Mr. Dinsmore," she said, giving her hand in a perfectly unconstrained manner to the blacksmith. "Walter ran away from me before I had hardly looked at him, and I knew he would go straight to your forge. Well, how does he look? Has he not grown! I really fear I am almost too proud of him!"

Dinsmore dusted a chair and offered it to the girl, who took it with a pleasant "Thank you." The addition to the group seemed to have a momentary effect upon his speech, for he only smiled assent to her words.

"To be sure I've grown," said the brother, looking

with a smile into his sister's eyes. "Did you think I was always going to be a little armful of a thing like you? New York is the place to grow. I shall be as big as John in two years more. Clara always did admire tall, strong men, John. Muscle and brawn are favorites with you; eh, sister?"

"I do like to see men strong and well," assented Clara. "It seems the right of their sex to be strong. But I do not despise the weaker ones. God does not make us all alike, and surely He knows what is best."

The blue eyes of the tall and brawny blacksmith brightened during Walter's speech and fell a little at the close of Clara's.

"If you want to see a perfect specimen of manly beauty," said Walter, "you ought to meet my friend Greyburn. I've been telling John about him. He is built like an Apollo, and they say he has the strength of a Hercules. His hand is daintier to look at than yours, Clara, and his grasp is like—well, like John's here—when he chooses to put forth his will."

"He has been very kind to you," said Clara.

"Indeed he has. I wasn't in the city a week, you know, before he got me a clerkship at the City Hall at one thousand dollars a year. In three months that was raised to fifteen hundred dollars, and in a year to two thousand dollars, with prospect of an increase in the near future. When I think it all over it seems like a fairy tale."

"I can't comprehend," said his sister, with a shake of her head, "how you can possibly be worth such a sum to anybody. My little brother earning two thousand dollars a year, while I can only get four hundred dollars for teaching thirty or forty children. You will certainly become rich and retire before long."

"Rich!" ejaculated Walter. "That's a very different thing, my dear. It costs a pile to live in the city, and a fellow must go around some, you know. I haven't saved a dollar yet, except what I sent to help you pay the mortgage off the homestead. When I get my salary raised again I mean to put by just so much every month, but I don't see how I can do it now. Living is very expensive, and there are so many things to get. Why, Mr. Greyburn insisted on lending me five hundred dollars to start with, as he said I needed that amount to fix myself up so that I could go to work at all. He said in the kindest way that my dress might look a little countryfied to the other clerks. It was a mighty good act of him. I couldn't have borne to be made fun of, you know, and I might have got into trouble."

Clara stared at him with wide-open eyes, but there was more astonishment than chiding in her expression.

"Of course you couldn't save anything until you had paid Mr. Greyburn his loan," she said, extenuatingly.

"But, to tell the truth, I've not paid it," said Walter, coloring just a little as he saw his sister's eyes open wider yet. "He told me not to mind it; that he was in no hurry whatever. So I gave him my note, and it hasn't seemed to come handy to take it up."

Clara's eyes encountered those of the blacksmith, and each read in the other the same sentiment. Dinsmore found his voice.

"Ye ought to pay that note, Walter, if ye'll excuse me for sayin' so. You an' yer sister have managed to get the mortgage off o' the old house. It was only two hundred and fifty dollars, but it troubled her, an' she looked like a new creature the day the debt was discharged. There were those of us who would 'a' paid it any moment, but she wouldn't hear to that. This note o' yourn ain't her affair, in one sense, but I know she won't feel easy till it's paid. Ain't I right, Miss Clara ?"

"John *is* right, brother," replied the girl. "You earn your own money, and are doing well, and I am very proud of you, but that note should not stand a day longer than you can help. I have a hundred dollars laid away that I will be glad to let you have toward the amount. Promise me that you will not leave it unattended to."

"Oh, very well," said Walter. "If you care about it, I will. It will put me out a little to do it this year, but let it be as you say. As to your money, Clara, of course I wouldn't touch that. My salary is large enough for my own debts. No," as the girl started to open her lips, "I should not think of it, so please don't ask me again."

Whatever further protestations the sister might have made were cut short by the sound of rapidly approaching wheels, and the quick, sharp steps of a horse coming at speed. A moment later the driver pulled up his animal at the forge door and leaped lightly to the ground.

Walter Campbell sprang from his seat and caught the hand of the new comer.

"Mr. Greyburn ! is it possible ? Where did you come from ? I supposed you were in the city."

Greyburn smiled pleasantly into the face of his impetuous young friend, and was about to reply, when he caught sight of Miss Clara, who had risen at the approach of the stranger and was preparing to depart. His broad hat of Panama straw was immediately lifted from his head, and he made a profound obeisance as the girl stepped from the doorway. His manner was courtly, but with no trace of anything offensive. It seemed like involuntary homage paid to beauty.

"Mr. Greyburn—my sister!"   *Page 19.*

"Clara," said Walter. She paused and looked up. "Mr. Greyburn—my sister."

He did not attempt to touch her hand, which, with country politeness, she half offered him.

"I am delighted," he said, "to meet any relation of a young man whom I esteem so highly as I do your brother. I was taking a drive through this part of the State, and learning accidentally that he had gone to his native town on a vacation, I directed the steps of my horse thither. The creature cast a shoe a little ways back, and I stopped here to get the damage repaired. I had no idea that I should meet him, and certainly not that I should have this additional pleasure."

Miss Clara listened to this speech with quiet attention. Dinsmore leaned heavily on one of his hammers, which he seemed to have picked up in a moment of abstraction, looking from the girl's face to Greyburn's and back again, as if he would read their inmost thoughts. Walter looked at Greyburn and him alone, with admiration written on every feature.

"I have often heard of you, sir, through my brother's letters," responded the girl, "and welcome you to our little village. You will find Mr. Dinsmore an excellent farrier. Our cottage is but ten minutes walk from here, and when your horse has been shod you will let Walter conduct you there. I will go in advance and be ready to receive you."

"Many thanks for your kind offer," said Greyburn, "but I had no intention of troubling you at all. The village hotel will answer for Robin (my horse) and me. However," seeing in Walter's face a decided negative to this proposition, "I will make you a call on my way to the hostelry. How long shall I be delayed here, sir?" he said, turning to the blacksmith.

Dinsmore did not answer immediately. He was

putting "Pet," Miss Clara's pony, which he had just shod, into her phaeton, which stood under a shed outside the door. He adjusted the harness with the greatest care, assisted the young lady into the vehicle, and placed in her hands the reins and whip. When she had bowed her good-byes to the company, and disappeared at the turn of the road, he deigned to reply to the question. Not in words, however. He took the blooded beast from the shafts and proceeded to the work required, without uttering a syllable. Greyburn, seeing that the shoe was being fitted, turned to Walter, and the twain engaged in animated conversation. When his work was finished the blacksmith put the horse back in his place, and re-entered the shop, still without speaking a word.

Greyburn stepped to the horse's shoulder. "Robin," he said, as if speaking to a child, "let me see it."

The intelligent creature lifted his foot and his master surveyed the shoe critically.

"That's well done, my man," said Greyburn, approvingly, turning to Dinsmore. "Not a farrier in the country could have set it better. In these days when there is so much bungling it's a pleasure to see a job like this. Nothing requires more skill than shoeing a horse, and nothing is done worse on the average. I thank you, and he thanks you, too. Don't you, Robin? Make a bow to the gentleman."

The horse immediately made several inclinations of his head. The action was executed so perfectly that Walter laughed aloud. The sight of Greyburn seemed to put him in excellent spirits.

"How much shall I pay you?" said Greyburn, taking out his pocketbook. "Charge enough, now. The job is worth it. I shall be satisfied."

"That is all right," said the blacksmith, gruffly, walking away toward the farther end of his shop. His manner was almost discourteous. Greyburn turned to young Campbell.

"Don't they charge anything for a job like that up in these parts?" he said.

"Oh, it's because you're a friend of mine," said Walter uneasily, for Dinsmore's curt words puzzled him not a little. "I've known him from childhood, and he never would take a cent from any of our family."

"But he mustn't do that," expostulated the other. "It's not right. The laborer is worthy of his hire. I'm going to leave this two dollar bill on the post here, with that bit of iron to hold it. When he comes to shut up shop he'll find it and think better of the matter."

Greyburn left the money as he had suggested, and entering the buggy with Walter, they drove toward the Campbell cottage.

After they had gone, John Dinsmore sat down on his lonely bench, and looked for a long time into the far-away sky. A tired look as of hopes unsatisfied marred the lustre of his blue eyes. Now and then his brows contracted, as unpleasant thoughts passed through his mind. Once he sprang up and grasped again his heavy hammer, as if to use it as a weapon of assault. Long after his usual hour for closing he sat there, and no one came to disturb his meditations.

When it was nearly dark he rose, fixed his fire, drew the large doors together, turned the key and started to leave the place. As he did so, he saw the paper money lying upon the post. He looked at it a minute and then the truth began to dawn upon his mind. Mechanically taking the key from his pocket he reopened the forge door. Stepping inside he picked up a pair of blacksmith's tongs and went back to the post. Then he took the piece of money with his tongs and buried it in the embers of the forge until it was reduced to ashes. He closed the doors again, locked them, and walked toward his home moodily, with slow and measured steps.

----●----

CHAPTER II.

HECTOR GREYBURN'S house on Madison Avenue was not the finest palace in New York, Walter Campbell's glowing description to the contrary. It was a modest residence, with an interior like that of many others, but with rather more than the usual amount of room within its walls. Its furnishings were all elegant, and nothing that could reasonably be asked to minister to the tastes or add to the comfort of its owner was missing. He was a good liver, happy and free in hospitality, with a carelessness of expenditure through which ran a grain of prudence. To be very wealthy had never been the desire of this man. To live at ease with a fair and certain income was all he asked. Had money flown twice as freely into his coffers, it had flowed twice as freely out. He was an enigma to all who knew him—at least, to all but one. Where he came from, who his people were, and whence his money, were the frequent cause of gossip among his acquaintances.

Some knew he had been, but a few years before, a mere clerk in the employ of the municipal government, with a salary no larger than his present monthly expense account. All at once he seemed to leap into opulence. Had some rich relative suddenly died and left him a fortune? Had he drawn the grand prize in a lottery? Was he a secret and successful gambler? Each of these propositions, with many others were advanced, and after investigation rejected as untenable. All that was known of

Hector Greyburn was that he was rich, liberal, and fond of pleasure.

Even in his vices he was prudent. No one ever saw him intoxicated, though he drank a glass of good wine when he liked. He was never excited at the card table, nor could he be persuaded to risk above a small amount on the turn of a game. He kept but one horse—his favorite "Robin"—which served equally well as a saddle or road beast, and to which he was devotedly attached. He had his dime always ready for the beggar, or his bankbill for the man or woman in distress, but he was never reckless even in his gifts.

If there was any place where Greyburn's generosity trenched on prodigality it was in the entertainment of his guests. Nothing pleased him better than to see gathered in his dining-room a set of good fellows who would do justice to his larder and sideboard. If the fair faces of women were scattered about the table on these occasions he was not less contented. For two years he had entertained on a certain day of each month such a party, and the gentlemen who met together had organized themselves into an association called the Greyburn Club, of which their host was perpetual president. There were but six members in the Club proper, but each one had the privilege of bringing any friend whom he believed would enhance the pleasures of the occasion. To the young men about town, and to some of the elder ones, nothing was more agreeable than an invitation to dine with the Greyburn Club. Reports of its gay character permeated all the other clubs of New York, and he who could boast of having attended one of its gatherings became at once a temporary center of interest.

As previously stated, the membership of the Club was limited to six. That number happened to be sitting at Greyburn's table one evening when the proposition to organize was made. It was voted then and there that the six gentlemen present should constitute then and forever the Greyburn Club, and that no other person should ever become a member except to fill a vacancy caused by death or resignation.

First of the six was the president, Hector Greyburn, already introduced to the reader, and sufficiently described in his young friend's eulogy to John Dinsmore. Next we may place Mr. Jacob Mendall, a banker and near friend of the host, aged about sixty, with a well-preserved frame and a ruddy complexion which, with the absence of gray hair, showed fine health and good living. Next, Clarence A. Perkyns, Esq., a lawyer with a lucrative office practice, a bachelor of five-and-thirty summers. Then Mr. Otis W. Middleby, an attaché of Mendall's, who owned to fifty winters and sported a sign in a down-town building announcing himself as a broker. Next Mr. Chester Bolton, twenty-five years of age, an attorney's clerk, who held a firm conviction that the fickle goddess had served him a shabby trick by sending him into the world with a hungry mouth and compelling him to undertake the job of seeing it filled. Lastly, Mr. Walter Campbell, who, when the Club was formed, had seen but three months of city life, and felt the honor of his selection more than all the others combined.

From the day Walter entered Greyburn's door, he advanced rapidly in the mysteries of those polite vices which are inseparable from life in a great city. He worked at his desk from nine to three each day, and did what he had to do well. The rest of the time was his own. He was entirely unsophisticated, and embraced eagerly his opportunities to see the gay side of New York life. At first its grosser forms repelled him, but step by step he learned to like what he could not once endure, and to endure what he could not learn to like. He found that his benefactor smiled upon such peccadilloes as came to his notice, and there was no one else in the city for whose displeasure he cared.

When Walter got so full of wine at one of the club dinners that he had to be carried upstairs to bed, Jacob Mendall interposed a mild objection.

"You should have put in a word, Greyburn, before he got so far as that. Such a boy as he is!"

"Oh, no," replied Greyburn lightly. "He must learn for himself. He's got sense enough to get tired of that sort of thing after he's tried it a few times. I'd wager a bottle of canary, Jacob, that you've gone under the table more than once in your time, and I can't see as you're any the worse for it."

Mendall joined in the laugh at his expense, and admitted the imputation. "But," he added, "it wasn't when I was a boy like him. I got my growth and saw my thirtieth year before I ever took enough liquor to down me. That was the way I built up my system. I'd like to see enough go down my throat to lay me out to-day, though."

He dashed down a bumper of brandy as he spoke.

"Early or late every young man of the present age, with any life in him, is going to drink something," said Greyburn. "He may begin at eighteen like Walter, or at thirty as you did, but he's going to do it. Let him take his own time, say I. Besides, I have some notions about hospitality, and I would see every one of you lose his power of locomotion and utterance once each month at this table before I'd say a word to influence what you should eat or drink here."

"Bravo!" cried Chester Bolton. "Three cheers for Hec. He's right, Jake, he's right. Let's all take him at his word, and get paralyzed to-night. Let's put what-you-call-its in our mouths to steal away our brains. Pour out one kind of wine at a time, and we'll all begin at once. He who goes down last will be voted to have the most sense. Come, let's begin."

But to this Mr. Perkyns instantly demurred. His tastes were moderate, and a couple of glasses in an evening satisfied his wants.

"All right, Perk," said Bolton, with that astonishing familiarity which follows a good dinner. "I know you and Oat," by which title he usually designated Mr. Middleby, "are light drinkers. Walt just pours it down and succumbs easily. Jake couldn't be filled up if he emptied the Prince of Wales' cellar, and Hec never takes enough to let us see how it would affect him. All right. I'll withdraw the motion."

Walter's constitution was so strong that an occasional indulgence of this kind was slow to make itself seen in his countenance, and he conducted himself so well on his visit to Springdale that his sister had no cause to suspect the truth. That her brother had drank to intoxication would have seemed impossible to her. She associated drunkenness with filthy hovels and bar-rooms. A drunkard could be known, she believed, by his bloodshot eye, his ragged attire, and his staggering gait. Walter was in danger from the vices of a city, she had no doubt. But not that, not that.

It was but a few weeks before the young man proffered his kiss to pretty Annie when she opened the door to let him in, as he had seen Greyburn do. He visited places of questionable repute, and associated with a gay set of dissolute young men who had more money than brains, and most of them not too much of either. It does not require so long as one might think to take the steps in a city education when one has good teachers and enough leisure in which to study. Clara's weekly letters proved a brake on her brother's progress for a little while, but their influence lessened month by month. As he had said to

John Dinsmore, he thought his sister, while the dearest creature in the world, a little old-fashioned.

At Greyburn's house he learned rapidly. The conversation at the monthly dinners was not always exactly what a young boy's mother might like him to hear or to join in. The women who generally formed a portion of the company were not such as he would have liked Clara to meet. "Fine girls," he would have told you, "full of fun and life, pretty as pictures, but, of course ——"

One evening he was sitting with Greyburn in the latter's cozy parlor, during his first few months in the city, when one of the housemaids entered, bearing a card on a salver. Greyburn took the card, read the name, and looked up as if a little in doubt.

"Shall I show the lady in?" asked the girl, seeing that he hesitated.

"Y-e-s," he replied slowly, as if in thought. "Where is she now?"

"In the lower reception room, sir."

"Very well. Show her into the library. Or, Susanne," hesitating again, "on the whole, show her up here. It will make no difference."

"Shall I go?" asked Walter, taking up his hat.

"By no means. I would much rather you would remain. If June is like what she usually is, you will be well repaid. Ah!" rising and extending his hand to his visitor. "To what am I indebted for the honor?"

The lady was of medium height, with dark hair and eyes, and what is often described as traces of former beauty. She was probably twenty-seven years of age, and still attractive. The look of scorn which she threw at Greyburn, and the gesture with which she declined his proffered hand, added to the imperiousness of her general carriage.

"You are sarcastic, as usual, I see," she said, taking a chair.

"I?" he repeated. "You mistake. I never am sarcastic. Least of all would I be so to a lady. But allow me to present you to my friend here, who seems quite amazed at your conduct. Mr. Campbell—Miss June. The one the solace of my youth, the other the companion of my declining years."

"God help you if you expect much from his friendship," said Miss June, bowing slightly to Walter as she spoke. "He professed it for me once, and it was all pretense."

"June," interposed Greyburn, "you are not fair. Upon my honor ——"

"Upon *your* honor?" she echoed.

"Well, upon my word, then."

"One is worth about as much as the other," said the lady, satirically. "Your honor or your word are things which, if you ever had them, were squandered long ago."

Walter looked with some astonishment at the never-fading smile which appeared on Greyburn's face under the harsh words and vindictive manner of his visitor.

"How very often you have told me that," said Greyburn, yawning a little. "Don't be prosy to-night, June. Have you nothing new?"

"To think," she proceeded, "that I could ever have loved such a creature! I despise myself for it."

"And that," he said, in the same bantering tone, "you have also told me before. If it was a matter of guessing, I should say I had heard it word for word— well—probably a thousand times."

She had risen and begun to pace the floor, but she turned fiercely at the last sarcasm. Drawing from her pocket a small ivory-handled pistol, she said :

"I bought that thing to kill you with, I don't

know what keeps me from doing it. I will some day.
Don't you believe it ?"

She flourished the weapon within arm's length of
his face. Walter started to intercept her, but was
stopped by a wave of Greyburn's hand.

"If that is a question," he answered, with the greatest nonchalance, "as much as I dislike to differ from
a lady, I must answer, No."

"You don't ?" she cried, approaching nearer, and
apparently beside herself with rage.

"You will certainly get hurt with that thing," he
went on, deliberately, "if you persist in carrying it.
Only last week I read of a man who was fatally injured by a revolver which he was handling. Take
my advice, June, and exhibit more prudence."

She put the pistol back in her pocket with a nervous action, and resumed her seat. Her excitement
showed itself in her nervous hands, and the pit-pat
which her feet kept up on the carpet.

"Do you know," she said to Walter, presently, not
deigning to address herself long to Greyburn, "what
sort of a man it is whose friendship you have been
honored with ?"

"Get her to tell you, Walter," said Greyburn.
"You will find it entertaining. It's a tiresome story
to me, but to you it will have the charm of novelty.
You see June is an old and dear friend of mine. Old
in the sense that we have known each other many
years, and dear in every sense. She is feeling a little
unhappy this evening over something, and when she
feels that way she always comes down here and be-
stows her charming presence on me. She'll tell you
the whole story of our early acquaintance, with plenty
of delightful embellishments of her own. If you're
not bored by that sort of thing, you'll find her interesting.

"He is a villain!" cried the lady, in great excite-ment.

"I don't deny it, Walter," said Greyburn, his smile broadening. "It may or it may not be true. But, coming with such unction from those charming lips, how can I dispute it. Excuse me. I interrupt."

"Listen to me, young man," said Miss June. "Twelve years ago I was an innocent girl living in a country town. I was fifteen. He was eighteen. He ruined and abandoned me."

"Triumphed over your virtue is the correct ex-pression," interposed Greyburn. "The other is obso-lete and never used now in polite circles."

"We came together to this city," pursued the lady, not noticing the irony which Greyburn used. "I trusted to his manhood and his honor to support and protect me here. We hired an attic, and lived for a week on what we could get. He never tried to get work. I knew that when our last penny was gone we must separate. I could not bear to lose him—wretch as he was—and I sold my soul to buy him bread."

"A fantastical expression," mused Greyburn, as if to himself, "and quite meaningless, but—*en regle*. Let it go."

Walter listened with eager attention.

"One evening I went out in the streets with the last dime I had in the world, to buy as usual a morsel of food for our breakfast. A man accosted me. I was desperate. After midnight I crept back to my room like a frightened criminal. *He was asleep!* In the morning when he woke (for I never closed my own eyes), I showed him money, expecting that he would rave and cry. *And he never said a word!*"

The lady rocked herself backward and forward for a minute, while a half sob issued from her lips. Wal-ter looked at Greyburn, and saw that the smile was still about his mouth.

"How I loved him then," she continued, raising her clasped hands, "you may guess when even that exhibition of his character did not induce me to leave him. When the money was gone I met the man again. He was rich. He gave liberally. Hector and I left the attic and took a pretty furnished room. We dined at restaurants. Though I knew he loved me no longer, those days seemed like heaven. Every dollar I got I gave to him ; and he took it. *He took it!* One night I came home and found that he was gone. He had left a note bidding me good-bye and saying that he should not return. I found out afterward why he went. The man to whom we owed our living had met him and *bribed* him to go. He got one thousand dollars for me. Good heaven ! A slave in a Turkish harem would have been valued higher !"

Walter looked at Greyburn, expecting surely now to hear his prompt denial. But there was the smile, just the same, and no sign that he questioned her statements.

"It is true, Walter, what she says," said he. "I did get one thousand dollars for her, and I considered it a good bargain. I wanted money. Her new lover had plenty of it. He wanted her. I didn't. What could be more sensible than an exchange ? I believe I had the best of it ; though, to do June justice, Mr. Moneybags didn't think so ! no, nor doesn't to-day ; for, would you believe it ? she is with him yet."

"I shall always wonder how I lived through the days which followed," continued Miss June. "For six weeks I was in a raging fever."

"And has been raging ever since," laughed Greyburn. "What do you think of it, Walter ? For these dozen years she has given her love to this man she speaks of, eaten his bread and worn the clothing and jewelry he provides, and you will see, if you take notice, that they are very good ones. How she must hate her 'Turkish harem!' How she must sigh for the little miserable hamlet from which I rescued her, and the attic where we went, and the penny rolls on which we tried to live. Ah! these women, Walter! Always complaining, always unhappy, always wronged!"

"If I have succeeded in saving myself from the street it is not his fault," said the lady. "What did he care what became of me? He was through with his plaything, and he tossed it away. Look at him now. Living like a Prince in a house which cost no one knows how much and on money got no one knows how! Is it not enough to make one doubt the justice of Heaven?"

"Well, if June has finished," said Greyburn, rising and walking meditatively up and down the room, "I'll say a word. Her story is substantially correct, in this way : If you look at anything with a colored glass the objects which your eyes encounter will be colored also. If I look at the sky with clear glass and you with black glass, and you say there is a cloud there, I will agree with you ; but if you say it is a dense, black cloud, and it appears to me a white, fleecy cloud, we shall disagree. She has put in the very darkest shade possible everywhere. When I was eighteen years old, Walter, I wasn't an unhandsome young fellow, though it may take a violent effort of your imagination to conceive it. She was a deuced pretty girl, as any one who sees her this evening will swear she must have been. She fell in love with me. I couldn't blame her. She wasn't the first girl who had done so, and she wasn't the last, by a good deal. Don't let me seem egotistical, my boy, but pretty women have always fluttered toward me as doves do toward their keeper. I never had to do more than stretch out my hand and they were there. When I concluded to start for New York, June must go too. Nothing would persuade her to let me leave her an hour. What could I do here, unknown and penniless? I went and looked at the wharves. Would she have had me a stevedore? I climbed stairs and asked for work. Doors were shut in my face. One man offered me two dollars a week to take care of a horse and cow in the suburbs. Should I have accepted it? I saw our pittance growing smaller and no prospect of more. What would have followed I do not know, but one morning I awoke to find money in my hand. Was I to ask questions which might prove unpleasant? One day old Moneybags met me and took me out to dinner. He had fallen in love with June and wanted her all alone by himself. He ended by offering me the thousand dollars. Was I to refuse it? Not I. I knew she was safe in his hands and I was glad when the money was safe in mine. I went my way. That week of poverty had taught me discretion. That discretion, properly applied, has brought me ease and comfort. As she says, Nobody knows how I get my money, but as it is Nobody's business, Nobody need not mind.

"Oh, he's a saint, there's no doubt of that," said Miss June, rising and arranging her dress for departure. "With a few pretty phrases he would tear down the wall of condemnation which I raised about him. I see by your face, Mr. Campbell, that you are converted by his sophistries."

"Must you go?" asked Greyburn. "So early?"

"I almost forgot to tell you," she said, evading his question, "that Mendall wishes to see you without fail at his office to-morrow morning by ten o'clock. Some business matter is troubling him."

"I will be there," said Greyburn. "I'm glad he makes the appointment at his office. I am horribly afraid every time he comes here that he will fall in love with one of my chambermaids, and that would put your nose out of joint. You see how thoughtful

I am for you, June. There! It's all out now! Walter knows who Mr. Moneybags is. Well, never mind. Mendall wouldn't care."

"If you must leave us, good-night," he added, as her touch was on the handle of the door. "But, June, you're not going to leave without a parting kiss. After all these hard words, just one little kiss."

She looked at him strangely for a moment, and then, as if moved by an impulse she could not resist, she stepped to his side and raised her lips to his. In her dark eyes the tears had risen till they nearly overflowed the lids.

"Oh! not for me!" cried Greyburn, with a light laugh, and retreating a step. "It wouldn't be right for me, June, under the circumstances, considering my relations with Mendall. I was only speaking for Mr. Campbell."

She dashed the tears upon the floor and for a moment looked as if she could tear him in pieces. He stood there with the provoking smile still lurking on his handsome mouth. Gradually she came to herself again, and turning away, hastily left the room and house.

"Come, Walter," said Greyburn, turning to his almost dazed companion, " let's go down to the parlor for a game of euchre." Adding, as they reached the staircase, " Do you like to see a woman in tears? I don't."

CHAPTER III.

IN one of Greyburn's many rambles through the country he met with a young gentleman lately graduated from the Andover Theological School, and intending after a short period of travel and rest to enter some pulpit of the Congregationalist denomination. This gentleman's name was Arthur Reycroft. He was the scion of a very old and wealthy family, and had been carefully trained from childhood with a view to the profession he was expected to embrace. Being gifted with superb health and excellent spirits, the course he had passed through did not succeed in making him a prig. Few better oarsmen lifted the blades. Few could leap a fence easier or ride a horse at a faster pace. In salt water or fresh he could swim an hour without fatigue. In short he was a likeable, athletic fellow, who seemed, when his spirits were aroused, as little like the conventional idea of a clergyman as it is possible to conceive.

Arthur Reycroft had never in his life committed knowingly a deliberate sin, and in this he did not consider that he had done anything entitling him to praise. He had after all acted out his nature in the school in which he had happened to be brought up. That there was such a thing as Sin in the world—and a great deal of it—he did not doubt, for was it not written in every line of his collegiate course? He had often argued to himself that in order to grapple successfully with this monster, a clergyman should obtain more than a superficial knowledge of the thing with which he had to deal. The minister who exclaimed against the theatre, for instance, never having been himself within one's walls, seemed to Reycroft like a man aspiring to teach navigation, never having been to sea. He determined before setting himself up as a preacher to take a look about the world and observe it awhile for himself. He meant to know what Sin was by actual observation, no matter into what places the necessities of discovery might lead him. It was not necessary that he should plunge into the mire, but he meant to see how and why others fell, in order to learn the best way to rescue them.

Some of these ideas Mr. Reycroft communicated to Hector Greyburn one evening as they were riding their horses slowly down a pass in the lower Catskills. They had become the best of friends and chatted with perfect unrestraint. Their views were diametrically opposed, but each gave to the other the same right of opinion which he himself claimed.

" Let me place myself at your service," Greyburn said. " With me for a pilot you will steer your bark among more sinful shoals than you ever dreamed existed. Pay me a visit in New York city for a month, and I will show Sin to you in all its forms, and I won't go outside of the Battery nor above Harlem river, either. Sin ! We'll revel in it. We will have Iniquity for breakfast, Wickedness for lunch, Crime for dinner, and horrors of all kinds to sleep on. Or, I could make you up a little special itinerary, like this : Sunday, Drunkenness ; Monday, Assault-and-battery ; Tuesday, Arson ; Wednesday, Burglary ; Thursday, Kidnapping ; Friday, Suicide ; Saturday, Murder. Bless you, Reycroft, I'll fill you full of it. It's all done within three miles of my house, every week the sweet sun shines on."

" I fear you are right," said Reycroft, with a touch of sadness in his tone. " And then there's another sin, worse in my mind than all the others, because more far-reaching and terrible in its results, that of unchastity."

" Oh! that ?" said Greyburn, with a laugh. " That you can have all the week. If you call that a sin, it never ceases."

" *If* I call it a sin," echoed Reycroft, stopping his horse short in the road. " Why, don't you ?"

" At the risk of your riding away like mad and calling for help, I must answer in the negative," said Greyburn. " It has only become a misdemeanor before the law on account of a puritanical folly which animates our statutes.   Anything can be made a crime by the consent of a few fools, with the aid of a sheet of paper, a drop of ink, and a bit of sealing wax, but that doesn't prove that it's a sin.   For instance : By one of the city ordinances it is forbidden to pick a flower in the park, and yet if I pick one when nobody is looking, I don't feel guilty of anything heinous."

"But you will admit that even this little ordinance against picking flowers in the park is a wise provision," said Reycroft, eagerly.   " Because, if it were not for that, the flowers would all be stolen, and the pleasure they give to so many would be destroyed."

"It's a bad simile," laughed Greyburn.   "For the women, though loved ever so incontinently, do not disappear, but continue to fill the earth with their loveliness.   We are born with a natural taste for beauty—at least I know *I* was—and has any one a right to shut me out of the whole floral kingdom when my senses long so eagerly for the rose and the lily ?"

"You can have your one rose or one lily, legally and honorably," said Reycroft, solemnly.

" Yes—one," responded his companion.   " Just one. And supposing I don't like it after I have got it.   Supposing I get a rose and discover that I should have had a lily or a violet or a daisy.   No escape for me ! No exchange with some man who has made a similar mistake.   It's too hard a condition, Reycroft; and flowers so plenty in this world, too."

"You are wrong Greyburn, quite wrong," responded the young clergyman, starting his horse again, "and your readiness of repartée won't save you.   If you will really spend a month with me investigating the sin of the metropolis, I think that I can show you that half of it all comes from violations of the SEVENTH COMMAND."

"All right," replied the other.   "I'll give you

leave. But you must be an honest, unprejudiced investigator. Throw your dogmatic notions one side and assimilate only what you actually prove worthy. Don't bring everything to your orthodox grindstone to sharpen, but take it as it is, and I will look for a fair verdict when you have examined the whole case."

"You're really serious in what you say? In your heart of hearts, removed from all considerations of personal desire, do you believe there is no sin in unchastity?"

"Just as much as there is in drinking a cup of this water," said Greyburn, dismounting and handing a dipper full of the clear sap of the hills to Reycroft. "In that draught you are taking, were a million—more or less—of little lives. They have been sacrificed to give you a temporary gratification. Their microscopic organisms have been ravished because you were the stronger and had the will to do it. If there is a God—and I won't say I doubt it—He cares as much for the smallest animalcule as he does for the Reverend Arthur Reycroft. He has created it with a wonderful organism, endowed it with life and liberty, and it was going on in the pursuit of happiness, when you—unfeeling creature—cut short its brief career."

Notwithstanding the gravity of the subject in Reycroft's estimation, Greyburn's apostrophe to the animalcule was too much for his gravity, and both men burst into a hearty laugh.

"We are taught," said the clergyman, presently, "that the lower creatures were made for the use of man. Their lives are not to go on through eternity like ours. They fulfill their destiny here and give way to new creatures who are to follow them."

"Made for man, are they?" echoed Greyburn. "All the lower animals made for man! What do you do with panthers and crocodiles and great crawling snakes. What particular good to man does the sand-fly do? Mosquitoes, gnats, and the red ants that crawl into your boots when you step into the woods to take a nap—mighty valuable they are to man's peace and comfort! Supposing you should meet a tiger, some fine evening, around these parts. Do you think that he would take your statement that the lower animals were made for man, or would he go to work like a sensible beast and stow you away in the interior of his striped body? It's an old fable, Reycroft, and a foolish one. It arose out of the vanity of man, and had no other inspiration than a desire to magnify his own importance. It took just as much time to make an anaconda as it did Adam. I believe every creature that was ever made was intended to go off and enjoy life on his own account. And, by that moon that's rising over there so clear and bright, I'm going to enjoy mine."

"Let me put it in this way," said Reycroft. "Do we not owe a greater regard to our own race than to any other? Would you think it as grave an offense to kill an ox as you would to dispatch a man?"

"Certainly not," said Greyburn, "and that is another instance of our cursed selfishness. Why do we not more frequently kill each other? The inclination is doubtless often felt to do murder, either for revenge, to remove unpleasant people from our path, or to secure goods which belong to others. But there stands in the way always, like a grim and watchful sentinel, the fear of punishment. Could oxen levy criminal process, impanel juries, and bring the destroyers of their race to justice, we should respect their rights as we do those of our own people. We take advantage of their ignorance to steal their labor and take at our pleasure even their lives. It is our cowardly method. We do to them what we would not dare if they could reason."

They rode on together slowly, in order the better to converse. The clergyman was astonished at the ideas advanced by his companion. While not in the least convinced, he was nevertheless much entertained.

"Do you dispute that the sin of which we speak causes distress and misery?" asked Reycroft.

"No. It may cause both. It may cause neither. Eating causes our teeth to decay, but shall we therefore never eat? This is a peculiar world. We must take it as we find it. If the fruits we like best are on the tallest trees we must climb. If they are on the lower branches and we can pluck them without effort, very well. Now, Reycroft, you are an honest young fellow, full of your mother's milk, and so dreadfully good that anything I say won't hurt you. What have I seen in New York since I have been there? This thing, forbidden by the Seventh Command, cursed by the church and condemned by the law, is as common as violations of the statute against profanity. Why, I know of a minister who denounces this sin with all his eloquence in the pulpit of a Sunday, and goes Monday to meet a paramour. I know a judge who executes the sentence of imprisonment on the hapless adulterers brought before him, and keeps his private mistress in the suburbs. The police, who are sworn to enforce the law, pat the pretty girls of the pave on the shoulder and accept their caresses in exchange for immunity from arrest. Society is honeycombed with it. To one like you it is almost past belief. Now what does it all argue? Why, that the law is against public sentiment and should be abolished. That's the way I see it. I would take it off the statute books and out of the church creeds, as a thing which can neither be prevented, nor, except in rare cases, discovered, and whose punishment is in consequence senseless and unfair."

"You would have a fine task before you," said Mr.

Reycroft. "The first thing you would have to get would be a message from Sinai, declaring that one-tenth of the law given to Moses has been abrogated."

"Oh, no!" laughed Greyburn. "Only that it had been suspended, like the commandment against covetousness ; or merely reserved for occasional use, like that against bearing false witness."

"You are incorrigible," said Reycroft, pleasantly. "But while I differ from you I quite admire your frankness. The vice of the time is deception. Nearly every one seems to think it necessary to ' assume a virtue' before men of my profession. This fact hides from us much of the true condition of the world. You are doing me a service in removing a part of the veil."

"Thanks," said Greyburn. "You're quite welcome, I'm sure. If you'll accept my invitation to spend a month in the city, with my house as the central point of observation, I'll lift all the veils you like. I'll show you, too, that they are all made of one material—illusion. When may I expect you?"

"You are very kind," responded Reycroft, "and I will accept your offer in the spirit which prompts it. Say the first of October ; how would that do? I think I shall finish my rambles by that time for this season."

"The first of October let it be then," said Greyburn. "You have a month yet to prepare your moral physique, for let me tell you it will receive some severe blows. For thirty days you must expect a series of shocks varying in intensity, and occurring on the average every three minutes. At my house there assembles on the first Thursday evening of each month a set of fellows who call themselves the Greyburn Club. You shall be introduced to them without a word in reference to your calling, and be a witness to their freedom from conventional restraints. You must receive what you see and hear as the young matriculate does the first blood which his scalpel draws, as a necessity to the end you seek. There will be ladies present also, oh ! yes !"—delighted at the young clergyman's sudden flush—" and plenty of the wine which maketh glad the heart of man. I pledge you my word that we shall introduce no novelties on your account, but shall have our dinner, wine and conversation exactly as we always do. I will show you the happy side of Sin—a side you ministers never allude to. If it be true that—

> " ' Vice is a monster of so frightful a mien
> As to be hated needs but to be seen,'

you'll find no vice there. Or if you do, you'll have better spectacles than the rest of us."

" Why don't you finish the quotation ?

> " ' But seen too oft, familiar with her face,' "

" Oh, yes !" said Greyburn.

> " ' We first endure, then pity, then embrace.'

" Well, that may have been Pope's way, but it isn't the style at the Greyburn Club. We have no trouble to endure after we have once embraced, and our pity is reserved for those foolish mortals who live in the hard, harsh atmosphere of the outside world."

CHAPTER IV.

THE first Thursday in October found the Rev. Arthur Reycroft installed as a guest at Hector Greyburn's house on Madison Avenue. He had passed the ordeal of seeing his host salute pretty Annie at the door and give a similar greeting to Nettie, Susanne and the rest, as they went upward to the parlor. He had had, in a hundred little ways, an insight into a life unlike anything he had ever before known. And within an hour he had admitted—to himself— that were it not for Conscience and its uneasy promptings, a man might be very comfortable indeed in those lodgings.

The first arrival of the party expected to dinner was Mr. Walter Campbell. This young gentleman grasped Greyburn's hand with great effusiveness, and Mr. Reycroft's with no less, on his being presented under the name of Mr. Arthur.

"You're in luck, Mr. Arthur," said Walter. "These little dinners are the pleasantest things in the world, and you'll never forget them. You're fond of the girls, of course? Always find plenty of nice ones here, sir. Each one a prize bird. Eh, Greyburn?"

Mr. Reycroft's embarrassment for an answer was relieved temporarily by the advent upon the scene of Mr. Chester Bolton, whose form appeared at the door, and whose voice called out, in tragic tones:

"How now, ye secret, black and midnight hags, what is't ye do?"

"Ah! Grabe, old boy," he proceeded, "excuse me. Didn't see there was a stranger present. Happy, I'm sure. What name did you say—Arthur? Ah, yes! I thought so. You must excuse my Shakespearean quotations. I am a lover of the stage, sir. An amateur actor, I may say. My head runs full of it. Do you admire the theatre, sir?"

"I admire Shakespeare," replied Mr. Reycroft, with pardonable evasion.

"Ah! Of course! Who doesn't, sir? Shake is the prince of the lot! Great mind, that Shake, sir. Poet, too. What a range! Rome and Jule. Mac. Three-Eyed-Dick. What a diff! and yet, in Shake's own words, " How express and ad ! Give me Shake, every time. Eh, Walt ?"

Mr. Campbell, being thus appealed to, expressed his preference on the whole for the ballet, and instanced the Black Crook as his idea of a first-class drama. The arrival at this juncture of Messrs. Jacob Mendall, Clarence Perkyns, Otis Middleby, and rapidly succeeding them, a dozen or more other gentlemen, put a stop to the discussion of theatrical subjects, in which Mr. Reycroft must soon have been hopelessly stranded.

Introductions were made in all directions, and the gentlemen were chatting familiarly among themselves, when the last guest arrived, Mr. William W. Pickett, a wealthy young manufacturer from a Massachusetts town, whose errand at the dinner was not wholly unlike that of the Rev. Mr. Reycroft. Mr. Pickett was a man of strong religious convictions, Superintendent of the Sunday School and President of the young men's Society for Religious Instruction in his village. He, like the clergyman, was a " chance acquaintance" of Greyburn, and had been invited to the dinner in much the same manner as the other. "Just to see and not to touch," as he expressed it.

At last Williams, the faithful colored steward-of-the-household, announced that the table was ready, and the party proceeded to the dining-room. Greyburn occupied the head of the table, with Mr. Reycroft on his right and Mr. Pickett on his left hand. When all were seated, he touched a bell which stood before him.

Instantly, at the signal, the door opened, and a line of handsome young women entered noiselessly, and took their places in the rear of the chairs. They were dressed in white muslin, adorned with ribbons of various hues, and in their hair the same colors were conspicuous. Well-rounded arms showed from beneath the short sleeves, and a glimpse of stocking was visible where the skirt just missed touching the slipper. The utmost propriety was observed by each as they proceeded to serve the dinner, and everything would have gone on without remark, had not Walter Campbell, happening to glance at the faces of Messrs. Reycroft and Pickett, been so struck by the expressions there, that a hearty laugh was forced from him in spite of himself.

"I beg your pardon, gentlemen, all of you," he said, upon recovering himself, "and especially of you, Mr. Arthur. It's an awful habit I've got into of laughing whenever anything happens to take me just so." And at that he went off into another spasmodic fit of merriment, in the midst of which he several times repeated his belief that he should die, and that he had better retire until he could get control of his risibles.

"You are perfectly excusable," volunteered Mr. Reycroft, "and I beg that you will not think of leaving the table on my account. I am entirely new to your circle, and shall doubtless give occasion for more mirth yet before we adjourn. Be assured, gentlemen, I take it all in good part."

At this, Walter sobered himself completely, and rising to grasp Mr. Reycroft's hand across the table, declared that gentleman the best fellow in the world, and the one for whom he entertained of all men the deepest affection.

"If I laugh again may I be—blest," he said. "I first sat at this table two years ago, and I was laughing more than anything else to think how it all struck me then. If nobody laughed at me it was owing to their better breeding. If Greyburn, here, wasn't a perfect prince, he'd have thrown me overboard months ago."

But the host immediately disputed this, and stated that he liked above all things to see perfect freedom among his guests. He hoped that every one would feel free under that roof to do exactly as he pleased.

"When a gentleman does me the honor to visit me," he said, in conclusion, "I put the house at his disposal. I say to him, Act yourself. Be yourself. If your inclination leads you to eat, there's the larder. If to drink, there's the sideboard. If you wish to smoke your cigar in the parlor, or put your feet on the piano, do it. You are here for your own enjoyment, not mine. Eat what you like, drink what you like, *do* what you like—kiss the waiter girls if you wish to."

Suiting the action to the word, he threw his arm around the buxom Susanne, who, as mistress of ceremonies, stood nearest him, and imprinted a warm kiss on her ruby lips, which she received as a nowise unpleasant gift. Nettie, who stood by Mr. Mendall's chair; Marie at Mr. Bolton's ; and each of the others in their several places, were treated in like manner without restraint. Little Annie, who was waiting on young Campbell, was half smothered in the impetuous embrace which he gave her. Allie and Florry alone doing duty at the chairs of Mr. Reycroft and Mr. Pickett respectively, stood with half-bowed heads, puzzled at their exemption from the general tribute.

"It's a forfeit for you both !" cried Walter, delighted, bursting into laughter again. "It's a rule of the house that we must follow Greyburn in everything. Allie, poor child, don't cry ! Florry, sweetest, I'll kiss you myself."

The laugh went round the table. Greyburn was regarding Mr. Reycroft attentively. The young clergyman was the picture of surprise and uncertainty. The rich blood flushed his cheeks, and his eyes sparkled a little, as if he had been drinking champagne. He half rose, and for an instant the host was afraid he should lose his guest. Indeed, the thought that he ought not to remain was formed in Reycroft's mind ; but, encountering Greyburn's smile, he seated himself immediately.

"You will excuse me, gentlemen," he said, "if I ask to be excepted from following this particular custom of the house, which has an entire novelty to me. Mr. Greyburn knows that I came here to see and to listen. I would not prove a damper on your festivities, but for myself I must ask some special exemptions."

"I ought to have told you," said Greyburn, looking around, "that Mr. Arthur is the most intensely moral man alive. While the best of fellows in most respects, his education in some important matters. has been sadly neglected. In fact, you will understand his position here better when I tell you that he has probably never kissed a girl in his life."

"Good Gawd !" cried Chester Bolton, striking an attitude. "An' dost thou think because thou art virtuous there shall be no more cakes and ale ! Such ignorance in this Nineteenth Century is positively shocking. 'Tis, 'pon my word. I'll betcher a fippenny bit there ain't a similar case down in the books anywhere."

"Yes, there is," spoke up Mr. Pickett. "Here is one ; and I trust to Heaven there are many more even in this city of sin."

"Doubtless you are right," said Greyburn, laughingly. "The sun has shone upon this earth with unabated heat for millions of years, and yet there are some places where eternal ice and snow continue to exist. Once in a while an iceberg breaks away from the frozen pack and floats southerly until it melts in the sweet bosom of the warmer seas. Such bergs are our two friends, and I trust that they will not invert nature by returning unmelted to their native north. I know them both to be, in the words of the dramatist whom our friend Bolton quotes so frequently, 'as chaste as ice, as pure as snow,' and I felt it my duty to show them the equatorial clime in which we dwell. I tried to begin in the mildest manner, when I instituted our game of forfeits. Gentlemen, I appeal to you, could I have commenced my treatment more delicately?"

"Impossible!" said Walter Campbell.

"Impossible!" echoed up and down the table.

"You see you are out-voted," said Greyburn, turning to his nearest guests alternately.

"We are crushed by superior numbers," admitted Mr. Reycroft, pleasantly, "but not convinced by any means that you are right and we are wrong."

Mr. Bolton thereupon declared that there were not two sides to the argument. "Oh, I could fight with you upon this theme until mine eyelids would no longer wag," he said. "That is Shake's expression, not mine, but it meets the case exactly."

"All is forgotten and forgiven so far as I am concerned," said Greyburn, "though it's the first time, I'll venture to say, that a woman was ever injured in her feelings by anything that passed at this table."

His tone was bantering, but good-natured, and Mr. Reycroft took no offense in the world.

"I have been taught," said that gentleman, "that undue familiarity between the sexes is harmful and unwise; that it can lead to no good. Hence my objection."

"All a mistake," interposed Mr. Clarence Perkyns. "I was taught the same thing, and had it drilled into me, *ad nauseum*. Those who say so are quite wrong, I assure you. We are nothing more nor less than animals of a higher order, with appetites and hungers which we seek to appease. Anything which reasonably tends to our happiness we have a right to partake of. Eh, Mendall?" he questioned in conclusion, turning to the banker, who had been a silent but interested listener.

"You've got my idea of it exactly," said Mendall. "The good things of this world are for them as can get 'em. That's my doctrine."

"Take beautiful woman out of the scale," put in Walter Campbell, "and you lower the gauge of life fifty per cent."

"A hundred !" cried Greyburn.

"Yes, undoubtedly—for you," assented Walter. "A sorcerer who can bring whom he pleases to his feet. A glance of his eye and they are captive. *I* know."

"And does Mr. Greyburn justify such wanton destruction ?" asked Mr. Reycroft, smiling upon his host.

"It's not destruction," he replied. "Walter's metaphor is too highly drawn. In fact, he overstates my capabilities. And yet," he added musingly, and half to himself, "I never tried for such game yet and failed to win it."

"He speaks truth," said Jacob Mendall. "I've known him a dozen years and he speaks truth. It's a gift. I never had it. Lucky for me, I always thought, that I got one after he was done with her."

"So it was," said Greyburn. "June is just the woman for you. Keeps you in place. You need a woman that's half tiger, like her. You are reasonable, too. When she shows her teeth you retire. Splendidly mated, Jacob, you and June."

"And are women really so easily won as your remark of a few minutes ago would seem to imply ?" asked Mr. Reycroft. "Speak guardedly now, and weigh your words well."

Greyburn glanced around the room and saw that his guests were all attention.

"I dislike to say anything that may seem like

boasting," he said, " but the truth is that the greatest fault I find with women is that they yield too easily. It takes all the sport out of the chase. You're a hunter, Mr. Arthur, and you will understand the simile. When you go after game what is it but the excitement of the run that sends the blood dancing through your veins? If, instead of the long chase over hill and dale, your game lagged for you and fell into your hands within the first furlong, would that suit your sportsman's ideas? I'll venture not. I am tired of shooting at domestic poultry."

" That's all right for you," said Walter, " but Venus is not so kind to the rest of us. It's over hill and down dale enough for me, I know that. There's one bird over on Long Island that I've tried to wing for six months, and I'm no nearer, as I can see, than when I started."

" That's because you don't understand the business," laughed Hector. " You rush in, raise a hue and cry, and frighten her into flight at the very outset. Women are like other fowl, and must be approached with caution. You lack coolness and nerve. When your bird comes in sight you go all to pieces, and lose your head at the very moment when what you need is calm deliberation. A young hunter, like you, should creep very near before he takes aim ; but away you go, banging at the air, and the creature takes natural alarm. The only way for you to hit anything would be for some one to hold it while you shot, and even then it is ten to one that you would kill your friend instead of the object at which you aimed."

Walter joined in the laugh which this raised, none the less because it was at his own expense.

" I get the fun of the chase, any way, which is what you were lamenting the loss of, " he said.

The wine was circulating pretty freely and was having its usual effect. On Greyburn it served to loosen his tongue and make him speak even more openly than usual.

"Do you mean to tell me," said Mr. Reycroft to him, "that you find the women of to-day, the respectable women, as easy victims as your words seem to imply; that it is as easy to overcome the virtue of the average woman as it is to shoot a wild fowl?"

"Right here, among friends at this table," replied Greyburn, "that is exactly what I mean. I am so confident of it that I will agree to put ten thousand dollars in Mr. Mendall's hands against a similar amount placed on a contrary proposition, that I will win any given woman within a year from this date or forfeit the stakes. I have made the offer before, and I make it now in the best of good faith."

"Yes," nodded Mendall, "he has made the offer in my presence time and again, and I never dreamed of taking him up. I'd like to make ten thousand dollars as well as another, but I'd as soon invest it in the mines of the Moon, as in such a wager as that."

"And I wouldn't bet a week's salary against those stakes," said young Campbell. "Of course he would win. Why, it's not a matter of common persuasion, Mr. Arthur. He uses necromancy, I tell you; clear diabolism !"

"I dislike to differ with you again," said the reverend guest, "but I am compelled to do so. I cannot, without more evidence, admit such a belief regarding the sex which I have ever credited with possessing most of the virtue and goodness in the world. There are women and women. Undoubtedly some would prove easy victims, finding in the attack upon them only what they had waited and hoped for. But your proposition would imply—God help us !—that there was not a woman of impregnable virtue in the country. That is preposterous. I could not subscribe to it for a moment."

"I would not mean exactly that," corrected Greyburn, pouring out another glass of wine. "I should wish for my own comfort to include in the wager only those women between the ages of sixteen and thirty. I wouldn't like to go on a quest for children or old ladies, so there would be a number left to whom you could pin your faith. And if I succeeded in winning the wager, it would after all only prove that that particular one was pliable. Put up your money, and let's have it tested," he added, toying with his glass and holding it between his eye and the light.

"Of course, I cannot do that," said Mr. Reycroft. "Even if there were no other reasons against it, I should not like to be a party to such an attempt, which seems to my mind nothing more nor less than a crime. To me it is a serious subject, and I do not feel like jesting upon it."

"Nonsense!" said Walter Campbell, who had drank very freely of the champagne. "You wouldn't dare risk a cent of the money. What's the use of pretending it's piety that stops you? Why, Greyburn could take in anything in petticoats just as easily as I could swallow this Heidseck."

The young man's words were sufficiently insulting to make the whole company wait with unusual interest for Mr. Reycroft's reply.

"I supposed every man had some woman," he said, at last, and with an expression of pain in his fine eyes, "whose name he held in honor. You cannot have a sister, Mr. Campbell, or you would not say what you have."

Walter started as if he had been shot. He turned as pale as a ghost, and took hold of his chair for support as he rose. In a second the blood came rushing back to his face again, and he hissed out:

"You coward! Do you dare mention *my sister* in such a way as that?"

" I mentioned no one," said Mr. Reycroft, quickly. " I did not know you had a sister. Your expression made me suppose you had none. God forbid that I should bring the name of any true lady into such a discussion !"

Walter had drank just enough to hear but not to understand the reply.

" True lady !" he cried again. " Do you mean to say my sister isn't a true lady ? I'll murder the man who says she isn't ! I'll——"

But Greyburn had him by the arm, and in a few moments convinced him that he was laboring under a delusion. Quick to apologize as to give offense, Walter instantly offered his hand. Mr. Reycroft accepted it, and the dinner proceeded in comparative silence. After a little while Mr. Pickett, who had hitherto said very little, began to grow loquacious.

" Gentlemen," said he, abruptly, " I'm a plain, blunt sort of a man, and I'm going to tell you what I think of this whole business. I think it's a direct branch of the Inferno."

" You flatter us," said Mr. Bolton. There was something in the frankness of Mr. Pickett which disarmed resentment.

" You are ruining your own souls, and those of God knows how many women," pursued the manufacturer. " You are wasting the precious moments which a kind Providence has given you to prepare for a future life. Like spendthrifts do you use the fortune Heaven sends you. Unless you repent, Satan will have you all."

" The devil, you say," put in a young man at the end of the table, not inaptly, as the rest seemed by their laughter to think.

" To these young women, your victims (cries of Oh ! Oh ! and derisive laughter), I have only to say, Leave this haunt of sin and secure yourselves honest labor; repent while there is yet time, or your end is not difficult to imagine."

"One minute," said Greyburn, soberly. "You are a manufacturer. You employ how many women—a hundred at least. What wages do they earn in your mill?"

"What has that to do with it?" asked Mr. Pickett, a little disconcerted at the change of subject.

"Never mind," said Greyburn, "I know, or approximately. They earn from three dollars and a half to six dollars a week. Very few indeed, the latter sum. Probably five dollars would be an average. Now, how many hours a day do they work?"

"All this has no reference to the matter," said the manufacturer.

"How many hours a day, that's the question," persisted Greyburn, not minding the interruption further than to pause while it was being made. "I know—about. I have ridden by your mills in the morning at a quarter past six and seen women hastening to the gates. I have passed at the same hour at night and seen it lit from top to bottom and heard the looms running. Twelve hours a day of such steady, confining work, for less than one dollar! That's the honest labor that is open to these girls if they choose it."

"I pay as much as anybody," said the manufacturer, a little warmly.

"To be sure," said Greyburn. "That's what I meant to say."

"And as much as I can afford."

"Excuse me," said Greyburn, "if I doubt that. You have been very severe on us, and we take it all in good part. Now let me criticise you a little. Your father left you less than five thousand dollars twenty years ago. You are now worth two hundred thousand dollars. How did you get it? You secured a mill privilege, so-called, a piece of water running through a ravine which the Almighty hollowed out for it in the creation. With the aid of many men, women, yes, and even children, you have built a mill, equipped it with machinery, and manufactured cloth until you are a rich man. Alone, you would have been worth little more than you were at first, but with all these people to aid you—that is, they and you together—you have amassed a fortune, and *you* have it all. To you, that mill has brought a splendid mansion, costly furniture, horses, carriages, bank stock, other real estate, in short, all that you could desire of the good things of this life. To them, the workers who have made your gains possible, it has brought long hours of unremitting toil, poor homes, scantily furnished, a crust of bread, and a grave in the cemetery over the hill. No more ! I challenge you to show me that it has brought them more than this."

"At least," said the manufacturer, pointedly, " they have not imperilled their souls there."

"I don't know about that," replied Greyburn. " I hardly see how they can have much soul to lose or save in that eternal treadmill of labor. Sunday is their only time for rest, and why you Puritans have left them that passes my comprehension, unless it be that they would otherwise wear out too soon, the same as your boilers, under perpetual strain. The offenses which are joined to poverty prevail in your village. Drunkenness is not uncommon. Theft is of weekly occurrence. And last year, when I was there, a woman lay in jail for strangling her infant, because, as she expressed it, she could not give up her loom to care for it without bringing her other five to starvation. Her husband was killed a few months previously by the falling of a piece of machinery, in your mill."

"You surely don't blame me for that," said Mr. Pickett, uneasily.

" I was blaming nobody," answered Greyburn. " I was only thinking. Here are these girls and there are your spinners. Have you one in all your mill who would not gladly exchange her life for the one these lead ? I doubt it ; I doubt it. Understand me, Mr. Pickett ! I am not finding any special fault with you, personally. But I do think the system under which one human being fattens out of all needed proportion, while a hundred or a thousand stay in perpetual poverty, is a disgrace to the age and a curse to society, compared with which the sentimental injuries of unchaste living are as a grain of sand to the whole globe."

The hour for separation came with this discussion unfinished, and all of the guests but Mr. Reycroft departed ; the manufacturer declaring, however, that he would meet Greyburn again and convince him that the mill-owners of New England were a great source of benefit to the communities in which they lived, and only received their just share of the profits arising from their business.

" May I ask you just one question ?' said Mr. Reycroft, as he seated himself in the library for a moment's conversation with his host before retiring.

" With pleasure," said Greyburn.

" Why do you not caution young Campbell about drinking so heavily ? It seems to me that he is doing himself an injury."

" I have done it at other places and times, but I cannot mention it at my own table. Rules of hospitality, you know. When I get the right opportunity I will offer a suggestion again."

" Thank you," said the minister. " And—ah—his sister. Have you ever seen her ?"

"Yes. He took me there a few weeks ago. A charming girl of eighteen. A little country school-teacher. Sweet as a strawberry."

"She comes within your limit—sixteen to thirty," said the visitor, sadly.

"Yes, and the very last one, you would say, to fall into the hands of sinful man."

"You—you are not trying?" said Mr. Reycroft in a constrained voice.

"There? Oh, no! not at all. You half believe in my power, I see."

The clergyman smiled a little.

"Good-night," said Greyburn, pleasantly, as Williams answered his bell and prepared to escort the guest to his room. "Sleep soundly, as I and all other men with clear consciences do. To-morrow we will commence the task of investigating the REAL sins of this modern Babylon."

———◆———

CHAPTER V.

LET us go out again into the air ; into that country which God made, and in which man was content to find his happiness long before he built himself the town. Let us go where the little country school-house stands on the edge of the maples. Let us see the little country school teacher—" sweet as a strawberry " —teaching the forty little children, bearing with their faults, soothing their griefs, interested in their joys and sorrows, loved by each, and loving each in return.

Every autumn afternoon, at four o'clock, the little school-house closed its doors, and the little teacher walked home, past the fields and meadows, past the loaded apple trees, past the little singing brook, and past John Dinsmore's forge. Each school day John hammered away at his anvil or placed the iron crescent on the hoof where it was to go, but stopped very often to measure with his eye the shadow of the forge door. For the shadow was his timepiece. It told him when it was the hour for Her to come, and this daily passing of Clara Campbell was more to the blacksmith than all the rest that came and went. Saturday, when there was no school, was a long and dull day for him. A close observer might have known when it came, only by the absence of the smile on John Dinsmore's face.

He had known her ever since she was a baby, and her brother Walter a toddling thing in petticoats. At that time Rev. Duncan Campbell and his pretty young wife were placed in charge of the parish of Springdale. Mr. Campbell, Sr., was a man of no great oratorical pretensions, but his piety and learning were undoubted. His wife was a lovable little woman, who did the whole duty of a country minister's consort, visiting the sick, comforting the distressed, breathing hope in the ear of the dying. When Clara was twelve years of age her father died suddenly of heart disease. The blow prostrated her mother, who had never been too strong, and within a year she followed him to the village cemetery.

Clara was thirteen and Walter fifteen, but the girl was the elder in all but years. The parish, with New England promptness, ceased to pay its minister's salary as soon as he was unable to perform his duties. The young girl and her brother were placed, theoretically, under the care of a guardian, but the gentleman selected did no more than follow Clara's directions. Every bill due was collected, and by the aid of a small mortgage on the homestead, was paid in full. Young as she was, Clara sought and obtained the primary school of the village, and set to work like a brave little woman to face the world. For two years she supported both herself and Walter, insisting that he should remain at school in order to fit himself for a position higher than he could otherwise expect. To do the boy justice, he protested against this arrangement, and yielded with reluctance to her superior force of will. He found light work for mornings and evenings and for vacations, and succeeded in adding a few dollars to the salary she received. But at last came the inevitable day, the day she had dreaded and tried to postpone, when he expressed the determination to go and seek his fortune. There was little to do in Springdale, that she well knew, and she had entertained the hope that he would settle in some of the larger towns within a few miles. When he declared that nothing would answer for him but New York city, she remonstrated at first and then pleaded with him. She begged him not to leave her so lonely ; she descanted upon the dangers, she pictured the evils of life in the metropolis ; she urged his extreme youth and the slight probability of his getting a foothold in a city where he had neither relations nor friends, all to no purpose. He had decided to go, and nothing could move him.

When she saw that he would go, she called up all her fortitude and tried to add to, rather than detract from, his stock of courage. She repressed the tears that rose to her eyes, and spoke hopefully, almost confidently, of his future. The good-hearted but stubborn boy had not that keen mental discernment which would have told him that each word of delight at his coming departure pierced his sister's heart like a knife. He kissed her a careless good-bye and departed, full of youth, full of animation, full of hope. Then she turned for consolation to the God of her parents, and left her brother in His care, with a somewhat lighter heart.

Two years had passed, during which she had not seen him. He had written often, and his stories of success, far beyond their dreams, had made her more content to miss his treasured face. Sometimes the feeling came very strongly that she ought to know from some other source just what Walter was doing. Not that she doubted him, but she wished to make assurance doubly sure. No way to do this seemed to present itself, however, as she knew not a soul either in or near the city ; and she had to wait until the two years had passed, when she had his positive promise that he would make her a visit.

Home at last ! The same dear brother. The same loved one—only taller and handsomer. A city young man, with a salary of two thousand dollars a year ! He had stayed a week, which went like a wonderful and impossible dream. And now he had gone again. She had seen him mount the stage box and wave his adieux as he rode away, the admiration and pride of the village. She had suppressed her sisterly tears— till he was out of sight. A stout-hearted little woman was Clara Campbell.

After Walter was gone, Clara liked more than ever to stop at the old forge and have a chat with John Dinsmore. John was interested in Walter, as well as she. John had carried him on his shoulders many and many a time.

"I had a letter from Walter this morning, John," she said, one afternoon, as she entered the forge and took the carefully dusted chair which the blacksmith handed her.

"Ah !" said John. It always took him a minute or two to get quite easy before this little woman, this child whom he had rocked in her cradle sixteen years before.

"Yes, John," pursued Clara. "And he asked particularly to be remembered to you."

"I'm thankful to him, I'm sure," said the blacksmith. "It's very kind of him."

Clara sat quite still for a minute after that, and he did not interrupt her.

"Do you know, John," she said at last, "that I wish I could go down to New York and see where Walter lives and how he spends his time? It almost frightens me to think of him there, in that great city, with so much money in his hands. It's a large salary he is getting. There isn't a man in this whole village, excepting Squire Singleton, who has two thousand a year. And you know, John, he acknowledged that he had spent so far nearly the whole of it. I can't think it is a good thing for a young man like him to have so much money. It opens every form of temptation, unless one is strongly fortified to resist, and Walter was always easily led. Not that I would say any harm of him, poor boy ; but he is so innocent, he seems to me in special danger."

The blacksmith paused a moment and then said:

"O' course, ye couldn't go, Miss Clara. It would be quite out o' the question. Some one else might go down thar an' look about quietly, but not you. Ye hadn't ought to think of it."

"There's one thing I might do," said Clara, thoughtfully. "I might write to Mr. Greyburn."

The blacksmith started violently.

"He has taken a great deal of interest in Walter," she continued, too much absorbed in her own thoughts to notice him, "and would do anything he could, I know. He said as much when he was here. Very delicately, to be sure, but I understood him. He thinks Walter needs looking after as much as we do."

"Did he say that?" asked the blacksmith, in a low tone.

"Not exactly. I can't remember just how he expressed the idea. It was in the evening, when Walter had gone to the office for the mail. I know he spoke very kindly. He is such a perfect gentleman, too."

Dinsmore stood very still, weighing every word. When she came to the end he glanced involuntarily at his own hard hands and at his workman's clothes.

"Money makes gentlemen," he said. Then, seeing that she looked up inquiringly, he added, "Fine clothes, diamonds, gold watches."

"Oh, no, John, it takes much more than those to make a real gentleman," said Clara. "It takes education, and politeness; yes, and goodness, too. A man must have goodness with all the rest or he is not a gentleman. And I think he had better have the goodness and miss all the rest than to have ever so much of the others and fail of that."

"It ain't the way o' the world, though," said Dinsmore. "It sounds very pretty in Sunday School books to read of honest hearts beatin' under rough jackets, but it's the fine feathers that make the fine birds. Now, look at me. I never wronged a man out of a penny. I've done my work in life as I found it to do without complaint. But do you think any one would ever point to me when I went by an' say, 'Thar goes a gentleman?' No. They'd be laughed at."

"But you *are* a gentleman," said Clara. "Honest, .upright; why, everybody around Springdale respects John Dinsmore. You know they do."

"Respects me? yes," said Dinsmore. "But when *he* was here they looked up at him as if he was a king. Why? What had he done? They'd heard he was rich, that's all."

"And that he had been very kind to my brother Walter," said Clara.

"Much that had to do with it!" cried Dinsmore, desperately. "What had he done for him, anyway? Got him a place, did he? Well, what did that cost him? Lent him five hundred dollars? The worst thing he could 'a' done. What was that to a man o' his money? But o' course, I hadn't ought to say a word. He's such a ' perfect gentleman.' "

The girl stared at him in the utmost astonishment.

"Why, John," said she, "I never in my life heard you speak so much ill of any one. You have no right to misjudge Mr. Greyburn. Perhaps it was not wise that he should lend Walter so much money, but we must look at his motive. It probably doesn't seem as great a sum to him as it does to us, and he lent it to my brother to enable him to dress as well as the other clerks in the office, and to get rooms in a nice locality. The motive was praiseworthy. John, you must at least admit that."

" How can you or I tell what his motive was?" said the blacksmith, doggedly.

" What could it have been except an honorable one?" cried Clara, impatiently.

" Oh, I don't know," replied Dinsmore, shortly.

" Then why do you speak as you did? You are not used to being so unkind in your estimates of people."

" I don't know what his motive was," repeated Dinsmore, slowly, but I'll wager my head it wasn't a good one. I'll wager my head that fine gentleman hasn't taken all this pains with your brother fer nothin'. It's agin the natur' o' things. Time'll tell whether I'm right or wrong. Fer your sake, Miss Clara," he added, in a softer tone, "I hope I may be mistaken, but I don't believe it."

"You're a strange man, John," said Clara. "When you get your mind once set there's no changing it. I don't think I ought to stay and hear you condemn Mr. Greyburn, unless you can give some reason except your intuitions and prejudices. This is not the first time you have taken occasion to speak slightingly of him to me. He is my brother's friend, and so far as I have seen, a gentleman. Yes, I repeat it, a gentleman. If you intend to abuse him every time I stop at the forge a moment on my way from school, I shall have to cease calling, that's all."

She rose as if to go. The blacksmith made a gesture of appeal.

"Oh ! Miss Clara !" he cried, "ye don't mean that !"

"I do mean it," she said. "Something seems to have come over you lately to make you act very disagreeably."

'Do you think," said the blacksmith, averting his face from her, "that I don't love your brother Walter ?"

"I know you do," said Clara, quickly.

"Don't you know," he said, dashing a tear from his grimy face, and speaking almost in a whisper, "that I haven't a friend in the world to claim my love, an' that it's all yours—an' Walter's ? Don't let me frighten ye, Miss Clara. I'm almost old enough to be yer father. Ever sence ye could creep—you two— I've loved ye both. An' now, fer an honest word, ye'll cast me aside."

"No, John, never !" cried the warm-hearted girl, with ready sympathy. "You have always been our friend, and you shall be. I will stop here every evening, if you desire. I spoke hastily. Forgive me."

The blacksmith brushed the tears from his blue eyes, as if ashamed of his weakness.

"Forgive ye!" he echoed. "Forgive *me*, rather. I was thoughtless. I allus am. I wasn't born a gentleman, ye see, an' don't know how to express myself. I won't speak o' him again. Ye'll stop at the forge evenin's, won't ye? Because," he said, pausing for a reason—" because I shall want to hear from Walter."

"I'll come," said Clara, "every evening. And I am sorry for what I said."

She gave him her hand in token of reconciliation. Had he been a " gentleman " he might have bent to kiss it, but he would as soon have thrust it into his forge's fire. To John Dinsmore, Clara was what a saint is to a devout Catholic, or as the mosques of Mecca to a Moslem pilgrim. Only she seemed farther from his possession than any heaven or any shrine. To have her shadow fall across his shop floor was all he could hope for, and on her frequent visits he existed. Had she stayed away entirely, a darkness like that of the Egyptian plague would have fallen upon his heart.

A few days later, without a word to any one of her intention, Clara placed this letter in the post-office :

SPRINGDALE, CONN., *Oct.* —, 188-.

HECTOR GREYBURN, ESQ.:

Sir,—When you were in Springdale you spoke to me very kindly of my brother, and as I understood, volunteered, should I so desire, to ascertain in what company he spends his leisure hours, and communicate the information to me. You will understand, Sir, that Walter and I were left orphans five years ago, and that, while I am the youngest in years, he has always seemed in a sense under my charge. I take the liberty of begging you to interest yourself to the extent of learning whether he is doing as a young man ought among the temptations of a city. Please do not let him know, in any way, that I have made this request, as he is high-spirited and might resent what he would call an interference.

By attending to this you will confer a lasting favor on

Your Obedient Servant,
CLARA CAMPBELL.

When Greyburn read this letter he burst into a hearty laugh. The ludicrous side of the notion that *he* should investigate the character of Walter's friends and surroundings struck him with full force. Then he read the letter through again, and somehow it did not seem quite so mirth-provoking. He recalled the little sweet-faced sister, living all alone and unprotected in the old country parsonage, and seemed to see her eyes fixed on him as he talked in her little parlor of Walter's successes. The wish that he could see her again came strong upon him. He answered her letter in a kind tone, bidding her rest assured that he would continue to do all in his power for her brother. He spoke of the pleasure his brief visit to Springdale had given him, and declared his intention of coming again to breathe the pure are of its hills and valleys.

"I shall stroll up that way another season," he mused, "and I must make a few days stay in that modern Arcadia. No," he added, as a new thought crossed his mind, "not with any special design upon the little schoolmistress. That would raise the deuce with Walter, and I couldn't afford it. And yet there's a charm in the girl that I can't rid myself of. Pshaw! This is treason to Gabrielle. What is it that Byron says:

> "'And Juan, had he quite forgotten Julia,
> And should he have forgotten her so soon!'"

CHAPTER VI.

FAITHFUL to his promise, Greyburn escorted the Rev. Arthur Reycroft for the thirty days next succeeding his advent at the Greyburn Club, through all the principal haunts of sin which the metropolis affords. They visited the slums by night and day, often under the guard of a police officer. They visited the criminal courts, the jails, the places of refuge and detention. They climbed the stairs of filthy tenement houses, they burrowed into the cellars where human vermin breed and die. They went to the gambling dens where the stakes are generally hundreds of dollars as well as those where a nickel or a dime meets the same grand passion for play. They entered the variety theatres of the lower sort, in which a small bribe admits behind the scenes, where the not over-particular ladies of the ballet disport themselves in abbreviated skirts. They went to some of those places which the French denominate *maisons de joie*, and which they found in squalor at Five Points and in splendor on Murray Hill. They went, in short, into the hidden places of New York, places which the ordinary traveler neither sees nor suspects, but which are to the body politic what the burning lava deep in Vesuvius' crater is to the people on the plain below— a never ceasing menace. It is not our purpose to follow them. Reycroft was sick at heart long before he had finished his self-imposed task, and when the month had expired he declared that he would under no consideration go any farther.

"When Dante walked the streets of Italy," he said one night, as they were taking a lunch in Greyburn's library, after a more than ordinarily unpleasant tour, "the people pointed at him and said, 'There goes a man who has been in hell.' I feel as if every person I meet might with equal justice call the same thing after me. I wonder how the Christian men and women of this city can let these things go on, year after year, without more effort to stop them."

"Why, they don't wish to stop them," said Greyburn. "If you will give me another month I will prove it to you. Who do you suppose owns the real estate where these dens, as you call them, are located? I wish I had time to show you the assessors' books. I wish I could take you where you could follow the profits made in these places and see into whose pockets they go. You would find that the dollars left in the gin cellar, the gambling shop and the house of ill-fame, go very often to purchase the horses and carriages, the velvets, laces and diamonds which stop Sunday mornings before the doors of our big churches. It would seriously lower the income of very many of your Christian men and women if the law were strong enough to enforce itself in the slums of this city."

"It is a terrible thought," said Reycroft. "But, Mr. Greyburn, excuse me for a personal question: How does all this array of sin affect you so little? You know what I mean. You are not partial to drunkenness, gambling, and all the horrors which we have witnessed. They can have no charms for you. In whatever light you may view the sins which have more alluring exteriors, these lower things must repel you. And yet you pass through it all as if the smell of the fire did not touch your garments."

Greyburn smiled at the serious face of his guest, and replied:

"A good deal of the reason is probably in the fact that I have seen nothing *new* in this month, which has opened so much of novelty to you. I have experienced no astonishment, which is one of the main elements of horror. I knew it was all there, as I had seen it a thousand times. As you say, I don't like it ; at least, most of it. I must have my sin gilded and well upholstered to make it palatable. The poison sold in the low dram shop does not charm me, while I like just the same my Maderia or my pale ale. The sight of excited men throwing their last dollar on a roulette table is unpleasant, and yet with a party of friends at piquet or euchre I'll none the less spice the game with a ten or twenty dollar stake. The drunken and bedraggled woman of the street might call after me in vain, but I would not turn away, for all that, from pink and white youth and beauty in the shape of Gabrielle Delaporte."

"It's none the less sin, though," said Reycroft, shaking his head.

"I don't believe you," replied Greyburn, gaily. "They say that conscience is to be our guide in such matters, and I never yet felt even the least bit of a twinge over anything of that sort. I bring everything up to that test, and the result is quite agreeable. Shall I do murder ? No ! Conscience tells me that without question. Shall I knock down my neighbor or burn his house over his head ? Certainly not ! I shouldn't enjoy it. Conscience would interfere with my pastime. Shall I make myself and the people around me happy ? Conscience immediately smiles her approval."

"I am afraid your conscience is not a true guide," said the minister, " if you find happiness in violating the express commands of Heaven."

"It's the best I've got, any way," laughed Greyburn, "and if it doesn't keep true time I can't be held to blame. Do you remember Mendall's expression, ' The good things of this world are for those who can get them'? I've thought it over a good deal and I believe he is right. Fourteen years ago I found myself in this city without a sou. A little later I discovered an easy road to luxury, and I've pursued it ever since. Perhaps if I had had too fine a conscience I might have denied myself my opportunities and starved on a clerk's wages till now. So, on the whole, I really can't regret that my inward monitor is a trifle elastic. You've heard the question discussed, no doubt, regarding my source of income?"

"No," said Reycroft. "I have met no one alone, you know, since I have been here, and the subject never occurred to me."

"Have you no curiosity?"

"I have no objections to hearing anything you would like to tell me."

"I shall tell you very little," said Greyburn, "because the value of my philosopher's stone depends largely on its remaining hidden from human eyes. It has amused me to hear the guesses which have been made and the deep investigations which have been set on foot to find how an unknown young fellow stepped so easily from penury to a competence, and no one is ever a bit the wiser yet."

"So long as it was done in an honest way, no one can find fault," said Reycroft.

"Ah! but the question comes, 'What is honesty?'" said Greyburn, "and a solution of that problem might take longer than you would think. Absolute honesty is, to my mind, almost an unknown quantity in this little world of ours. Take any sphere of life you choose, and you will find a vein of fraud running through it. It's all I can do to get pure articles even when I am willing to pay the highest price. Take the professions, too. Supposing I go to a lawyer and put a case in his hands. Will he try to settle that case for my best interest, or will he study out what he can get for himself? Say that I feel slightly ill and call a doctor. Will he say to me, 'Greyburn, you must drink a little less sherry and get to bed at eleven o'clock;' or will he shake his head and look grave and scare me, if he can, into paying him for a dozen visits? Why, even the pulpit is just as bad. When I ask my-self. Do I get my money honestly?' I answer, with such examples all around me, 'Yes, more hon-estly than most of your neighbors, for your method causes no heart-breakings, adds no sting to poverty, and poisons no one's system with adulterated food or drugs.' Honest! I'm a paragon, compared to most men."

As he did not seem inclined to pursue the subject farther, silence fell on the pair for a few minutes.

"You spoke of a Miss Delaporte," said Reycroft, finally.

"Gabrielle? Oh, yes! You haven't seen her, have you? She has been quite forgotten in the mul-tiplicity of other investigations which we have been making. She must be produced, for to visit my house and not see Gabrielle, would be like climbing the Swiss Alps and missing the Jungfrau."

"Must I? Had I better?" said Reycroft. He knew from experience what to expect from his host's female divinities.

"Must you? To be sure! You will see the prettiest creature in all New York. You will find her interesting, too. Scold her, if you think proper, for not hiding the light of her pretty face under a bushel, but don't miss seeing her, or I'll never forgive you. Susanne," he continued, as that young creature responded to his bell, "ask Gabrielle to come here."

The young minister was not made of stone, and he

could not suppress a murmur of admiration as Gabrielle appeared. She was a blonde of petite, but well-rounded, form. Her wavy hair fell unconfined about her shapely shoulders. Her eyes were of the deepest blue, and her mouth, which parted to show two white and even rows of pearly teeth, would have driven a painter to distraction. She came directly to Greyburn and stood looking into his face as if for instructions.

"Gabrielle," he said, "my friend, Mr. Arthur."

She put out her hand and he had to take it. She had a momentary surprise when he did not carry it to his lips, but she did not lose her self-possession.

"I am *so* pleased," she said, in soft and liquid tones, more musical than any instrument except the human voice ever produced.

She took the chair assigned her and sat down, looking alternately at the gentlemen.

"Isn't she pretty?" said Greyburn.

Mr. Reycroft started a little. The words were but echoes of his own thoughts.

"She is indeed a perfect specimen of the handiwork of God," he said, reverently.

"And of man, also," smiled Greyburn. "For in these days of prudery the handiwork of God alone is not considered presentable before a miscellaneous audience. I will say this for Gabrielle,'however. She is less beholden to the arts of man for her good looks than any girl I know of. She's all genuine. It doesn't take a lady's maid and a milliner to make her over every morning. She's all there, Reycroft, with no deception. A diamond of the first water, without a flaw."

A good deal of extra color rose to the face of the young minister during this rather bold description. The fact that the girl's eyes were on him, and the intuitive knowledge that she felt no answering blush, did not lessen his uneasiness.

"I am going to ask you a few questions," said Grey-burn, after a slight pause. "I want my friend, Mr. Arthur, to hear your answers. You must speak with perfect freedom. Are you ready?"

She smiled a sweet affirmative.

"Your name?"

"Gabrielle Delaporte."

"Your age?"

"Twenty years."

"Whom do you love best?"

"The man who asks me the question."

"How long have you known him?"

"Six months."

"Answered like a professional!" laughed Greyburn. "Your witness, Arthur. I believe you appear for the prosecution."

Mr. Reycroft hesitated and then fell into his vein.

"This lady is ——"

"My sweetheart! Certainly."

"Do you love her?"

"Of course."

"As you have others before ; how many?"

"Oh! it would be impossible to tell that," said Greyburn, lightly. "Go count the sands of the sea."

"And as you will love others after her?"

"Probably, yes. I'm not a seer into the future."

"How long did you love this lady's predecessors?"

"Different lengths of time. Sometimes an hour, sometimes a day, sometimes a week. Once I loved a woman almost a year, but I was very young then. Not often have I loved one so long as I have *ma belle* here."

Turning to Gabrielle, Mr. Reycroft said, very soberly :

"My child, does this satisfy you?"

"Perfectly," she replied.

"Do you think his love and protection will last forever?"

"I've no idea that it will," said Gabrielle.

"And when the bond between you breaks, as it may any hour ——"

"Ah!" she interrupted, "'Sufficient unto the day is the evil.' What shall we dwellers in this world do? Must we never inhale the fragrance of the spring flowers or taste the luscious fruits of autumn because we know there is a winter to come after? Must we not enjoy the glorious sun's painting of the western sky because darkness treads close on his skirts. In a few days or years the mould will surely cover us three, and yet we sit here and smile and chatter."

"It is infatuation!" cried the minister.

"Why, then, I beg you not to disturb me," she laughed. "If I am happily-demented, I am better off than if I were melancholy-sane. If I am insane, let us be thankful for insanity. Yes, and for love, that pleasing 'delusion' which you evidently would have us abandon."

She came to Greyburn's side and clasped her round arms affectionately about his neck.

"She's enough for you," said Greyburn, returning the embrace, and looking with mingled love and pride upon the fair being whom his arm encircled.

"The life you live will shorten your days," said the clergyman. "Have you thought of that?"

"Will it? Well, what of it?" retorted Gabrielle. "We live too long and too slowly. Five years of real *life* is worth a century of vegetation."

"Right again!" put in Greyburn. "Women are like strawberries, only good in their season. I don't want mine green, nor yet old and shriveled up.

' Whom the gods love,' you know. And if the gods don't love young and pretty women, I haven't much to say for their judgment."

" You are a handsome woman," pursued Mr. Reycroft. " Do you know why? It is because generations of your ancestors lived honest, sober lives. They bequeathed you health, good blood and a strong constitution. Your descendants, if you should have any, would inherit the seeds of deterioration."

" I did not make the world," she responded, as if tired of argument. " Most people are slow enough to keep it going. If my ancestors have been content with an ox-team gait, I can ride a few miles at a faster pace without much harm. As to my descendants," here she looked archly at Greyburn, "they are not near enough to excite either my sympathies or my interest. What is he trying to get at, Hector? I never was asked so many queer questions in my life."

Greyburn laughed loud and long.

" Why," said he, " Mr. Arthur is a man with very peculiar notions. He is the best fellow alive, but practically demented on one or two points. He thinks, for instance, that it is just as wicked for me to place my arm around you like this, as it would be if I drove a dagger into your heart."

" Oh, no !" corrected the clergyman. " Not quite so bad as that !"

" Why not ?" said Greyburn. " Sin ought to have no relative sinfulness. There is nothing in the decalogue which you receive as divine which intimates that violations of the Sixth Command are greater than lapses regarding the Seventh."

" You reason speciously," said the clergyman. "All violations of God's law are undoubtedly hateful in His eyes, but they are unequal in their effect on his creatures. Of course one would rather be told a falsehood, or have his property stolen, than to lose his life. Though, to put it plainly, and with no desire to speak harshly, if that young lady were a relative of mine, I would rather she fell by a dagger's blow, than to be the mistress of the kindest man alive."

"Why, you cruel thing!" cried Gabrielle. "You would be just as bad as that horrid Roman which Hector and I saw at the play, who stabbed his daughter because one of the great generals wanted her. I was glad the brute went crazy in the next act and died before the curtain fell."

"Served him right," added Greyburn, "though to be sure he had some provocation. The triumvir didn't go to work fair to get the girl. It was a shame, though, to shed her innocent blood. That Virginius should have lived some centuries later. He would have made an excellent member of Cromwell's parliament. But it's nearly two o'clock, my charmer, and those bright eyes of yours should be closed. A kiss and good-night."

Gabrielle kissed him. "I would do as much for you, sir," she said archly to Mr. Reycroft, "if I wasn't afraid you had a dagger or pistol concealed about your clothing. I don't mind anything you said, though, and I hope I didn't speak too sharply, either, I think I will kiss you, after all, just to show that I quite forgive you."

St. Anthony might have taken the salute from those rosy lips and soothed the years of after penance by the memory of its fleeting bliss. Reycroft felt for at second how much the transgression of Adam has left in his remote descendants.

"No, I thank you," he found strength to say, at last.

"Well, it's the first time *that* ever happened," said Gabrielle, with mock pique. "Just wait till you're offered it again ! Hector, will you not revenge me ?"

"Yes, by taking what he refuses." said Greyburn, snatching kiss after kiss from her unresisting mouth. It's a revenge which I would take on every man in Christendom if he treated you in like manner."

"A nice revenge on *him*, that is !" said the girl. " It seems more like levying tribute on *me*."

"Not so," he replied, "for I take no more than I leave. Go, now ; and may Venus watch over and keep you."

She ran laughing from the room, and Greyburn turned to Reycroft.

"You are indeed adamant," said he, "if such a creature as that does not charm you."

" I am not adamant !" cried the minister, his voice trembling slightly. "I almost wish I were. I have the harder task of struggling against temptations and conquering them. Adamant has no such duty."

"Then you *are* human ?" said Greyburn. "It is really blood and not vinegar which flows in your veins ?"

"Such blood," responded the minister, "that were I to give way ever so little it would hurl my soul to ruin. Were I to stay here under your roof a month more I know not what would happen. How can the ' livery of the court of heaven ' be given to the messengers of the devil ?"

" Do you call Gabrielle a messenger of the devil ?" laughed Greyburn. " By Beelzebub ! The fellow has exquisite taste ! And she has affected you, has she ? Pierced your heart through all its coats of orthodox mail ? Come ! We are friends. There are plenty more for me. You may have her for your own. Shall I call her back ?"

He laid his hand on the bell rope.

"No !" cried Reycroft, in a tone so loud as to be

almost ludicrous under the circumstances, and reaching out to stop him.

" You're half inclined," persisted Greyburn, tantalizingly. " Really, you're very welcome if you want her. She won't care. Hadn't you better ?"

" I beg of you," said the clergyman, excitedly, " don't tempt me further. To-morrow I will leave this city for my country home. I have realized in time the danger of going too close to the edge of the pit, where, in a moment, one may be overcome by its fumes and fall headlong. The moth's wings are singed just when he thinks the light most beautiful I thank you heartily for your generous hospitality, but I must trench on it no longer. I will go home, where, in the atmosphere I am used to, I can inhale a full breath and regain my moral strength."

" And in the meantime we poor victims of the pestilence must care for ourselves ?" said Greyburn. " Very well. Only after you get your 'moral strength' let us see you again. To me your visit has been extremely pleasant and I much regret to lose you."

" There is one thing heavily on my mind," said Reycroft, changing the subject : " Young Campbell."

" That little fool ?" said Greyburn. " Well, what can I do with him ?"

" Do you set him the best possible example ?" asked the minister, with a shade of reproach in his manner.

" Example ! He don't follow *my* example in anything. I take a glass of wine or a mug of ale. He takes a dozen and gets drunk. I enjoy a quiet evening with a party of friends. He paints the town in a hack, and goes home exhausted with what he is pleased to term 'fun.' I take Gabrielle to the theater, return when it is over, take my little supper and retire. He gets a front seat at the ballet, runs around to the stage door, gets an actress whose shape has fascinated him and rushes off to a private dining-room. For goodness sake, Reycroft, 'an' you love me,' don't talk about that young idiot following any example of mine."

"He is going down hill fast, at any rate," said the minister.

"I'm sorry, but I don't know what to do about it," replied the other. "He has been placed under my guardianship lately, too. Did you know that? His sister wrote me a letter asking me to look to his companionships and surroundings."

"Wrote to *you ?*"

"Yes, why not? I am a very particular friend of the family, now."

"And what reply did you make ?"

"Well, of course I didn't wish to hurt her feelings, and I smoothed things over pretty nicely. She's as innocent as a bird—in fact, much more so than some birds—and it will do her no good to know the truth. When I go up there again, I'll talk it over with her."

"You ought not to go there again," said the minister.

"Oh, I'll do no harm. She's quite captivating, though, in her quaint, country way."

"Greyburn, have you a female relative in the world ?"

"Not one," he replied. "I am all the sisters of my father's house and all the brothers, too."

"If you had a sister like this Miss Campbell, would you like to see her thrown into the company of a man like—well—like Hector Greyburn ?"

"My dear fellow, I haven't the slightest idea. I never had a sister, and how I should feel is more than I can tell. I never was what is called jealous, and I hope I should be reasonable. Good night. Don't let Gabrielle's face come between you and slumber."

Arthur Reycroft tried in vain all the rest of that

night and late in the morning to sleep, but he could not. The face of Gabrielle did come between him and slumber. The scene of the previous evening was enacted over and over again, and her blue eyes seemed always fixed in softest languor upon him.

When he rose to dress, late the next day, more tired than when he went to bed, a thought of Clara Campbell came into his mind, and he half resolved to make a visit to Springdale and give her a quiet warning. Upon consideration, he decided that he would seem contemptible as a revealer of secrets, and he changed his mind. Had he not done so this history would never have been written.

CHAPTER VII.

WINTER has passed and it was summer again. June, the month of roses and of love, is almost ended. Springdale lies in its valley, wearing its dark-green garment like a maiden who is unused to suitors, but who waits patiently the call inevitable whenever it shall please Heaven. The scent of newly mown hay fills the warm air. The village school is closed. The little village school mistress wanders along the side of the half-mountain which looks on Springdale from the north—and she is not alone.

Their journey was made ostensibly in search of strawberries, but the fruit was not plenty, and their baskets were nearly as empty as when they came. Slowly they walked, pausing often to note some especial object in the scenery, or to mark the sudden uprising of a startled bird, which they had unintentionally alarmed. Strangely familiar they seemed for people who had met but once before that week, but the perfect innocence and confidence of the girl, and the well-bred ease of the man, accounted for that. To her brother's kind friend Clara felt that she owed every possible attention. He found at first a novelty in the very *naiveté* of the child, for so he called her, which charmed and held him. But almost before he was aware of it, there arose a new feeling. He began to think with uneasiness of going home. He liked to hear the voice and to watch the movements of this rustic beauty.

Early each morning he left his room in the village tavern and strolled down to the old parsonage with some ready excuse for a brief call. Sometimes he caught her at her household duties, and she never seemed a bit ashamed. Not the less charming did he find her when her sleeves were rolled up at the dish-pan or the oven, and the dress of printed muslin fitted loosely about her girlish figure. Every afternoon, as early as he thought it reasonable, he went for his formal call ; and after tea they walked together up the hilly road to see the sun set, and wandered slowly back in the twilight. Very pleasant was all this to the man of thirty-two, this fellow who had seen his cup of life brimming and had almost drained its pleasures dry.

What they talked of neither could have told an hour after. It was of as much consequence as of what the robins twittered about in the trees overhead. But, on the last day which he was to spend with her, he grew more sober as they walked over the hills. He felt that he must say something more than the ordinary simplicities. Again and again he essayed the task, but words failed him. What was the matter with this roué, this man of the world ?

The knowledge that he was hopelessly entangled had been dawning on him gradually. At first he tried to laugh it off. He ! It was ridiculous ! In love with a girl who had never been ten miles from her own doorstone ! In love, as novels picture love, with all its elements of fear and doubt and faintheartedness ! What would Mendall say, and Perkyns and Middleby ?

He could not throw his snares one by one around this creature and watch with unmoved brain her pretty struggles to escape. He could not dazzle her with the prospect of a gayer life in the city. He could not undermine her womanly virtue by making light of purity in his old, easy way. Those women who capitulated under a week's siege were not at all like Clara Campbell.

" I go to-night," he said, as he half reclined on the ground near where Clara sat braiding leaves and flowers into a garland.

" To-night ?" she repeated, with a little start.

" Yes. I have been here a week. Does it seem so long ?"

" Is it a week ?" she answered, incredulously.

" Yes, just seven days. I came on Thursday. Friday I called on you the first time. Saturday I came again, Sunday I went to church to hear you sing. Monday ——"

" You should have gone to church to hear the sermon," she interrupted, in a manner that was meant to be impressive.

" Probably," he replied. " But being a truthful man, I must repeat that I went there to hear you sing. As witness the fact that I recall the words of the hymn very well, while I cannot remember even the text of the sermon."

" Then you did wrong," said Clara.

" I fear I do wrong very often," he said. " I have no one to tell me when I stray. It would have suited me better to lie in some shady nook by the little stream which flows through the valley down there, than to have heard the best sermon ever written.

But to hear you sing I endured the close air of the church, once, twice, yes, I really believe, three times that day."

She was silent. He wondered if he had said too much. He had not meant his words for flattery, but he feared they would sound like it, and hastened to break the stillness.

"I was born in the country, and it seems very natural to be there again. I feel, while climbing the hills and treading the valleys, like a traveler who comes to his home after many years of wandering. When a boy I liked nothing better than to go alone into the woods and stay there days and nights together. The earth seems to me now as it did then, the kind bosom of a mother, to which we can always fly when the vexations of life oppress or discourage us."

"And in whose arms we are at last enfolded for an eternal sleep," said Clara, gravely.

"Have you ever read what Walt Whitman says about that?" he asked. "He calls grass the uncut hair of graves."

"I never read it," she said, "but I think the expression is very beautiful."

"There is one thing I can't understand," he continued, "and that is, while I find the country in one sense as it was in my boyhood, in another there is a great change."

"In what way?"

"I can hardly tell. It is as if something had gone out of it. Here it is June. The sun shines hotly. The insects drone sleepily, the grass is green, the sky is blue. But let me lie here a moment and give myself up to reverie and I am transported back to the old days. I feel a warmer sun, I hear a louder hum as the insects pass, I see a greener grass and a bluer sky. Then I rouse myself and it disappears. I cannot understand it, but the rivers are not so clear, the birds sing less sweetly and the air of the hills has lost its exhilaration. I suppose it must be because I am growing old."

The last expression drew from the girl a light laugh.

"Wrinkled and gray as you are, how can you expect to see and hear?" she said. "You do very well to walk without a cane."

"It is no laughing matter," he responded, "to have passed your thirty-second birthday. The fourteen years before you reach that advanced period, Miss Campbell, ought to be worth more than all the rest of your life."

"Thirteen years," she corrected, "for I am now nineteen. They will soon be gone, and I shall not regret them if they are wisely spent. That is the main thing after all."

"Supposing that one has passed those thirteen years and cannot look back upon them with satisfaction from your point of view," said Greyburn, looking earnestly at her. "Supposing he sees little there but what he ought to regret."

"Then I should pity him very much," she answered, "and advise him to be careful of what was left—the future?"

"I wish I were a Roman Catholic!" he burst out. "I should feel easier after a confession."

"Let me be your priest," she answered, and instantly repented having done so, when it was too late.

"If you only could!" he exclaimed. "And when I had finished, if you could say, 'I absolve thee.' But I fear you would like me less afterward. You do like me a little now—Oh, yes! you needn't deny it—and I couldn't afford to lose it, little as it is."

"I certainly respect you," she said, in some doubt as to whether it was exactly what she ought to say.

"Then I will not give you cause to lessen that respect by unveiling my life," said he.

"You go to-night, remember," she replied, "and whether you will ever see me again is doubtful. Leave me the hope that whatever has been wrong in your life will be amended."

"Never see you again !" he exclaimed, starting to his feet. "Do you place a bar on my ever coming to Springdale ?"

"I thought—I only meant ——" she stammered.

"*Never see you !*" he went on, wildly. "You, who are all I care for now in the whole world ! Clara, I love you—I adore—I worship ! Do not let me frighten you. I know it is hopeless. You are too pure, too good, to link your life with mine. My love is beyond control. It has taken my tongue out of my possession. I beg of you, do not weep." Her tears were flowing freely. "I will try and say no more. Why did I throw myself between you and your peaceful, innocent, happy life ?"

She looked up through her tears and he saw with inexpressible relief that her features bore no trace of anger.

"Do you forgive me ?" he entreated, humbly.

"I have nothing to pardon," she said in a low voice, "but I fear from your words that God has. His smile is much more needed by you than mine. I do not believe you are the greatest offender in the world, but if you were you might go in trust to Him who has said : 'Though your sins be as scarlet they shall be white as snow; and though they be red like crimson they shall be as wool.'"

He uncovered his head in no pretended reverence as she repeated the sacred words.

"I have heard that before, more than once," said he, in a low tone, "but to me it has no meaning. I have so little spiritual nature. Everything in me has been subordinated to pleasure. I have lacked nothing that money could procure, and I thought that included all. Until this week I believed myself the happiest man in the world. Now I would give, oh! so willingly! everything I possess if I could say, 'Clara Campbell, I am an honest man; I have lived a life worthy to join with yours; will you be my wife?' I cannot say it. Like a man drowning within sight of the harbor, I can only regret the folly it is too late to undo. I am sinking! sinking! sinking!"

There was an agony in his voice that went to her heart.

"Speak not so hopelessly," she said, gently. "You are yet young, with long years of life probably before you. What is past cannot be helped, but all in advance is yours."

"And you will not hate me?" he cried.

"Surely I would never do that. You have the ability to win my highest regard, and I hope, I trust, I pray that you will do it."

"But never your love?" said Greyburn. "Never, never, whatever happens, your love?"

"We will not speak of that," said the girl, a shadow coming over her features, and the tears rising again. "Let us speak rather of the resolutions you are to make and fulfill. You have talents and should find a noble place in the world. But we must be going. As we walk toward home promise me that you will respect my request."

"When may I come and see you again?"

"When you can say, 'I have done as you advised.' But you had better write at first. I will answer, and I may be able to help you in that way."

"If I had any faith in myself," said he, with a disheartened sigh, "I would promise whatever you might ask, but I have no confidence that I shall persevere when I am away from your influence. I will try, however. Yes, I will *keep* trying, and at least I will write, for that I shall consider a great privilege."

They walked on, and when they reached the gate of her cottage he said, suddenly :

"If suffering and regret would blot out recorded transgressions, the page where mine are kept would be virgin white to-day. I am going from all I love back to the place where lies all I have learned to despise. I turn from the gates of Paradise to seek again the portals of Hades. Give me some hope, ever so little, and I will rest content. Clara, some day, if I become what you would have me ——"

"Hush !" she said, softly. "Say nothing in your present impetuous mood. Remember that I am an orphan, without a protector in the world. Good-bye ! Write to me when you reach home. And—don't forget !"

She was gone. He walked back to the hotel and ordered his horse to be saddled at once. The landlord endeavored to persuade him to eat some supper, but he said he had no appetite.

"Do you ride far, to-night ?" asked the landlord.

"To New York," he replied, absently.

"Forty miles !" exclaimed mine host. "Say, this won't do. Besides, you are not looking well. You won't take a bite ? Well, at least let me get you a tumbler of brandy. I have some in the cellar thirty years old, that my father bottled. Just one glass. It'll do you lots of good."

Greyburn turned from the man almost angrily and sprang into the saddle. His intelligent animal set off at a brisk trot, which he soon exchanged for a canter, and horse and rider disappeared down the road in a twinkling.

"I would like to know what that means," said the tavern-keeper, nodding his head sagely to his wife, who stood in the doorway to witness the guest's departure. "That fellow has been here a week and has spent the most of it at the old parsonage or walking around by-roads with Miss Campbell. They say he's a great friend of Walter's, but I'm thinking he hasn't stayed here a week on *his* account. Did you see his face? He looked like a ghost, and I know they was off together all the afternoon. By hokey! Do you suppose he asked her to marry him and got the mitten. I'd bet that load of hay standing under the shed there that's just what's happened."

"Bah!" exclaimed his wife. "Don't be a fool, Judson. Do you suppose Clara Campbell is a born idiot! Without a cent of her own, except that little tumble-down house, do you thing she'd refuse a man who's rolling in money? No, sir, it's something deeper than that."

"Well, perhaps you'd better tell us all about it, if you know so much," said the husband, ironically. "I'm sure of one thing, the fellow looked all broke up, and he'd just left Clara at her gate, for I see 'em myself as I was driving up the road. And I know another thing, he was as bright as he ever was at one o'clock, when he eat his dinner, and went down the lane whistling like a boy. Now he's rode off like a wild man, and if he don't kill that ere hoss before he gets to New York, I miss my guess; that's a blamed fine hoss, too," he added, regretfully.

"Don't ye fret about that hoss," remarked the stable boy, who came up just in time to hear his master's closing words. "Mr. Greyburn thinks more o' that Robin than he would of a child. I'll bet that hoss would go on a canter all the way to York an' not hurt him a bit, an' he'd do it inside o' three hours, too."

"Probably he thinks more of that hoss, Sam, than he does of the minister's darter," said the landlord, with the view of ascertaining whether any ideas worth having could be got out of the boy.

"I don't know nothin' about that," said Sam, "but if that ere Robin was mine, I wouldn't swap him for all the gals this side o' Kal'mazoo. An' he's the gentleman! See what he chipped me as he was startin' off."

The boy exhibited a five dollar bill, to the amazement of the innkeeper and his wife.

"See here! Part of that belongs to me," said the landlord, advancing suddenly, as if to claim his rights, then and there, *vi et armis*.

"Don't ye wish ye may get it," said the youth, derisively, springing out of reach. It was as useless to follow him as to try to catch a squirrel. He went down the lane singing, and the landlord sorrowfully followed his wife into the house.

But Greyburn! where was he?

———◆———

CHAPTER VIII.

FAST and faster through the cool evening air sped Robin and his rider. Greyburn's brain was all in a whirl. For the first few miles his rapid thoughts seemed to be leaving his old life behind him and speeding onward to a new one. Then it changed, and every step seemed taking him back to the scene of all his sin, made doubly hateful by the awakening he had just experienced. Involuntarily he slackened the pace of his beast, until at last, ten miles from Springdale, he came to a walk and then to a dead stop. Indecision took possession of the rider. He dismounted and threw himself on the ground under a tree near the roadside, leaving the horse to crop the rich herbage which grew by the fences. The moon rose early and found him there.   A terrible conflict was going on in his mind.   At last a town clock in the distance broke the stillness by sounding twelve strokes.   Greyburn stepped slowly and mechanically to where Robin awaited him.   Mounting the faithful beast again, he turned his head once more in the direction of Springdale.   He rode slowly at starting, as if not yet quite decided.   Then, suddenly, he burst out with the exclamation :

" I must do it !" and giving the word and rein to his horse he rode at great speed toward the village he had quitted five hours before.

Clouds crossed the moon's face.   A quick, sharp summer shower came on and drenched him to the skin.   His clothing was splashed with mud.

Entering the village, he reduced his horse's pace to a walk.   He turned into a lane and slipped to the earth.

" Wait there, Robin, till I come," he whispered, and walked slowly across the field until he could see the old parsonage.

Everything was as still as death, save the soft drippings from the trees and the old house as the remains of the shower fell drop by drop to the grass below. The clouds across the moon favored his purpose, and made him less likely to be observed.

He knew the house well.   A giant elm stood close to one side.   He climbed the tree as quietly as a cat could have done.   When even with the attic window, which stood open, he passed his body from the tree to the inside of the house.

Was he bent on burglary or murder ?   Either might have been suspected from his actions.

Stealthily he glided along the floor.   The house was built with solid oak timbers and no sound betrayed his presence.   He reached a stairway.   Descending slowly he came to a door.   Until this moment he had

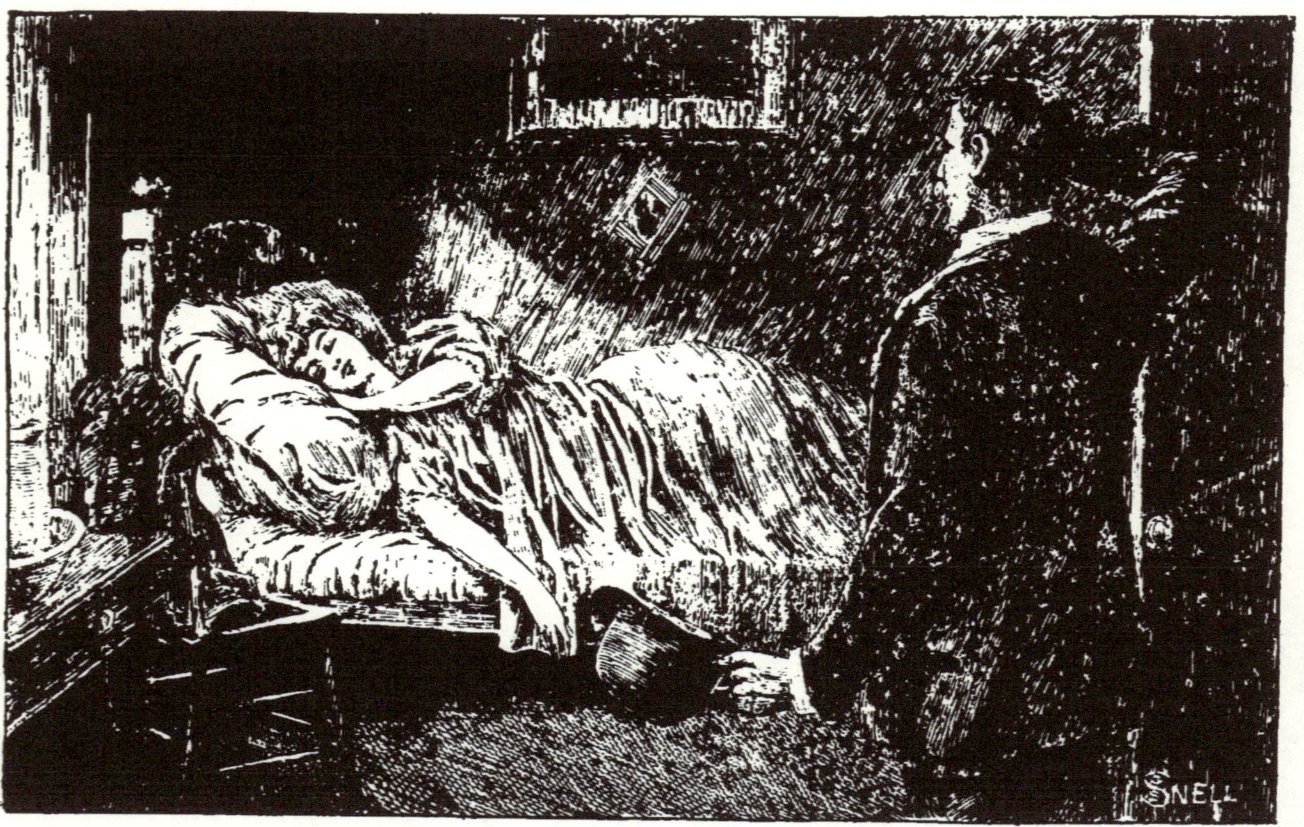

"Upon the little cottage bedstead, lay the school teacher." *Page 91.*

lost no time. Now he hesitated. Only for a moment, however. Then he turned the knob and without a sound stepped into the room.

It was Clara Campbell's chamber. The moon stealing out from the clouds at the moment, threw its light upon the scene. In her snowy drapery, upon the little cottage bedstead, lay the school-teacher. Her pure, almost angelic face was turned to the light. One white arm hung over the edge of the couch. Her quiet breathing was all that suggested life. Otherwise she might have been a wonderful statue of marble.

Greyburn stood for some minutes gazing upon the scene. His mind was torn by conflicting emotions. At one moment he wished he had not come. At the next he banished all such thoughts and tried to think how next to proceed. A slight rustle decided him, and with two steps he was at Clara's side. He hastily planted himself upon the edge of the bed, and with a quick motion covered her mouth with one hand, at the same time holding her so that she could not move, and whispering excitedly that it was he—that it was Hector, and she must not be afraid.

Clara Campbell was intensely startled when she awoke and found herself thus clasped in Greyburn's arms. She had always felt as safe in the old house as though a regiment of soldiers guarded her. She knew it contained nothing in worldy wealth to make it a likely place for robbers to attack, and in her pure soul she never dreamed it necessary to have another person on the premises as a protection to herself. After retiring the previous evening she had lain awake for hours thinking of Greyburn and his strange confessions. Until that day she had never thought of him as an evil being. His goodness or badness, morally, had never entered into the account. She had supposed from the generosity which he had showed to Walter that he was one of the few, better than the average, and had respected him accordingly. During the visit he had just made to Springdale he had done his best, until the very end, to convey a good impression, and Clara had learned to like him extremely well. Unpleasant as were the events of the day, they had not served to take this "liking" from her heart. After he left her, her whole thought in regard to him took the vein of sympathy. He seemed to her like a soul under conviction, as her father would have said, and the religious element was so strong in her that his condition, seen in that light, over-balanced all other considerations. She dropped asleep with his troubles deep upon her mind, and when she awoke it did not seem so strange as it might have been to find him before her eyes. Still the time, the place, and her own unprotected condition served to fill her with instant alarm. She reflected that he had accused himself of being sinful almost beyond his own control. His present conduct was not calculated to inspire confidence. Her maidenly modesty joined in the protest made by her fears and even overbalanced them She struggled for a minute, in spite of his repeated protestations that he meant no harm and would release her the instant she would consent to hear quietly what he had to say. Finally her reason returned and she lay passive.

"Clara, darling Clara!" said Greyburn, speaking rapidly, in a tremulous voice, "do not fear me. I would not harm you for a million worlds. I know I should not have come here, and I do not expect you will ever forgive me for it, but my feelings overcame me. I love you so, my dearest, that I could not resist spending one more hour with you—an hour that everything seems to tell me will be the last. I rode as fast as I could away, but your face kept calling me back. To go on was to reach again my old associations, and I did not dare go among them as I felt to-night. Here, under this roof, I knew dwelt purity, innocence! everything with which life should be adorned. I felt that I must see you. To ring at the door would have been worse than useless at this hour, and I entered—like a thief—at the attic window. I came not to profane, but to adore. I came to get strength to meet my adversaries on the morrow. Do not drive me away. Forget the hour and your attire, and remember only a distracted fellow-creature, who craves your pity and begs your sympathy. If I seem rude, it is not because I would be so, but to prevent you from alarming the village, and thus bringing a worse fate upon yourself. Darling Clara—Miss Campbell—say that you will answer me in your ordinary voice and I will gladly let you speak. You will? Then do so, and let your first words deal as gently with me as they may."

"Mr. Greyburn," said Clara, her voice trembling in spite of her attempts to force it into calmness, "in the name of all that you hold dear I ask you to leave this house as quickly as possible. Every moment you stay is fraught with the most terrible danger to us both. Were it known that you came here my reputation would be forever blasted. If you care for me as you say you do, lose not an instant in complying with my request."

She saw his flushed face pale in the moonlight and witnessed his teeth set themselves together.

"Clara," he said, "if to stay doomed me to the gallows I would not—could not—go. I have forfeited everything now, and I will not be driven away by any such argument as the one you advance."

"Then," she said, her voice growing stronger as she proceeded, "do at least this thing for me. Go down to the parlor and wait there until I can dress and join you. If you cannot do that, never let the word 'love' pass your lips again."

He looked into her face doubtfully.

"And if I go," he asked, "have I your word of honor that you will join me there? Will you promise not to make any sound to alarm the neighbors or try to escape? Pardon me, my best-beloved, if I make conditions. You see I am desperate. If you will give your word to what I ask I will go. If you break it after it is given, God only knows where this will end."

"I promise," said Clara. "Now hasten—go—do not delay until some new fancy seizes you."

"I will go," he replied, "but give me one kiss. I *must* have that. I ——"

"*Hector Greyburn !*" She tore herself from his arms with extraordinary strength. He quailed before the look she gave him and stole like a guilty creature from the room.

The instant he closed the door, she sprang and bolted it, and then fell on her knees. Her lips moved a moment in prayer. Then, hastily dressing herself, she sought Greyburn down stairs.

"I am here as I promised," was her greeting, as he sprang up to receive her. "Now once more I beg —I implore—you to go."

"Not until I have talked with you," he said. "Not until you give me some hope. Clara! If I knew you would be the reward at the end—no matter how long or how hard the road—I could persevere. But what have I to look to? This night makes or unmakes me. Clara! If you knew my life! I cannot bear the thought of going back to it, and yet without you I must go back. To win you I will do anything. I know that what I said yesterday, and especially what I am doing to-night, cannot raise me in your estimation, unless you look beyond appearances into my heart and see how wholly desolate it is. Say that you will be my wife ! I will never be harsh with you. I will love you as no other woman was ever loved. I will abandon all evil and at your feet learn to do well. Do not say no."

He turned his white face toward her and she pitied him from the bottom of her heart. If she had felt aversion it was all gone now.

" Hector," she said, softly, "you should not yield to such tempests of passion as this. I could not have one particle of respect for myself if I answered as you wish under such—what shall I call it—compulsion. Think what you are being led to do. Out of what you believe is your love for me, you are possibly inflicting an injury which you can never live long enough to efface. Should it become known to a single person that you were in this house at this hour, I am ruined. Do as I tell you. Go back to the city. Strive to do what is right. Send me letters and I will answer them. Curb your rashness and remember that you are a man ?"

Greyburn sat like one dazed. She saw that he was yielding and pressed her advantage.

" Mr. Greyburn—Hector—for my sake, go at once!"

He rose mechanically and followed her to the rear door. She unlocked it and he stepped out into the night. Something in his face told her he would not break his resolution. She bade him good-bye in a low voice and turned to close the entrance, when a new sound stayed her. It was a noise as of scuffling on the lawn. She stepped outside again and saw two figures engaged in a passionate struggle. One of them was Greyburn. She sprang to the place where the fighting was going on. Then she saw that the other was John Dinsmore. It was no child's play that was taking place. Two athletes had met and the quarrel was not a light one.

"*Stop!*"

At her voice Greyburn, who had the advantage of hold at that moment, released it, and both men stood confronting each other and her.

"What does this mean?" she demanded, looking from one to the other with imperious glances.

"Ask him," said Greyburn, alluding to the blacksmith. "Ask him why he sprang on me like a tiger and tried to strangle me."

"John Dinsmore, is this true?"

The blacksmith disdained to reply directly. "Let it pass," he said. "He and I'll meet ag'in."

"No, you shall not go," said Clara, stepping in front of him. "I wish to know who gave you authority to assault my guest."

"Your guest?" repeated Dinsmore, looking at Clara and then at Greyburn. "Your guest! At two o'clock in the night! and you alone! and with a man o' that character! Do you own it?"

Greyburn did not allow Miss Campbell to reply to this.

"If it were not for arousing the village and bringing a scandal on this house," he said, "I'd teach you manners. I will, as it is, if Miss Campbell will permit me."

He actually looked at her for consent, as if he half expected it.

Dinsmore replied by a contemptuous glance.

"Once more I ask you," said Clara, "why you trouble my guest? Why do you constitute yourself my guardian? Why do you spy around my house in the night time? Answer me, John Dinsmore!"

"A perfect gentleman!" he ironically muttered. "White hands, diamonds, money. Any hour will do for *him*."

He strode off across the fields.

"You see what trouble you bring to me," said Clara, looking after the retreating form with tears in her eyes. "Do not waste another instant in going. Get to the city as fast as you can. And another thing," she continued, as she saw him preparing to obey, "look out for that man. He bears you no good will and I am afraid he is dangerous. He has known Walter and I ever since we were babies and he will not tolerate anything which he thinks will harm us. Many a night I have known him to get up from his bed and come and watch my house. Had he been early enough to see you enter he might have done you serious injury. Hector—I mean Mr. Greyburn—don't treat this matter lightly, but have a thought for your safety."

"You would care, then, if he killed me?" said Greyburn, a look of joy stealing over his face.

"How shocking! Of course I should care," cried the girl; and then she added in a sort of sad half-earnest tone, "You must not die until you are better prepared than now."

"Never so well as when the brightest of all the angels stands ready to receive my soul," he replied, with affected gayety. Then seeing that the levity of his answer pained her, he added: "Farewell, my guardian spirit. I will try to become worthy of you."

She walked with him to where Robin stood waiting, and bade him good-bye as he rode down the lane.

"Don't forget!" were her last words. "John is a desperate man."

She ran as far as the high road to see him safely beyond the little bridge at the forge, and returned with her eyes blinded with tears.

"Wicked as he is—wrong as he was to-night," she sobbed, "I would not like any harm to happen to him." And kneeling once more by her bedside, she prayed:

"O God! dear God! bless Hector and keep all evil from bringing him to hurt."

CHAPTER IX.

GREYBURN rode until sunrise, and then, bethinking himself that his horse had gone quite far enough since yester eve, he stopped at a country hotel for rest. The day which followed was very warm, and he kept indoors until evening, when he remounted and finished the journey to his city home. His mind was in a tangle. He almost wondered as he ascended the high steps of his residence whether this was the man who used to occupy that house or some stranger who looked enough like him to pass the doorkeeper. He went to his room, vouchsafing the briefest answers to the "Good-evenings" of the servants. Throwing himself heavily into a cushioned arm-chair, he sat for a long time in silence.

"A week ago,"—so his thoughts ran—"I left this house a happy, careless, contented being, for a run into the country. I was going to have a little visit with a girl who was nothing to me, and whom I did not expect I should ever wish to be anything. I intended to pass a week in the fresh air, with country living, good scenery, and a cheerful, pretty companion. Now I return, dispirited, unhappy. Something without a name has taken control of me. I have avowed the possession of a pure love—I, Hector Greyburn, the libertine, the practiced seducer, who have always boasted a contempt for everything called virtuous. I have promised a little, unpracticed country girl to leave all my former habits, and embrace others which I have hither to despised, all in exchange for *her love*. Am I mad? Is this myself? Is this my house? Am I the man I was, or has something changed me into another? Give up wealth ease, all for one pair of bright eyes! Impossible!

And yet, I do love her. Clara Campbell, deny it as I may, it is true. I love you! I love you !"

A knock came at the door and Nettie's face peeped in.

"Mr. Walter Campbell is here, sir. Will you see him ?"

"No ! No ! Wait ! Let me think. Walter here ? What time is it ? My watch has not been wound to-day."

"It is about one o'clock, sir. Mr. Campbell wished particularly to see you."

"Shall I ?" muttered Greyburn to himself. Then raising his head he said, "Show him into the back parlor and say I will be there presently."

He turned up several of the burners in the dimly-lighted chandelier and took a survey of himself in the pier-glass. He was white, tired-looking, almost haggard. His raiment still showed the marks of the muddy ride, for in his rest at the hotel his mind had been too busily occupied to think of his personal appearance.

"I look more like an escaped lunatic than a city gentleman," he mused, and proceeded to make the necessary alterations in his attire, stopping at the end to apply cologne to his face, and especially to his eyelids, in an endeavor to take away the weary expression. He also essayed a brighter look, and practised a smile or two before the mirror ere he turned away.

"Ah ! Walter," he said, cordially greeting the young man as he entered the room where he waited, " I did not expect a caller to-night, but I am glad to see you always."

"I rang and found that you had returned," responded Walter, "and thought a brief call would not be out of place. I'd been to the theatre and after that had a game of billiards with some fellows. Come to start home I felt confoundedly dull, and thought you might cheer me up a bit. You're always so full of spirits, you know."

"Yes," said Greyburn, absently, and hardly bearing out the description. How much the lad looked like Clara !

"Where did you go?" queried Walter, after waiting in vain for his companion to say more.

"Where?" repeated Greyburn, with a slight start. "Oh, into the country. Up among the hills. Just for a run. Nothing special." His voice would have betrayed him with a more experienced judge than young Campbell.

How much Walter looked like his sister !

"I wish I had been with you," said the other. "Terribly dull here. The theatres are positively awful. Nothing on but trash, you know ! I've run down to Long Branch, but there's no fun there. The beaches around here are insufferable. The country would do for a change, but I probably sha'n't go anywhere this year for long. I wish winter was here again. There's always something in the winter."

"Yes," assented Greyburn, again. It was Clara's face, but not her voice. Their eyes were very nearly alike. He was considerably the taller.

"Come, what's up, old fellow?" said Walter, with the familiarity which boon companionship had taught him. "You're not as cheerful as usual to-night. One would think—ha ! ha !—that you'd fallen in love ?"

"I have," said Greyburn, desperately.

He spoke with such a peculiar intonation that the young man ceased to smile and looked deeply interested instead.

"You !" he exclaimed. "You in love ! And sober as a church deacon over it, too ! What's the matter, old man ? You haven't met your match at last, have you ? Don't tell me that the girl has sent you flying.

What would the boys say if I should bring them such a story. No, I don't believe it myself."

"You will oblige me, if you please, by telling them nothing. It's not their business."

"Probably it's not mine, either," said Walter, hotly. So Clara's eyes had flashed when he asked her to kiss him !

"Walter, my boy," he said, very gently, "I only meant the others, not you. If I had not wanted you to know, would I have told you ?"

The young man was mollified instantly.

"I was too quick !" he said. "I always am. No one but you would bear with my temper. But I am all curiosity. Tell me about it. It seems so incredible. She is handsome, of course."

"The fairest creature earth ever beheld," said Greyburn, reverently.

"To be sure. And young, of course. Virtuous to the core and lovely to distraction. All this goes without saying when she has captivated you. But how was it that your arts didn't work ? Did your magic power lose its efficacy ? Did the evil genii steal your fairy wand ? Or was she protected by bands of bright spirits, who came in just at the wrong moment and overcame your charms ? You see, I have been to a spectacular play to-night and these things suggest themselves perforce."

Greyburn heard this ironical speech with strange feelings. What would Walter say if he knew of whom they were speaking ?

"You jest almost too much," he said, presently. "You see I am not in your mood."

"I see it has hit you hard," replied Walter, "but it will be sure to come out all right in time. When you get over your blueness a little you will go to the attack with renewed courage. It will be hard for me to believe a woman lives who can withstand you, when you really try. Tell me more about her."

"She is nineteen," said Greyburn, looking the lad in the eyes like one fascinated.

"Just the age."

"Fair-haired."

"The sweetest kind."

"An orphan."

"Excellent !"

"Poor."

"Best of all."

"And very beautiful." .

"So you said before. Well, Hector Greyburn, if you can't win a girl of that description to your will, you ought never to show your head at the Club again. An orphan, did you say ? Any old uncle or guardian about ?"

"Not a soul," said Greyburn, with startling distinctness. "Not a protector in the world. Nothing but her own strong sense and innate purity to guard her."

Would not Walter understand ? It seemed as if they had almost spoken the name.

"It's your lucky star !" cried the visitor. "Such chances only fall to those who are under the guidance of the beneficent planets. And you can't bend this girl ! *You* give her up ? *You ?*"

Could it be that this man was her brother ?

"Supposing," said Greyburn, very deliberately, "that I had fallen so deeply in love that I could not bear to think of profaning my idol ! Supposing that I had decided to offer her marriage !"

Walter burst into a wild laugh.

"I beg your pardon," he stammered, as soon as he could control himself. "It was d—d impolite, but if I was to die I couldn't help it."

"What would you say were I to tell you in sober

earnest that I shall do exactly that?" pursued Greyburn, entirely unruffled by the outburst.

"Why, what everybody would say!" cried Walter,
"if you'll excuse the expression; that you were a
fool!" He laughed again.

"Why!" persisted Greyburn.

" Haven't you told us a hundred times why? Must
I go on and reiterate to you your own arguments?
Marriage, the grave of love! The cursed compact
which ties two souls in lingering agony until blessed
death cuts the hated cord! The humdrum-life which
only idiots will consent to lead! Or shall I draw the
contrast, as you so often have done for me, between
that state and the blissful, ecstatic, etherealized loves
of the unwedded? Loves which can be broken at
will and resumed at pleasure! Loves like those of
the feathered songsters of the air, the variegated
flowers on the hillside, or the evening dews which
greet the summer grasses at sunset and hie away at
daybreak! Marriage, the miserable dregs of the
tapster's ale-barrel! Love, the champagne spark-
ling from the vaults of the Widow Cliquot! Why,
indeed!"

Greyburn recognized each of the expressions thrown
at him with such reckless audacity.

"Do you deny the truth of the lessons you have
taught your pupils?" laughed Walter, with a mock-
serious air. "Will the teacher tell his class that he
was wrong when he said that the earth was round,
and that it went every year of its life on a pleasure-
trip about the sun?"

Greyburn scarcely heard him. He was thinking
how much there was like Clara in the way he carried
his head. The eyes were the same. The hair a little
darker. The mouth—yes, there was the difference.
When Walter ceased to speak, his challenging words

seemed to come back like a dim echo, and the burden of them penetrated Greyburn's mind at last.

"You will perhaps admit," he said, "that if I have taught you wrongly, I ought to set you right now. Not by precept only but by example."

"And do you really seriously think of getting married?" asked Walter.

"If the woman I love will marry me."

"Oh, that's in doubt, is it?"

"Yes."

"She is poor, you say?"

"She is."

"With no expectations?"

"None."

"Does she know you have money?"

"She knows it all."

"Then she doesn't think you are in earnest," said Walter.

"She knows I am fearfully in earnest; that I would marry her to-night if she would let me."

"She hasn't refused you?"

"She has done just that."

"She will repent and change her mind."

"If I thought she wouldn't—" began Greyburn; and then added, with a look and tone which removed the last trace of doubt in Walter's mind, "No matter what I've said in the past, I mean what I say now. I shall quit—entirely, absolutely and forever—the life I have been leading."

Walter hesitated.

"Will you leave this house?"

"Most certainly."

"But—Nettie—Susanne—Gabrielle."

"I will think of those things by-and-bye. I am resolved to go. The detail I can arrange later."

"It quite startles me," said Walter. "I can't comprehend it. I only wish I was able to step in when you step out. If you sell the furnishings, save me a piece or two of bric-á-brac. By Jove! A happy thought! Commend me to Gabrielle." He broke into a snatch of song :

"I'm dying for some one to love me !"

" Are you ever serious ?" said Greyburn, looking at the young man with something indescribable in his eyes.

"Oh, don't you begin to preach !" cried Walter, with a little laugh. "Don't enter the pulpit just yet. If you're determined past all remedy to go to the dogs yourself, don't scold your friends quite so soon for following your old ways. Well, it's after two, and I must be going. Good-night."

"Good-night," replied Greyburn. He held the extended hand an instant longer than usual.

" I'll not speak to any one about what you've told me," said Walter. "You may let it out when you please. I shall still hope for your recovery. There is to be a meeting of the club next Thursday, you know. Don't throw that up as your parting act. It wouldn't leave a good impression. Think this matter all over—candidly and prayerfully, as they say—and, if you're still of the same mind, break it to us dramatically at the dinner. Put out your best wine and let us take leave of you in the correct style. And say ! Don't forget to speak to Gabrielle. I'm first, you know."

Greyburn went to his room, threw himself on a sofa and burst into tears.

Yes. He couldn't help it. It seemed so much as if Clara had been there—there in that house—which the gold of the Orient would not have induced him to let her enter even for a moment.

CHAPTER X.

WHEN Greyburn awoke the next morning he lay for an hour or more in bed, thinking. His intentions of reform were still strong in his mind and made the basis of his calculations ; but now more than a day had passed since he left Clara, and her influence was not quite so strong as yesterday. He still meant to leave his old associations, but there seemed no need of undue haste. He thought, on reflection, that he had better not be rash about it. Last night he would have sacrificed every dollar he had and have been quite content with an empty pocket and Clara Campbell's love. This morning it seemed to him that money was not so undesirable a thing after all, and that a fellow to whom fortune had given a share of it, ought to treat the gift with becoming respect. All his plans still centered in Clara, all his hopes were in her coming to like him after he had made himself what she would have him be. The difference in his mood was this. He was less under the control of excitement and more under that of ordinary reason.

He ate the eggs and coffee which Nettie brought him, and went down the street for a walk. Passing near his banker's he bethought himself of an errand there. Taking a check-book from his pocket he inserted figures for a small amount and passed the paper in to the cashier. That functionary turned to his ledger, then said :

" Your account is already overdrawn, sir, more than a thousand dollars."

" Impossible !" ejaculated Greyburn.

" There is no mistake, sir. See—June 20, four hundred and eighty dollars—June 26, eight hundred and seventy-six dollars—July 1, one thousand six hundred and twenty-five dollars —— "

"Let me see the checks," said Greyburn. The cashier brought them to him.

"Here they are, sir. You see they are all right, 'Pay to order of self—480–876.'"

Greyburn looked a good deal puzzled as he surveyed the checks and saw his signature so plainly written at the end of each. He could not remember ever having drawn or signed them, and the last two were dated while he was in the country, when he knew he had drawn no money.

"You see they are all right," repeated the cashier, for want of something else to say. It was quite evident from Greyburn's look that they were *not* all right.

"They all seem to be here," he said. "I must have forgotten some of them. Let me see—who came for the money?"

"A young man about twenty-one or twenty-two, who has been here for you before, drew some of them. Mr. Johnson ! You know that young man who drew the money on the check for Mr. Greyburn the other day. You spoke to him, you remember."

"Mr. Campbell ?" queried the person addressed.

"Yes, Mr. Campbell. He's a clerk at City Hall, I believe. Of course it's all right, sir."

"Oh, certainly !" said Greyburn, with perfect calmness. "I recollect now. It's not like me to overdraw. How much am I short ?"

"Just one thousand and thirty-seven dollars and twenty-six cents, sir."

"Very well. I'll turn some stocks and cover it in a day or two. I must have lost my reckoning."

It's no matter, I assure you," said the president of the bank, who had overheard the conversation from an adjacent desk, and now came forward with a smiling countenance. "Don't incommode yourself, I beg. Take your time, Mr. Greyburn; take your time."

"Thank you," said Greyburn. He walked out on the street, with the checks in his hand. Hailing a passing carriage, he drove straight to City Hall and entered the office where Walter Campbell sat writing.

"Can I see you alone for a few minutes?" he asked.

"Certainly," said Walter. "Here, step in this way." Then, when the door was closed, "You're looking better than you were last night, old fellow. I knew sleep would bring you around. Have you given up the crazy scheme you unfolded to me, or are you still determined to wreck your life on matrimonial shoals?"

"Do you see those checks?" demanded Greyburn, paying no attention to the young man's speech.

"Do I see them? I see something; yes, they are checks. Paid checks. Been through the bank," said Walter, taking them and eying them quizzically. "Like squeezed lemons. You couldn't raise much on them now."

"Who filled them out? Who wrote that name at the end? Who collected the amounts specified in the corners?" demanded Greyburn, getting out of temper.

"Well, I should say," said Walter, turning and holding one of the checks to the light, that the name at the end was 'H. Greyburn.' Not very clear, and yet tolerably distinct. I presume he could tell you all about them."

Greyburn gave a gesture of impatience.

"I've just come from the bank," he said, with rising voice, "and the cashier tells me you drew this money, two thousand eight hundred and twenty-five dollars. Do you deny it?"

"Does he say so?" queried Walter. "The cashier? What's his name, oh, yes! Mr. Stedman. He says that I drew this money, does he? Well, I would not like to dispute him if he is sure of it. These cashiers are pretty good at remembering, you know."

Greyburn was rather taken aback at this tacit confession, and still more so at the cool, unconcerned way in which young Campbell made it.

"Drop your nonsense, Walter," he said, "and tell me what this means. You have forged my name for two thousand eight hundred and twenty-five dollars and drawn the cash. Why did you do it? You knew I would have lent you money if you had asked for it, as I have so often done before. Why take and steal it behind my back? I did not think you were a thief," he added, becoming exasperated to see that Walter gave no sign of appreciating his position.

"Didn't you?" said Campbell, with a mocking smile. "Thanks for your good opinion, I'm sure. Wish I could return the compliment."

"What do you mean by that?" demanded Greyburn, advancing toward his companion. "Is it not enough to rob me without adding insult to it?"

Walter looked perfectly unmoved.

"No hard expressions, my friend, if you please. They won't settle a thing like this. If they would I could meet words with words. The place we are in is not the best one in the world, either, in which to come to an understanding. I called at your house last night on purpose to tell you about these checks and save you trouble at the bank. You were not feeling well, and so I passed it for the time. Let it go now until this evening and I will call up and explain it to your satisfaction."

"You will explain it, as you call it, now and here," said Greyburn, "or you will explain it to the Tombs judge. Say what you have to say quickly or I shall call an officer."

Walter laughed discordantly.

"If he takes me he'll take you, too," he said. "There'll be a pair of us. I'll take pot luck with you." Greyburn hesitated.

"Arrest me, would they?" he queried. "You for the forgery and me for being victimized, I suppose."

"Bah!" cried Walter, throwing off his mock levity. "Do you want me to talk? Shall I tell you why you don't dare have me arrested? Do you think I don't know all about you—how you've made your money—how you and Mendall have grown rich? Did you suppose I would be blind forever, a mere mole toiling in the earth to make it produce for you, and I get nothing?"

"I don't understand you," said Greyburn, coldly.

"No, I suppose not," replied Walter, ironically. "You wouldn't like to understand me. It would have suited you better if I had never understood you, either. But I have the secret now. I know as well as you or Mendall how to coin money at my will. I know more than either of you, for I now have both ends of the puzzle, and you will have neither unless I choose to give it to you. And to think that I have been drudging here at fifty dollars a week while you have spent your twenty thousand a year! You the prince—I the serf. You the giver of the feast—I the humble recipient of the crumbs that fall from your table. Have me arrested, will you? Try it on! By turning State's evidence against you I should be bailed, pardoned, and fêted like a king. Don't I know? A petty forgery of three thousand dollars against frauds of millions. Ha! ha! Why don't you call your officer?"

The angry look on Greyburn's face changed to an expressionless one as his companion continued his speech. He evidently did not know exactly what reply to make.

"You would have a nice time convicting *me* of

fraud," he said, after a pause. " I'm not the fool you do me the honor to think. No one can lay a finger on anything criminal in my career. Possibly I've taken advantage of situations, but never in a compromising way. However, Walter, we won't quarrel. Let the checks go. Only don't repeat it."

"You'd better call the officer," jeered Campbell. "You'll be sorry if you don't. It would be so exciting ! Think of the newspapers to-morrow, with big head-lines, ' Hector Greyburn Arrested—Frauds in the Millions !'"

"One would think I had been your worst enemy," cried Greyburn, the perspiration breaking out all at once on his forehead, "instead of a steadfast friend, always trying to get you advanced in position and ready to bear with every caprice. Walter, what has come over you lately ?"

"You'd better call the officer," repeated Campbell. "You said you'd call him. Why don't you ?"

"Enough of that !" said Greyburn. "I've said you are welcome to the value of the checks. Of course we must part after what has passed, but we'll part as friends. Go your own way and I'll go mine. If you were in the mood to listen to advice, I would give you some ; but you are not. Let me say only this—there are ways of doing certain things, and there are other ways. One way is safe, the other dangerous. In one way, a man may go on to fortune and never risk his liberty. In the other, the slighest misstep will send him behind the bars. I wish you well, Walter, upon my word I do. And all I have to say to you in parting is, ' Be cautious.' "

"Never you fear," replied the young man. "I understand the ropes now as well as the next one. I'll take *my* turn at ease and luxury. Fine houses, fast horses, rich wines and pretty women will suit me as well as another. I've been stifling in boarding-house quarters long enough. I've counted my cash for the last time to see whether I could afford an opera box or a *petit souper* for two. Now I am made. The doors of fortune are open to me. It is just as easy as saying it. On the whole, I'd just as lief you *wouldn't* call an officer. My liberty even for a week would be worth too much to me now."

"Walter," said Greyburn, whose mind became lost on Clara again, "I wish I might talk to you a little before I go."

"Say what you please," said Walter, very much mollified. "I'll listen."

"I've trod the path you are entering," pursued Greyburn, "for fourteen years. I entered it a boy and I am now almost thirty-three years old. I have had all that money could bestow. I need not tell you the life I have led. What I wish to say is, I would give half the days I have left to blot out those which I have wasted—worse than wasted—since fortune found me. Pleasure is not everything. Gratification of each desire is not all that a man wants to make him happy. There will come a time, my boy, when an unquiet conscience will make all your pleasures seem as naught. That time has come for me. Walter, you are young. The world is before you. You have talents. Let me advise you to live in such a way that you will never look back upon any act with shame and sorrow."

Walter closed his eyes in mock solemnity.

"We will close with the benediction," he said, laughing. "Greyburn, it is quite providential. You have lived this gay life, and now wish to step out of it. I haven't lived it, and I wish very much to step in. You got your funds in a way which your conscience will not allow you to continue to practice. I will get mine in the same way, having no conscience to trouble me. It is excellent. You will dispose of your house, because it is associated with deeds which you desire to efface from your memory. I will buy it, because I purpose entering the same road that you are leaving. You would throw Annie, Nettie, Susanne, and that seraphic Gabrielle out on the cold, cold world. *Tres bien!* I will take them all. If there were a hundred I would take them. Your taste has never been impeached. Pass everything over to me for so much cash—all in a lump, as it were. Pull down the old sign, put up the new : " Walter Campbell—successor to Hector Greyburn. Business Carried on as Usual at the Old Stand.' "

Walter paused to break into a laugh which lasted for nearly a minute.

"Greyburn," he went on, when he could catch his breath, " I forgive you. Upon my soul I do ! Everything—that threat to call the officer, and all. I will be magnanimous with my predecessor. You say you've tried it and it has palled on you. Well, I'll try it too. As you say, we won't quarrel. That little matter of the checks was not strictly *en regle*, but it was all right, after all. We had been business partners— Mendall, you and I—and you didn't divide fair with me. The little amount I raised on your credit doesn't settle it, either, but we'll let it go at that. I shall soon have enough to supply all my wants. There is a big scheme on foot—the biggest yet—and I am solid on every detail of it from beginning to end. I could sell the information outright for enough to buy your house and furniture and put a deposit into the bank big enough to keep me going a year. It's a regular bonanza. I don't mind telling you, as you are going out of the trade, but I don't say where it is, and nobody else who could tell would tell. Oh ! I'll fix myself up in a few months, old fellow ! I'm going to live for a little while—live like a lord !"

It was of no use talking to him, Greyburn felt that,

and they parted. One all elation, the other more de-
pressed than ever.

Crossing the square, Greyburn met Jacob Mendall.
He drew that individual into a neighboring restaurant, and sought a private room upstairs.

"The game's up with young Campbell," he said,
the moment the door was closed. "He's got the
whole thing through his head and proposes to go it
alone—or at least independent of us—hereafter. I
don't care for myself, as I had determined to quit
anyhow, but the boy will certainly go to the devil if
he follows the ideas which he has got, and I wish
something might be done to stop him."

Mr. Mendall received this intelligence in blank dismay.

"How the mischief did he get on to it?" he said,
after a stupid pause.

"I don't know, but he's got on, sure. The worst
thing likely to happen is, that with his juvenile im-
petuosity he will give the whole thing away in a
short time and make trouble for you. You'd better
see him, Jacob, and try what influence you have on
him. I think you might scare him out. But you'd
better do just as I shall, drop the business from now
on. You've made money enough and so far you've
been safe."

Mr. Mendall's cunning face did not brighten much
at this proposition.

"I shall *have* to give it up, if it is as you say," he
said. "That boy is a perfect mule, and if he's got it
into his head that he can get along without us, nothing will turn him."

They talked for half an hour longer upon the subject, and when they separated, Mr. Mendall said, "I
think I won't go near him. It would do no good.
Cuss the luck! Whoever thought he would tumble
on to it!"

Greyburn took a carriage for home, and Jacob Mendall went out and met Walter as he left the City Hall for his two-o'clock lunch. In the same room where he had talked with Greyburn, Mendall set himself to convincing Campbell that their interests were identical. For a while Walter proved obstinate, but at last he made a partial concession :

"I tell you what I will do, Jacob, rather than have any falling out with you. I'll give you one-third and keep two-thirds myself. I could make better terms with plenty of men about town, but there may be an advantage in keeping things as quiet as possible. You must not forget one thing—I've had nothing out of all that's been made in the last three years. It's my turn now for a while."

Mendall assented to this with not a very good grace, and both rose to go.

"Don't forget the dinner Thursday night, probably the last we'll get at Greyburn's," added Walter. "I suppose he told you he was going to become virtuous. Speak to any of the fellows you see, for we want a nice party."

"All right ; good-day," said Mendall, graciously. But he felt like a man outwitted, and did not intend to let this boy beat him to the end without a struggle.

———◆———

CHAPTER XI.

THURSDAY night came ; that Thursday night when the final dinner given by Hector Greyburn to his jolly companions was to be celebrated ; that Thursday night which was to witness his closing hours as a man of the world, and immediately precede his entering upon a career of virtue and uprightness.

Greyburn stood in his reception room and welcomed

the guests as they arrived. He bore their good-natured railleries as a host should do; he smiled at each sally of alleged wit, and joined—mayhap a little absently—in each laugh which was raised. But his mind was elsewhere. He played his part, but his heart was away out in the little village of Springdale, where, under a humble cottage roof, reposed the one in all this world who had charm for him now.

All were finally gathered at the table. The dinner—never better—was disposed of. The wines and cigars were brought.

"Gentlemen," said Greyburn, when it became time for him to speak, " this is probably the last time we shall ever sit at dinner together. I expect to sell this house and move away from New York. The reasons which actuate me are known to some of you, and *I* have no scruples in telling them to the others who do not know. For almost fourteen years I have lived what is called a life of pleasure. It has lost its charms for me within the past two weeks. I shall retire into the country and devote the balance of my days to undoing what I have done during the previous part of my life."

Walter Campbell burst into one of his long and irresistible laughs. The rest of the company tried to frown him down at first, but peal followed peal until it became contagious, and in a few moments the drollery of the affair seemed to possess all present.

"I beg ten million pardons," gasped Walter, with his first breath, "but it's so dreadfully funny, you know. So like a prayer meeting. It's hard to believe that he's in earnest. I expect every minute to have him own up that it's all a sell and that he's only been play-ing a trick on us. The idea of *him* preaching! The idea of it's being *him* who is going to repent and be saved, and we minor sinners who are left to destruc-tion ! It's really quite too comical !"

Greyburn's brow contracted a little. Had he not been playing the part of a host he might have replied angrily. The occurrence of the forgery was too recent to have lost much of its insolence. Things which Greyburn would not ordinarily have noticed grated on him at this time.

"Mr. Campbell is disposed to be humorous," was all he said.

"But there *is* an odd side to it, you know," put in Mendall, who was inclined, for business reasons, to keep on the right side of Walter.

"In what way?" asked Greyburn.

"Why, it's a love disappointment, of course, that's at the bottom of it all. Nothing else would set you so agog. Now it would be my way, in a case like that, to let the matter drop and try elsewhere. That is, if I were sure I could not succeed in the first place. This going to the dogs for one woman, more or less, is not what I should expect of you, Mr. Greyburn."

"I'm not going to the dogs," said Greyburn, a little irritated. "I shall *quit* ' going to the dogs.' That's the difference."

"Depends on how you figure it, I suppose," said Mr. Middleby. "When I was a young fellow I got into a faro bank one evening and lost all I had ; only a few hundred dollars, but a good deal to me. What did I do? I waited until I got another hundred and tried it again. I lost that too. The third time I had a change of luck and broke the bank, coming out with fifteen thousand dollars in my pocket. Did I go back to faro playing after that? Not I. The time to quit is when you've won. Now, if it were a case like that which Mendall hints at, I wouldn't quit until I had succeeded. That's the true policy. Stop when your luck is at the full, and not when it is at the ebb, and may be just turning. Luck is like the tides—it will flow both ways, only give it time enough."

Walter Campbell nodded, with a wise air.

"He's right, Greyburn. 'There is a tide in the affairs of men,' you know. But, after all, you've had your share of life. Why should you go on absorbing all the good things forever? It's better that you step out in this magnanimous way and give some other poor fellow a chance. When you are gone the field will be open, and we can all try for the prizes."

Greyburn sipped a goblet of wine and did not look toward his voluble and over-free guest. He really had begun to hate him.

"Come, gentlemen," broke in Mr. Clarence Perkyns, "this is dull music. We are not here to criticise our friend. As Bolton would say, 'We come to bury Cæsar, not to praise him.' However we may feel in our minds regarding his intentions, it is not the part of courtesy to air our opinions here. We ought rather to make a jolly ending of an association which has been so pleasant to us all. This good wine should be supplemented with bright sayings and good stories."

"Bravo! Bravo!" cried several guests from the lower end of the table.

"My idea exactly," chimed in Walter Campbell. "I never did go in for serious things. That is why Greyburn's first speech this evening set me off into a roar. I know him so well, you see. He could tell us the tales, if he would. All the Decamerons and Heptamerons together would not parallel his adventures. He ought to write an autobiography. It would sell like wildfire. Do it, Greyburn! Put in places, names and everything. Then give me the copyright, and, by the memory of De Montespan, I'll never ask a cent while I live, beyond the profits of it."

The room rang with plaudits, and the glasses rang with the blows showered upon them.

"No doubt I could write some interesting things," said Greyburn, with a muffled sneer in his tone, "but perhaps the suits for libel would make a hole in the receipts. Some very respectable names might get tangled into the narration."

"By Gad!" cried Walter, "there ought to be a law against libels in such a case. Every one should take his own risk and the devil the rearmost, say I. 'Let the galled jade wince,' you know. What a country this is! There are laws giving a man the right to hunt every kind of game during certain seasons, except the most entrancing of all. That is barred the year round. It's a d—d shame."

The speaker dashed a glass of brandy into his throat as if to take out the unpleasant taste, and Greyburn felt his detestation growing stronger than ever.

"I'm still of my opinion," said Mr. Middleby. "A man ought not to quit anything when his luck is against him. It must turn. 'Back to the charge,' is the motto to be followed. But perhaps I am wrong, Mr. Greyburn, in supposing that you are quitting under such circumstances."

"No, you're not wrong," put in Walter, before Greyburn could open his mouth to reply. The brandy was telling upon his tongue as usual. "He's told me all about it. The fact is, he met his match during his last visit into the country. It broke him all up. He never'll try again. He's going as a missionary to China now. All the money he's got he'll put in the conscience fund. By Gad! if I had a mind, gentlemen ——"

"*Will* you shut up!" whispered Jacob Mendall in his ear. "Don't you see you are going too far?"

"Why, what am I afraid of?" cried Walter, rising. "Of him? Do you think you can muzzle me? You'd better have a care, Jacob. By Gad, I'll let you out too, the next thing you know."

Everybody looked at Greyburn, who forced a

cheerful expression through the dark clouds which had gathered upon his face.

"Please be seated all," he said, noticing that nearly every guest was upon his feet in anticipation of imminent hostilities. "Our impetuous young friend doubtless forgets the time and place."

"So I did," ejaculated Walter, pausing a moment to catch the idea. "And you're the prince of fellows, Greyburn, to put it in that way. I'm a fool, and only such a man as you would ever have got along with me. Gentlemen, I drink his health."

The health was drunk in silence. The proceedings had not added to the festivities of the evening. To Greyburn the apology was, if anything, more disagreeable than the affront. The familiar air with which the young man treated him had become particularly distasteful. Still he sacrificed everything to his duty as a host, inwardly thankful that this could never occur again.

"But do you really intend to live 'a life of perfect virtue?'" queried Middleby, with a smile.

"I do," said Greyburn, soberly.

"And—pardon me—is this at the end of a career during which you have never been disappointed in achieving the woman you sought? I don't wish to be too personal, but you know there are privileges which we always take with each other around this board."

"I never attempted to win any woman from virtue and failed, if that is what you mean," replied Greyburn. "Mr. Campbell seems to have misunderstood me, but, be that as it may, I am the one now asked the question and I have answered it."

The whole tenor of the conversation disturbed him, and he longed for the hour when his guests would depart.

"You have offered a wager, often, we all know," put in Mendall, who had recovered his serenity since

Campbell had relapsed into silence, "that we could not name a woman whom you could not win."

"Time and again," said Greyburn, wearily. "In any sum you pleased."

"Has that offer ever been withdrawn?" asked Middleby, cautiously.

"Withdrawn!" echoed Greyburn, a little of the old light coming into his eyes. "Withdrawn? It were not well hinted, Mr. Middleby, that Hector Greyburn made offers and then withdrew them. No, the offer has always stood, these eight years past. Why did you ask if it were ever withdrawn?"

"Because," said Mr. Middleby, slowly, and weighing each word as he spoke, "because I wish to take it up."

"You jest!" cried Greyburn. "In another hour all such thoughts are to be banished from me. You are not serious."

"He has taken your offer, Greyburn," put in Mendall, "and is entitled to fair usage. If you decline to accept, there is no law to compel you, but it is not like you to do a thing of that sort. Mr. Middleby states that he is ready. I really do not see how you can escape."

Greyburn looked at Mendall sharply. He then glanced up and down the lines of men at his table, and saw that all held the same opinion. "At the worst," he thought to himself, "it is only to lose a little money. Probably the sum to be wagered will not be large."

"Oh," he said, haughtily, as Mendall finished, "I don't wish to escape. I thought it odd to propose a thing like this an hour before the time when you knew I had decided to change the whole course of my life. There are strong reasons, which I cannot explain, why I object to altering my plans, but my last act with you shall not be a craven one. Prepare your papers. In what sum do you wish the wager made?"

"Fifty thousand dollars," said Mr. Middleby.

Greyburn was visibly startled at the figure. He saw in an instant that more than the broker were in the affair, and the blood began to rise to his brain. It was a plot, then, was it, to fleece him out of a large sum of money while sitting at his table and enjoying his hospitality? His resolutions, his love, his intentions for the morrow, vanished with the rapidity of thought. The Greyburn of the last few days was gone. The Greyburn of the ten preceding years had returned. He turned to Mr. Middleby with an air that was almost gay.

"I accept your proposal, sir, and will take care that you never see your money again. I am sorry to say that I shall be obliged, however, to ask your indulgence for a couple of days, as I have not the sum you mention in bank. It will, in fact, compel me to part with some of my real estate, as my method of living has never allowed me to accumulate a large fortune. I do not speak of this with regret, as I intend to sell everything I own in New York within a short time. If you desire, I will put up five thousand dollars in city bonds to-night as a pledge of the rest. I assure you I am only too desirous to complete the wager."

"I am very sorry," said Middleby, "but I had arranged to start to-morrow for a six-months' trip to Europe. Unless the matter can be arranged to-night, I do not see what I can do about it."

Greyburn thought he saw in these words an intention of withdrawal, and became more and more determined to revenge himself on those who had tried to take this large sum from him.

"When did you decide upon this European trip?" he inquired, with a touch of irony in his tone,"

" More than a week ago," replied Middleby. "Do you doubt me? Here, I will show you the tickets."

"No, no!" interposed Greyburn, refusing to examine them. "Of course I believe you. We are all of good intent, but what can we do?"

"What is this house worth?" inquired Mendall, as if the matter had just occurred to him.

"I suppose about thirty thousand dollars," said Greyburn. "Why?"

"And the contents?"

"You mean the furniture," cried Walter Campbell. "You forget Gabrielle. She is part of the contents. Don't include her. I want a chance to bid on that article, myself."

"Perhaps ten thousand dollars more," said Greyburn, paying no attention to this interpolation. "That is, they cost me that. They wouldn't bring so much, now, probably."

"If you would take thirty-five thousand dollars for the whole," said Mendall, " I will send out for a conveyancer and you can transfer them to me at once for cash. That would enable you to close the wager to-night. I don't see any other way."

Greyburn looked around the room, and his thoughts traveled rapidly over the house. It had been his home so long. Hours he had then esteemed the brightest of his life, he had passed there. As he saw them going from him, the walls took on a new beauty. Then he looked again at Middleby, at Mendall and at Campbell. There was no escape. They had hedged him in.

"Call your conveyancer," he said. "Excuse me till he comes." And he left the room.

The wager became the subject of conversation among the little knots which gathered in corners, the table being abandoned by everybody. " Middleby's a fool." "No, he isn't, he knows what he's about,"

"Greyburn will win," and similar remarks were heard in all directions.

Jacob Mendall took Walter Campbell by the arm and led him to a window opening upon a balcony. They stepped outside.

"In half an hour," said the older man, "these premises will be mine."

"What's that to me?" cried Walter, impetuously. "You know it has been the desire of my heart to own this place myself. It is just what I want. Just the cage for the birds I mean to have, and half full now of the sweetest ones imaginable. The place is of no use to you, while to me it would be worth everything."

"Would you really care so much for it?" said Mendall, with affected surprise. "Well, that's easily arranged. Only use me fair in the business we are in and I will make this crib over to you the first minute you get the money to take it."

"Will you?" cried Walter, in ecstacy.

"To be sure. I'll even do more than that. I'll install you at once as a free tenant until you are able to buy it, or as long as our relations are amicable. I only took the house to help Greyburn out of his difficulty. I don't want it for myself, and if you do, it's the best thing in the world that I've got hold of it."

Vowing that Mendall should never lose anything by his kindness, Walter proceeded with him to the library, where a well-known real estate lawyer was examining a lot of old deeds and papers.

"Everything seems to be all right here," he said, as Mendall entered. "Mr. Greyburn gets his deed from old Marples, whose titles were perfection itself. I can't say, of course, whether there have been any mortgages or attachments on the premises since Mr. Greyburn bought them, but otherwise they are all sound and right."

"Oh, I'll risk the mortgages," smiled Mendall.

" Mr. Greyburn is too honorable a man to leave any doubt on that score." Then, turning to Middleby, he whispered, " I had it looked up to-day."

The deed of the real estate and a bill of sale of the furnishings were signed and witnessed, and Mr. Mendall paid over his check for them as agreed. This being done, the conveyancer withdrew.

" And now," said Mr. Middleby, " for the referee, and the writings. Have you any choice for referee, Mr. Greyburn ?"

" Mr. Perkyns will be agreeable to me," was the reply.

" The very name I should have proposed," said Middleby, not a little vexed, nevertheless, that he could not find an excuse to change the name to that of Jacob Mendall, whom he had supposed would of course be selected. " Mr. Perkyns, will you please take these writing materials and draw up the document ?"

Mr. Perkyns had done this sort of thing before, and proceeded to his task without hesitation.

" Let us understand everything before I begin to write," said he. " The wager is to be for fifty thousand dollars a side."

" Yes," assented Middleby.

" And that sum from each of you is to be put into my hands, the joint amount to be paid by me to whichever I shall decide is entitled to it under the terms of the contract."

" Exactly."

" The wager really runs from you, Mr. Middleby, as you are placed in the position of betting that Mr. Greyburn cannot win over a certain woman whom you will name, within a given length of time. Now, what shall be the time allowed ? That is very important."

Mr. Middleby hesitated to reply. Greyburn hesitated also. The referee turned to the assembled guests.

"What do you say, gentlemen ? What would be a fair time ?"

"Half an hour ?" ventured Walter Campbell.

Everybody laughed.

"Shall we call it a year ?" said Mr. Perkyns.

"A year ?" cried Walter. "To win over one woman ! How long was the Son of the Morning, when he drew after him the seventh part of the children of light ? No woman who lives could withstand Hector Greyburn a year. Give Middleby *some* chance."

"Mr. Middleby is to stay in Europe six months," suggested Greyburn, impatient at Walter's interruptions. "Let that be the time. Then, when he returns, he can call for the amount in your hands—that is, if he wins it."

The sarcasm in the last few words decided Mr. Middleby, who said that six months would suit him very well if it was satisfactory to his opponent.

"There is but one thing more, then," said the referee, "and that is—the proof."

"The proof ?" repeated Greyburn.

"Precisely."

"I do not understand you."

"Why, how am I to be satisfied at the end of the six months who has won the bet ? How shall I know to whom to pay this money ?"

"I supposed," Greyburn replied, haughtily, "that my word would answer for that."

"Well, hardly," replied Mr. Perkyns, while Middleby and Mendall shook their heads decidedly.

"Quite out of the question," said Mendall.

"What is it to you ?" said Greyburn, rather warmly. "It's not your bet. Mr. Middleby won't say, I'll venture, that he'll dispute my word."

"But this is not the way bets are decided," interposed the referee. "There must be some proof, outside of the word of either of the parties interested, be they ever so honorable. Mine will be a delicate position. There will be no appeal from my decision. It is most important, therefore, that the proof shall be complete. You gentlemen must agree on that point, as I do not care to decide it for you, possibly to your subsequent dissatisfaction."

There was a pause, and then Mr. Middleby ventured: "If the referee is satisfied that the parties have passed the night together in the same chamber with the consent of the lady, that will satisfy me. I realize the unreasonableness of asking for more."

"Will that suit Mr. Greyburn?" asked Perkyns.

Greyburn thought a moment and then said, "Yes."

Mr. Perkyns took his pen, and in a few minutes produced the following:

"The undersigned, residents of the city and county of New York, do each deposit with Clarence Perkyns, Esq., the sum of fifty thousand dollars, upon the following conditions:

"If, on or before the sixth day of January, 18—, at twelve o'clock, noon, the undersigned, Hector Greyburn, shall satisfy the said Perkyns that he, the said Greyburn, has occupied during one night the same chamber with ——, by the free and full consent of the said ——, then the said Perkyns shall pay to the said Greyburn the joint sums so deposited with him, viz.: the sum of one hundred thousand dollars. In case the said Greyburn shall not so satisfy the said Perkyns, then the said sum of one hundred thousand dollars shall be paid to the undersigned, Otis W. Middleby.

"To all these stipulations the undersigned set their hands and seals, and also agree that the decision of the said Perkyns in the matter described shall be final, and that this shall be his release from all claims whatsoever arising out of his actions in the premises."

" Is that satisfactory ?" asked Mr. Perkyns.

Both gentlemen assented and signed their names.

" Now, when you have placed the money in my hands," he continued, " I will insert the name which Mr. Middleby will give me. But first, for the witnesses."

" Mr. Mendall can witness for me if he pleases," said Middleby.

" And Mr. Campbell ?" asked Mr. Perkyns, turning to Greyburn.

" No, not he !" cried Middleby, almost with a scream.

" Why not ?" said Walter, turning black in the face. " Why not, I'd like to know ?"

" Let him sign !" whispered Mendall in Middleby's ear. " What are you thinking of to interrupt like that ! You'll spoil all."

" I consent," said Mr. Middleby, paling under the fire of the eyes which were turned on him.

" I will pay you for this," said Campbell, as he finished writing his name. " There will be a place where I can do so, if not here. My blood is not the kind which allows insult heaped upon it. I will see you elsewhere, Mr. Otis Middleby."

The broker did not reply, though he was visibly disturbed. Mendall tried in vain to rally him, but he grew no better, and presently muttering that he was a trifle faint, he walked to one of the open windows. In a moment he was recalled by the voice of the referee asking for the name of the lady with which to fill the vacancy.

Middleby's hand shook like an aspen when he drew the name from his pocket, written on a piece of white cardboard. He looked at Mendall for help, and that gentleman said :

"Of course the name must be known only to the parties in interest. That is reasonable. I would suggest that even the referee had better not know it at present. Let Mr. Middleby write it in the blank space and show it to Mr. Greyburn. Then Mr. Perkyns can seal it up without inspecting it and will not need to examine the document until one party calls on him to claim a forfeit."

"I am satisfied," said Perkyns. "I have no curiosity in the matter, and, in fact, would rather not know who the lady is. What say you, Mr. Greyburn?"

Greyburn would have objected to the plan had any ground for so doing presented itself, merely because Mendall proposed it. Within the last two hours he had learned to hate him as well as the rest of them. It seemed incredible that he could ever have liked the society of such creatures. He consented to Mendall's proposition.

Middleby took a pen and went across the room to put the document on another table. It was only with the greatest difficulty that he could hold his hand steady enough to write. After a little, however, he inserted the name, and leaving it there for Greyburn to see, crossed to the opposite side of the room.

Greyburn sauntered carelessly to where the document lay. He had little curiosity about the name. What did it matter to him what particular form of combined consonants and vowels might be there written out. But when he glanced at the writing, he turned whiter than the marble on which it rested. For an instant lights danced before his eyes and he respired with difficulty. He grasped the paper in one hand, closing his fingers upon it with a dim idea that he could hold his secret from the rest if he became unconscious. It was but an instant, however.

In a second more he recovered and turned to his guests, most of whom had been astonished witnesses of his emotion.

"I have signed," he said, huskily, "and I shall win the wager. Good-night, gentlemen."

Slowly the guests departed.

The name on the paper was, "CLARA CAMP-BELL."

CHAPTER XII.

A WEEK after the events narrated in the preceding chapter Walter Campbell was sole master of Hector Greyburn's late city residence. The property stood on the books of the registry of deeds in the name of Mr. Jacob Mendall, but that honest gentleman had installed Walter upon the premises in the character of lessee, and had also furnished him with a reasonable, and even liberal allowance of pocket money with which to support his new dignity. Mr. Mendall was at first well satisfied with the course affairs were taking. The potent springs under whose touch gold had been wont to flow so plentifully were now in his hands. Walter had been only too willing to exchange the information which he possessed for the pottage of a temporary lease of the house and the sum requisite to keep it up. There was a sort of understanding that the profits were to be equitably divided in the end, but Mendall determined to put the day of reckoning far off into the future. As long as he could keep Walter amused with baubles and trinkets the young man would not be likely to make trouble.

The wager with Greyburn added also to his satisfaction. As has doubtless been suspected, Mendall had the heaviest share in the venture of which Mr.

Middleby was apparently the sole owner. By an accidental meeting with the landlord of the Springdale House, who was an old acquaintance of his, Mendall had learned that Greyburn had visited Miss Campbell, and had left the village in the deepest despondency. Further investigation into the young lady's character convinced him that here lay the opportunity which he had long sought to make a wager with Greyburn. Not liking to have it appear that he was seeking to make money out of his quondam partner, Mendall made use of Middleby as a cat to save his chestnuts from burning. The crafty banker believed that he had made sure of his wager. That Clara was of a high order of purity he had made sure by the testimony of several persons who had known her from infancy. Then, she was Walter's sister ; Walter, the impetuous, whose fiery temper would stand as a menace to Greyburn, he knowing well that in case of harm happening to the sister, the brother would more than likely require his life in answer. Besides this, Mendall was convinced that Greyburn was sincere in his intention to leave all his old habits and associations. Fourteen years of acquaintance with him had convinced the banker that his word was to be relied upon. There seemed every reason to believe that even for the sum of fifty thousand dollars Hector Greyburn would not turn back from any path upon which he had determined to enter.

Of the half-dozen fair creatures whom Walter found in the house, only one of them—Gabrielle—could be persuaded to remain after he took possession. This gushing young creature seemed to transfer her affections from Greyburn to Campbell as easily as Greyburn transferred the real estate to Mendall.

"You loved Hector yesterday," said Walter, with a look of mock reproachfulness.

"Ah, yes !" sighed Gabrielle, winding her fair arms

around his neck, "but that was so long ago! I love you now—you and you alone."

And he believed her.

In some respects Gabrielle was pleased at the change. Walter was more easily managed than Hector. Almost every hour, when not compelled to be at his desk at City Hall, he was by her side. He came home at four every day. Generally they went for a ride in the Park. Evenings were often spent at the theatre, followed by supper at Delmonico's or in their own cosy apartments.

Hector had been a cold lover of late. Walter was devotion itself. As for the rest, Gabrielle was not of a nature to mind the difference.

"I would be quite content now," said Walter to Mendall, "but for the slavery of six hours a day at that miserable desk. I wonder if we could not find the right sort of a man to put there and relieve me."

"Impossible!" was Mendall's very positive rejoinder. "There is a thorn to every rose, my boy, and this is yours. If we were to put some one else there—provided we succeeded in doing it, which is not certain—we should run the risk of wrong information and perhaps get ruined in one operation. Or, again, our clerk might get a notion into his head that he could run the business on his own hook—as another one did—and I should have to get *him* a house and sweetheart. So we might go on, with never a rest. No, my dear boy, you must bear the few hours of treadmill and trust to Gabrielle's smiles to repay you when you reach home."

Gabrielle's smiles were all right, but they began before long to cost Mendall a good deal of money. She developed a *penchant* for diamonds and other jewels, which kept Walter busy calling upon his patron for funds. Walter would not have questioned her right to the Koh-i-nor, had she demanded it, but

Mendall felt obliged to protest. This led to some scenes, Walter declaring that he would have more money or dissolve the partnership, and Mendall expostulating, only to make a whole or partial concession at last. Gabrielle put out her lily-white hand for all the money she could get Walter to give her, and it disappeared with magic swiftness.

"My angel," he would say, "where is the thousand dollars which I gave you last week?"

"I don't know, pet," she would respond. "Only I'm sure it's all gone. I can't spend the same money twice, you know."

And Jacob would have to find another thousand, which would go as rapidly as the first.

It was not long before the banker himself began to fall under the witching powers of the fair girl. Under the pretense of business, he got to calling upon her in the morning after Walter left the house, and soon found it hard to leave much before it was time for the young man to return in the afternoon. Williams, the observant colored man who officiated as steward-of-the-household, remarked that the same lovely creature who tripped to the hall door at nine o'clock in her white breakfast wrapper and showered her passionate kisses on the lips of her younger lover, met the elder one half-an-hour later at the head of the stairs and permitted him, not unwillingly, to touch her soft cheek with his bearded mouth. It was not the steward's business, and he was wisely content to notice but not comment.

There was soon a very good understanding between Gabriel and Mendall. She knew that he was the source from whence the money came, and deemed it best to be on the right side in case there should ever be a crash.

One day when they sat tete-a-tete in Gabrielle's boudoir, Williams knocked at the door.

"There's a man down below," he said, as she responded, "who is determined to see Mr. Greyburn, whom he will not believe has left here. What can I do about it? I don't like to call a policeman, as he looks honest enough."

"What kind of man?"

"Well, a rough fellow, a laborer or something of that sort. He won't do any harm, but he is set on staying until he can see Mr. Greyburn, and all I can say won't move him."

"I'll go," said Gabrielle, and like a bird she flew down the steps to where the man stood waiting.

"You wish to see Mr. Greyburn?" she asked, eying the man with interest.

"Yes," said the stranger, "an' I sha'n't leave till I do see him." This was spoken earnesly, but with perfect politeness of manner.

"But he has left here."

"Excuse me," said the visitor. "I must see him."

"You look like a sane man," said Gabrielle, "and should exercise reason. Mr. Greyburn has sold this house and removed from the city. Where he has gone I do not know. If you doubt me you can go to Mr. Brown, the grocer, or Mr. Jones, the provision dealer, who used to supply him with goods, and they will tell you the same thing."

The man colored a bit.

"Excuse me ag'in, he said, "if I doubt ye. I know Mr. Greyburn. I know he lives here. I know yer face, too; I've seen ye out ridin' together."

"But not for several months," said the girl, nowise abashed. "Not since last June."

"My name's John Dinsmore," said the stranger. "Mr. Greyburn has seen me afore. I've only a few words to say to him. I'm not an eddicated man—not a polished one—I don't claim to be what they call a gentleman. Fer all that, I know there's respect due to a woman, an' I'm tryin' to show that respect to you. But I can tell ye, if ye'll let me, why I'm sure that Mr. Greyburn hasn't moved from this house."

"Why?" said Gabriel.

"Because you're here."

"That is a strange reason," said Gabrielle. "I was not his servant."

"No," said Dinsmore, looking her full in the eye, "you are his—I beg pardon—at least, if he'd gone ye'd 'a' gone with him."

"Are you ready to go now?" said Gabrielle, smilingly.

"Not till I've seen the man I asked fer."

"Well, Mr. Dinsmore," said the fair creature, with a laugh like the trill of a robin, "if you are determined to stay, please step upstairs and make yourself at home. William! Open the shutters in the parlor, please." She added in a lower tone, "Tell Mr. Mendall to wait in the boudoir, and if he hears any disturbance to come to my rescue." Then, laughing all the way, she led Dinsmore to the parlor and offered him a chair.

"You are a curious man," she said, as he refused to take it. "Can't you accept the word of a lady, or would you rather search the house? I tell you again, Mr. Greyburn has sold this place and gone away."

"If he's gone," said the blacksmith, measuring his words slowly, "why do ye remain? If he's sold this house, why are ye in it? Surely you were his——"

"Sweetheart?" suggested Gabrielle, as he seemed to pause.

"Yes. He was your lover. Isn't it so?"

"Certainly," said the girl. "He *was* my lover, as you say. But that was two months ago. He is gone now, and it is unlikely that I shall ever see him again."

She smiled and showed her pearly teeth.

"Is that the way city folks love?" said Dinsmore, rather to himself than to her. "If you stick to it that he isn't here, I must go. But let me leave a message for him, and it's this: 'If he harms a hair o' Clara Campbell's head I'll kill him the first time we meet as I would a wolf!'"

The man's voice was not raised above his usual tone nor was he unduly excited. But he seemed very much in earnest, and she had no doubt that he meant every word he said.

"Who is this Clara Campbell?" inquired Gabrielle, with suddenly aroused interest.

"He knows," said Dinsmore, doggedly. An' he knows her brother Walter. One he's ruined, or will ruin, but he sha'n't touch the other. If he does, God witness fer me, it'll be his death!"

"How do you know these people?" asked the girl, "and what is your interest in them?"

"How do I know 'em, miss? Why, ever sence they was little bits o' babies I've knowed 'em. I've seen 'em grow up, hansum an' strong. I've seen Walter start off to York with the bloom o' innocence on his cheek. I've seen him sence with the flush o' liquor on him, reelin' into a carriage at midnight. I've seen Clara go her way singin' to her school, loved by every child an' every man an' woman in Springdale. I've seen this Greyburn there, bewitchin' her with his di'monds, horses an' fine clothes, an' his smooth tongue. Her father died long ago. Her mother sleeps beside him in the little churchyard. Who is thar to look arter her, miss? I owe it to the DEAD to see that no harm comes to her, an' I mean to do it."

Gabrielle could not help being affected by the sadness of the speaker's manner.

"Do you think this girl is in danger from Mr. Greyburn?" she said.

"Do I think—?" he began. "What do *you* think? Is he a fit companion fer a virtuous woman? Forgive me, miss, if my words seem to reflect on ye; but tell me, is that man the sort you'd like to see with *yer* sister, if ye have one?"

Gabrielle's lips formed themselves into a little pout.

"Every woman must judge for herself in such things," she said. "If your Miss Campbell is not able to take care of herself, I fear your kind guardianship over her will be wasted."

"Oh, he'll never ruin her in any fair way," said Dinsmore. "She was too well taught by her mother for that. What I fear is that she'll let him get on such terms that he can take her at a disadvantage." Then he added, pleadingly: "But surely, miss, ye wouldn't wish Mr. Greyburn to ruin this young lady. Ye'd help me in gettin' him to quit her acquaintance."

Gabrielle tapped her dainty foot inpatiently on the hassock where it rested.

"You really forget," she said, "what I have told you. I have not seen Mr. Greyburn for many weeks, and never expect to again."

"You quarrelled then?"

"We did not."

"Why did ye part?"

"Because he was going away."

"And wouldn't take you?"

"I didn't ask him to. I stayed with the house. Went with the furniture. The new owner took me at an appraisal. Don't you see?"

Gabrielle laughed sweetly and softly, and Dinsmore, partially convinced, turned to go.

"God forbid!" he said, lifting his eyes toward heaven, "that she should ever come to be like this!" And without even saying good-bye, he went down the stairs and into the street.

Jacob Mendall came out of the boudoir where he

had been a most interested listener to the whole conversation. He had written down in his diary a name which he meant to use some time, if necessary : "John Dinsmore." He was in excellent spirits ; so much so, that when the fair Gabrielle sat on his knee, and with her cheek to his, told of a set of jewelry at Tiffany's worth fifteen hundred dollars, which she was dying to possess, and which Walter declared that he could not afford, the worthy banker drew his check for the amount, without a word of protest.

CHAPTER XIII.

WHERE was Greyburn all this time ?

He was riding from town to town and from city to city, vainly seeking in change of scene relief from the torrents which swept over his soul. Writing long letters to Clara Campbell, tearing up nine out of every ten, and sending the tenth one in fear and trepidation, lest something in it should be taken amiss. Clara had written to him once, giving him leave to continue writing, but saying that she could not promise regular answers until she saw the tenor of his communications. The first letter that she received read as follows :

ON THE ROAD, *July* 10, 18—.

MY GUARDIAN ANGEL :

Yesterday I sold every article which I owned in New York city and shook off forever the dust of the place where the most regretable part of my life has been spent.

From this hour I exist because *I love you.* All else is gone. If it is your will that I should die, write that you can never care for me, and it is done.

To-night I am at a miserable little country hotel. Robin is stabled in the barn, which I can see from my window. He is the only friend upon whose perennial affection I can now rely.

Where is this to end? I am perishing for your presence; may I not come to you?

If you could love me, what a life might open up before me! I would take you where you willed and learn from your dear lips the way I ought to live.

Do you know, Clara, it seems to me that if I had never told you of my sins you might have been at this moment my true and loving wife, with your sweet face pressing the pillow I find so sad and lonely now. I could have undeceived you after the ceremony, little by little, when your love had grown so strong that you could bear it. Must I suffer because I was too honest with you?

My dearest one, you *must* let me come to you! I have so much to say that pen and paper will not tell.

If I grow desperate, my love, and do some terrible act, you will be all to blame. You can mould me as you will.

Clara, my angel, write that I may come, and I will fly on the wings of the wind to your side.

HECTOR.

Letter after letter of the same tenor did he write and send. Very few answers came, and these were very brief. He travelled on. At times it seemed to him that he must fly to Springdale and put himself again upon her mercy, but before he could put this scheme into execution, he realized that to go without her permission would probably prove fatal to his success. Not to go was terrible; to go was madness; what could he do? Each day the separation became more and more unbearable.

One day he picked up a city paper and read the following item :

" The Manhattan Island Improvement Company sold a large tract of land recently to Mr. Jacob Mendall. Mr. Mendall disposed of the entire lot yesterday at an advance of ninety-two thousand dollars. The lucky financier is one of our most successful business men."

This apparently innocent paragraph was enough to fan the nearly dead embers into a blaze.

" So," said Greyburn to himself, " our friend Jacob is making fortunes, and I am to lose everything. The money I was inveigled into risking, is probably most of it to fall to him. He shall not win it ! And yet, how can I prevent it ?"

Three hours of brown study followed, and then Greyburn started to his feet with an oath.

" By all the gods ! I have it. I might as well make a trial for my life as to endure this any longer. If all works right, I shall win the wager. The rest will take care of itself."

The next express for New York bore him toward the metropolis. Reaching the city, he went quietly to a hotel and wrote a letter to Mr. Stedman, cashier of the bank where he had been used to deposit, asking that gentleman to call upon him in the evening, at nine o'clock.

Punctual to the hour, came Mr. Stedman. The result of their conversation was such that early the next morning a warrant was in the hands of a Tombs officer, authorizing him to take the body of one Walter Campbell, clerk, and convey him before some competent magistrate, that he might be committed to jail on the charge of forgery. No mention of Greyburn's name as prosecutor appeared in the document, as Mr. Stedman had agreed to let the bank take the entire honor upon itself.

The officer who was to serve the warrant was given careful instructions and knew his business well. He broke in upon Walter's osculatory exercise at the door of his residence by giving a vigorous pull at the bell just as the master of the house was getting ready to leave it. The young man paled a good deal when he learned the nature of the officer's errand, but he kept up a reasonably good front, after all.

"It is damnable," he said "but I know better than to make any trouble for *you*. It will get my name in print, I suppose, and all that sort of thing, and probably make me no end of annoyance. But that doesn't interest you. Where am I to go?"

"Just down to Jefferson Market," said Mr. Bilks, the officer. "I suppose you'll waive examination and get committed for the next term of the upper court. This court can only bind you over. It's a ticklish thing—this forging. The judges are getting very severe on it lately. The highest penalty is twenty years at Sing Sing."

With such enlivening conversation did Mr. Bilks beguile the trip down town, made in a carriage which he had brought for the purpose. When his thoughts began to run in normal channels again, Walter inquired if he could not see a friend—a very particular friend—who would probably become surety for him, before they went to the court. Receiving an affirmative reply, he directed Bilks to drive to the office of Mr. Jacob Mendall.

Mendall was a good deal disturbed when he learned of the course affairs had taken. Walter's reputation was a very delicate piece of mechanism just now, and very valuable to him. He knew enough of the law to keep on the blind side of the woman who holds the scales, but he was not sanguine as to the success which his young friend might have. If conviction followed, the term in state prison would be long enough to put all prospects of any immediate return from their financial partnership out of the question ; unless, indeed, Walter purchased his pardon by revealing, as he could, the deeper rascalities of others. At all events, a published announcement of his arrest would entail endless complications.

"My good fellow," said Mendall to the officer, "is there any way in which you can help my friend in this matter ? If so, I shall not forget it."

"There is something that could be done," said Bilks, all primed as he was at the instigation of Greyburn, "in this way : I could get Mr. Campbell arraigned on the quiet and a few dollars would prevent the papers in the case getting within reach of any of the newspaper reporters."

"That would be immense !" cried Walter. "But they would get it all sooner or later," he added, with an uncomfortable shrug.

"Then," said Bilks, "after arraignment, if the gentleman would pay liberally for the privilege, I could take him in charge in his own house, instead of locking him up in Ludlow street. It's a little irregular, of course, but it has been done and can be again. It would have to be a real watch, you see, no fooling about it, as I should have to bring him into court whenever the case was assigned. It would take a day and night watch; my partner, Mr. Haney, half the day and I the rest. I don't suggest anything, but things *have* been done like that."

Walter looked at Mendall.

"You could bail me, I suppose, and save all that trouble," he said.

Mendall was thinking. He had expected this very question, and it worried him not a little. If the bail was high, the fear of sentence would be proportionate, and the accused might be hard to find when wanted. He was wondering what answer to make when Bilks came to his rescue.

"Bailing makes publicity," he said. "You can't avoid it. There must be two sureties on the bond and a notary to witness it. That makes three or four people to keep quiet, and it would be next to impossible to stop the thing from getting known."

"I was thinking of that, Walter," said Mendall, much relieved. "Your best way is to let this gentleman exercise a watch over you at your house until we can see what to do. Send word to City Hall that you are sick and cannot be there for a few days. In the meantime I will get a good lawyer and do the best I can for you."

Walter acquiesced in this arrangement and was driven to the court-house, where, in the most quiet and confidential way, the judge put him under bonds for his appearance at the next term of the upper court, and committed him into the hands of the sheriff for safe keeping. Half-an-hour later he was with Gabrielle, telling her the story, while Bilks sat at a respectful distance keeping guard.

"Isn't it funny!" was Gabrielle's comment. "A real policeman and a real judge! Do you think they will send you to Sing Sing? It must be awfully romantic there! I've seen the place from the steamer. Can I call on you and bring you bouquets and books?"

Toward evening came a note by a messenger. Walter opened it and read:

CITY, Aug. 13, 18—.

MY DEAR BOY:

·I have just learned in the most accidental way of your trouble. I do not see what possessed the bank officers to prosecute the case when they knew I should not, and they had not lost a cent out of it. I hope, however, through my acquaintance with influential parties, to relieve you of your embarrassment. It will not be wise for me to call, but if there is anything I can do, write, and you may rely on my efforts.

Truly,

H. GREYBURN.

P. S.—You need have no fear that others will learn of the matter. I am sure no one in the world but myself would have heard what I did. It was the purest accident.

H. G.

Walter took his pen and wrote hastily and impulsively ·

IN BONDAGE, *Aug.* 13, 18—.

MY KIND FRIEND:

Your generous letter fills me with gratitude. I was as much astonished as you could have been when the officer called at my house this morning and took me into custody. You may imagine my feelings. The sentence is twenty years, which would in my case mean death, as I neither could nor would serve it out. You have placed me under repeated obligations, which I have ill repaid. Save me this time, and if I ever treat you unkindly again may that act be my last.

Yours ever,

W. CAMPBELL.

Greyburn received this letter with unbounded delight. "It is perfection itself!" he cried. "Now let me try the other." And he wrote :

CITY, *Aug.* 13, 18—.

MY DEAR SIR :

A young friend of mine, Mr. Walter Campbell, has been held in the Jefferson Market Police Court to-day on a very serious charge—that of forgery. The offense, if any there is (which I dispute), is against me, and not against the Bank which enters the complaint. It will be easy for you to *nol. pros.* the case and throw it out of the files without publicity. This you can well do, as the accused is a mere boy, and the alleged crime merely, at the worst, a too free use of the permissions which I gave him. Do this in the name of Mercy. What say you ?

H. GREYBURN.

H. R. SPAULDING, Esq.

The next day came this answer :

CITY, *Aug.* 14, 18—.

DEAR FRIEND :

Your good temper has led you to ask too much in the case of young Campbell. Unpleasant as it may be to your feelings, he will have to take his trial. If convicted, the court will deal harshly with him, as the judges are all determined to make an example. These things are not pleasant to me, but I am an officer of the law. The young man is only an acquaintance of yours, after all. Were he a relation, so that the injury to his name would hurt yours, I would do my best. As it is, with great regret I say it, I can do nothing.

HENRY R. SPAULDING.

P. S.—Come up and play a game of whist with me some evening. I am at home nearly always.

As Greyburn read these lines the joy they gave him showed in every lineament of his face.

"Fate smiles on me at last!" he said, half aloud. "Spaulding has worded his letter in a way which I could not have equalled even in imagination. It will remove the necessity that I should appear harsh with Clara, demanding her sacrifice in return for saving her brother's life. With this letter in my hand I can offer myself as the door through which she can assist him to escape. Capital! Excellent! If this fails I am no prophet. Hector Greyburn, you are in luck! You will outwit your Mendalls and your Middlebys after all!"

Springdale in not on the line of the railroad. Six miles from the village is the railway station at Brewster. Toward dark Greyburn alighted at Brewster and ordered the first carriage he met to convey him with all speed to Springdale. Arriving on the outskirts of the village he told the driver to wait there for him, no matter how long he was gone. In ten minutes more Clara Campbell opened the door of her cottage and, to her intense surprise, beheld him standing on the threshold.

A half indignant feeling rose in the breast of the maiden that he should have ventured to come without leave, but mingled with it was a deep sense of joy that he was there. All the time that Clara had been writing to him in the curtest of letters that he must stay away, she had longed for the hour when he would be again at her side. Her heart was persuaded, if not her reason. As she opened the door and bade him enter, she experienced a mixture of sensations which brought the high color to her cheek. She motioned him to a chair and sat down without speaking.

Greyburn stood with hat in hand, not less excited than was his hostess. He was the first to find words:

"Have you no better welcome than this for me, Clara? After all these weeks, when one glimpse of your face would have been worth all the rest of the earth?"

A forced smile came into her flushed face. There was no cynicism nor anger in its expression, and it flashed upon him that her astonishment at his unexpected advent was the cause of her reticence. He sprang to her side and addressed her again :

"My life! my angel! you are not sorry I came? You have a thrill for the poor wanderer, have you not? You will not send me away without a word of comfort? I frightened you by appearing so suddenly. I was inconsiderate. Pray forgive me."

She smiled into his eyes in a way which set his heart to beating rapidly, and motioned him to be seated.

"I do forgive you," she said. "But you should have let me know. I don't think I am quite well to-day."

"I would not have come," he replied, "if I could have helped it. I have an errand for you."

"From Walter?" she almost screamed.

"From Walter."

"Is he ill? Let me fly to him!" cried the girl, rising. "He is not dead!" she cried again, as a new and freezing horror came over her.

"Not dead—not even ill," said Greyburn, with great solemnity. "Calm yourself and I will tell you."

Clara stood before him with her lips quivering and her eyes distended.

"Tell me instantly!" she said, unconsciously taking hold of his sleeve. "Instantly! He is my only brother! I love him as I love no other earthly thing! What has he done?"

"He is under arrest for forgery," said Greyburn,

despairing of finding words to make the statement easier.

It seemed as if she would faint then, but she did not. She staggered a little, and he willingly lent her the strength of his arm until he could persuade her to sit down again.

"Poor boy! poor boy!" she moaned, while the beaded drops rose on her fair forehead. "It seems as if even death would have been better. Our name was never tarnished before." She was silent a moment and then asked, "Where is he now—in jail?"

Then he told her the story: How it was his own name that had been forged, and how after he had passed it over, the bank officials had procured the warrant; how Walter was under guard in a private house; how he had tried to save him and how the friendship which he had relied upon with Spaulding had proved insufficient. The stricken sister blamed herself during this recital for her harshness to this kind benefactor of her brother, and when he had finished she expressed her thanks with great warmth of manner.

"I have Walter's letter here," said Greyburn. "Would you like to see it?"

The young girl kissed the missive and read it through several times.

"He would do it!" she said, musingly. "Walter would never stand the disgrace of a felon's sentence. As he says, when they send him to Sing Sing they send him to the grave."

Her feelings overcame her and she sobbed for several minutes. Greyburn did not interrupt her. Not now could he kiss those tears away! Not now!

"He speaks so kindly of you," she said, presently, "that he almost accuses me."

"Not a word of that," interposed Greyburn. "I am your slave. Do not reproach yourself for anything that is past. We have enough to do in thinking of the future. Would you like to read Mr. Spaulding's letter? It may not give much comfort, but you might like to see it."

"I will not believe that the case is hopeless," said Clara, when she had perused the note which he handed her. "It is evident that he would like to oblige you. See what he says: 'Were he a relation, so that the injury to his name would hurt yours, I would do my best.' Surely the man who wrote that has a kind heart. You can move him. I know you can!"

Greyburn shook his head.

"I know him thoroughly," said he. "He is, as he says, an officer. The conviction of felons is his daily avocation. He would go far to oblige me if the case were the one he cites, but to him my interest in this matter seems purely sentimental, and he would not interfere. Look at the postscript: 'Come up and play a game of whist?' You see it is all business with him."

"You could try," said Clara.

"Yes, and I will try—try all I can—with every argument I can bring, rest assured of that. I shall try for your sake, Clara, as under other circumstances Spaulding would try for mine."

For an hour more they talked together, and then Greyburn said that he must start for Brewster in order to get the night train for home. It was agreed that Miss Campbell had better remain in Springdale, as she could do nothing in the city, and Greyburn promised to send her daily bulletins of the latest news in the matter which concerned her so deeply. When he left he did not offer to kiss or even caress her, but lifted his hat in the old-time fashion. The grief which rested on the little house would not admit of anything lighter.

Every day, after his return, he wrote a letter to

Clara. With all the skill of which he was capable he continued to present the disheartening features of the case in their full light. When a week had passed, believing that the time was ripe for the next move, he sent the following letter :

New York, *Aug. 22, 18—*.

Dear Miss Campbell:

Within a few days your brother will be called for trial unless a miracle interposes in his behalf. That miracle, strange as it may seem, it is in your power to bring about.

The more I have worked upon your brother's case, the more discouraged I have become. I can see but one way to save him, and that, I fear, will require too much sacrifice on *your* part.

You will remember that Mr. Spaulding wrote me that were Walter "a relation" of mine, he would interpose. Despairing of any other argument, at the close of a long conversation to-day, I told him that Walter's sister was dearer to me than life itself, and that his fate was therefore as much to me as if he were really my kin. Mr. Spaulding said : " I will keep my word. The day he becomes your relation I will save him."

Clara, as my wife's brother, Walter would be easily freed.

I have no more to say. Your answer must decide.
                    With love and regard,

Clara's answer was to immediately make arrangements for an indefinite stay from home and take an early train for New York city. Apprised by a telegram of her action, Greyburn met her at the station. He found her very pale but calm.

"Has anything transpired since you wrote ?" she asked.

"Nothing."

"Then I am ready."

"To be my wife !" he cried.

"To save my brother," she said. "There is no time for preparation. You must take me as I am. I feel as though Walter was in the quicksands and every hour's delay dangerous."

They entered a carriage.

"To the Hampden !" was the direction which Greyburn gave.

The girl's face was fixed immovably at one of the windows. He knew better than to disturb her, and when they reached the hotel he quietly escorted her to her room. It was in the early evening, and as he whispered to her to await his return, she hardly seemed to notice what he said.

In an hour he came back, accompanied by another gentleman.

"The clergyman," he explained, briefly.

Clara rose and said the necessary words, and then sat down again. He whispered to her that he must again be absent for a few minutes, and departed— this time to the residence of Clarence Perkyns, Esq.

"I've come to say that to-morrow morning I shall claim the amount of the wager," he said, as Mr. Perkyns showed his smiling face in the drawing-room.

"Indeed ! and the proofs ?" said Mr. Perkyns.

"Are for you to be satisfied of. In the first place, here is this telegram from Brewster, stating that Miss Clara Campbell would leave there on the three o'clock train and meet me at the Grand Central Depot. Next is hackman No. 1826, who brought us to the Hampden, where we are now staying. Thirdly, Miss Campbell's trunks, marked with her name and address, which I am going to show you. And fourthly, the young lady herself, a glimpse of whom

I suppose it is necessary you should take. Can you go over with me now ?"

"At once," said Mr. Perkyns, taking out from his safe the document which Greyburn and Middleby had signed, and glancing through its contents. Let me see the telegram again. That's all right. Now let us go."

The hackman and trunks were inspected, and Mr. Perkyns ascended the hotel stairs and saw with his own eyes that a very charming young lady occupied the room into which Mr. Greyburn passed and locked the door.

But he was a careful fellow, was Perkyns. So it happened that he sent a dispatch to Brewster, within the next hour, asking the telegraph operator at that place for a description of Miss Clara Campbell of Springdale, and whether she had left there on the southern train that day. Both replies being satisfactory, Clarence Perkyns, Esq., took a turn or two up and down the street, muttered a few words to the effect that Greyburn was d—d lucky, and went to his club and played billiards till past midnight.

CHAPTER XIV.

WHEN Hector Greyburn passed into his room and locked the door behind him, Clara sat at a window, pressing her face against the pane, with her eye fixed on the evening sky, which was lit up by thousands of those spheres of light which may be, for all we know, the homes of beings with their own joys and sorrows, hopes and disappointments. She was wrapped in thought. Walter, her only brother, was the subject which agitated her mind. She forgot all about herself; forgot where she was; forgot the vows she had just taken ; forgot everything but Walter. So completely was she lost in thought that Greyburn had been in the room for some minutes before she noticed his presence. He stood gazing upon her with a strange look on his handsome countenance, for handsome it was still, though sorely distraught on this memorable night of his life, long before he broke the silence and recalled her to herself.

"Clara !"

She turned with a start, and for the briefest possible moment seemed not to realize where they were. Then the knowledge came like a flood, and the color rose to her pure white cheeks

" Clara !"

" Yes, Mr. Greyburn."

" Not *Hector*, Clara ? Not even *now ?*"

He said it reproachfully, and the look which she gave satisfied him, though she spoke no word.

" Do you remember where we are ?"

She bowed her head mutely, and he saw that she understood.

" This is the Hampden."

" Yes." Her lips silently formed the words.

" You are my wife. It is our wedding night. This is our bridal chamber."

" Mr. Greyburn—Hector—spare me !" she cried. " It is the saddest hour of my life. My brother—my darling brother—is in prison. His release, while probable, is not certain. I am alone with you in a strange city, almost for the first time in my life out of sight of the home-roof."

He looked at her almost coldly.

" Not a loving word ?" he said. " Not a fond look ? Not one kiss ?"

The conscientious little Clara was upon her feet in an instant.

" I was wrong. Say no more. I am your wife."

She had never looked so beautiful to him as at that moment. Still attired in her traveling garments, with no ornament to add to her charms, she seemed like an angelic being. It was her action, her words, and the bright flashing of her blue eyes. All seemed to say, "Here I am, my husband. Take me."

"Will you obey all my commands?" Greyburn asked, fixing his eyes searchingly upon her face.

She glanced for an instant about the room as if to collect her thoughts.

"I must—yes—I *will* obey you."

"You have not removed either your bonnet or your cloak," he said.

"I—forgot," she stammered, making a movement to untie the strings of her bonnet.

"*Stop!*" cried Greyburn.

She ceased at once.

"Not for the world!" he cried, with passionate vehemence. "for a *thousand* worlds would I permit you to finish that?"

She looked startled. His manner was so at variance with the apparent unimportance of the subject discussed, that she had a momentary fear that she was locked into a room with a madman.

"Clara!" he contiuued, "listen! You have promised to obey me. It is my desire—nay, my command—that you will sit here all night long without removing one article of clothing. Not a button of your cloak must be touched. Not a glove on your hand."

She regarded him with wonder, but the suspicion of insanity faded away. And there came another feeling to this guileless child—a feeling that perhaps she was somehow to blame, and that, however foreign it might be to her mood, she owed him a better reception.

"Hector," she said, moving toward him, "forgive

me if I have done wrong. I am not quite myself to-night."

He started and moved further away.

" Will you obey me ?"

" I have promised to do that !"

" You promised, also, to love and honor me," he said with suppressed bitterness, "two things you can never do. Why should you obey a man whom you neither love nor honor ?"

" Obeying is an easy thing," said Clara. " I will obey you from the first. I will honor you as fast as— as you will make it possible for me. And I will love you at least so much as this, that no other man shall ever touch my heart. Hector, let us be honest with each other."

He renewed that searching look, and then like a despairing man he broke out :

" Don't you love me at all, Clara? Not even a little ? Am I wholly hateful to you?"

" Hush !" she said, soothingly. " Do not make my position harder than it need to be. You are a man and should be magnanimous."

" You will obey me ?" he asked the third time.

" Assuredly," she answered.

" Then resume your seat."

How strange he was ! She was almost frightened again.

" Listen to me," he said. " To-night you must not for your life remove one article which you wear. You must not touch me. If you are tired, you may lie on that sofa. If you are not tired, we will sit where we are. I have something—I do not know how much—to say to you. When I am ready I will tell you."

It was an hour before he spoke again.

" Do you remember what I said that day we were walking on the hillside at Springdale—that I was the greatest villain the sun in heaven saw in all his rounds ?" ·

"I remember it," she said. "I also remember that I told you I thought you were much too severe on your own follies when you made so extravagant a statement."

"After you have heard the story of my life," he replied, "you will say that I have described my character mildly. You have heard of sea-pirates who rob ships of merchandise and throw the passengers into the ocean ?"

Clara gave a little scream of horror.

"Don't tell me," she cried. clasping her hands over her eyes, "that you were ever one of those !"

"No," said Greyburn, "not I. They are gentlemen—honest, Christian gentlemen—compared to what I have been."

He spoke so earnestly that she instinctively drew her chair further away.

"Worse than sea-pirates, yes ! And, until within this year, Clara, I never dreamed that I was doing anything wrong. Shall I tell you what I have been ?"

"If you desire, I will hear," she answerd, "but if I become too much affected give me time. I am very nervous."

"Oh, it's not a tale of blood and knives, pistols and cutlasses," he said. "I am no murderer. But listen :

"My mother died when I was born, my father not much later. A guardian undertook to expend on my board and education the little sum which was left to me. As a boy I went to school when I pleased, and stayed away when I liked. I had only to look at a lesson to know it. In the hands of a careful tutor I might have learned anything. Reading was my main diversion when indoors. Everything in print fascinated me. I read all kinds of books, devouring them with a ravenous appetite,

"At eighteen I was a handsome boy. I have a right to say it, for every one said it for me. A lady who came to stay that summer in the town where I lived, told me so, among others. She was a beautiful woman in all that goes to make up physical perfection. Only twenty-five years of age, she was tied to a man of seventy, a rich old fellow who was almost, if not quite in his dotage. Riding through a lovely bit of woods on horseback alone one day, she met me. I was not too young to notice her charming face, and the red lips, dark eyes and rosy cheeks flashed on me like a vision. The lady stopped and made some trivial inquiries, and in a few minutes we were fast friends. She asked me if I often walked on that road, and I told her that I should always do so if I knew that I could meet her there. She replied that she might be there at the same hour any day. The next afternoon I wandered to the place and found her before me.

"I can tell little of what we said. I remember that she asked me why I stayed in that little country village, and that I, feeling piqued, retorted by asking why she had married that little old man whom I had seen with her at the hotel. She laughed, and asked me if I would leave the village if she would leave the old man.

"'Why, you goose!' she said, looking me boldly in the face, 'he's not my husband. His money is all that keeps us together, and I'm tired of him. Go with me. Let us fly the town to-night while every one is asleep.'

"The idea of an elopement fascinated me. When morning came we were here in New York. Our life together lasted a month. I suspect she tired of me even sooner. As for me, I was charmed both with her and the gayeties of the metropolis. One morning she left me a note, saying, 'Dearest, we must part;

enclosed is one hundred dollars ; I have a new lover with plenty of money. Good-bye.' I went away with a feeling as if I had been violently struck upon the head.

"I wandered about the suburbs and then further away into the country. It was autumn. My friends, the squirrels, were putting in their winter's store of food. The trees I loved had arrayed their forms in darker shades. I spent my days clambering over the hills, and my evenings talking nonsense to a young feminine creature in a farm-house where I slept. Tiring at last of the solitude, I began to long to see the city again. I told her I must go and she begged me to take her. She has told the story often, and much better than I can. When we reached here our money was nearly gone. In an attic, on Eighth avenue, we starved for a week. I knew no more how to earn a dime than how to reach the moon. She did, however. One night, very late, she came in and gave me a ten-dollar bill. A man had exchanged it for a few hours of her company. It lasted us a week, and then —she got more."

Clara's lips formed the word " Horrible !" but she spoke not.

"One day I met my lady-love's masculine friend. He was twice my age, in sin as well as years. Finding that I was penniless, he made me an offer. ' Leave the girl to me,' he said, ' and I will give you a thousand dollars.' I closed the bargain."

" Hector !" cried Clara, "tell me no more to-night. I cannot bear it."

" If it is hard for you to hear, what must it be for me to repeat," said Greyburn, with a shade of tenderness. " I look upon the record as you do, and extenuate nothing. The Evil One himself has always stood my counsellor, and I have listened to him, never suspecting whose was the siren voice, until I can no longer say him nay."

"Not now, Hector!" said Clara. "Not now! You have repented these things and will never sin again."

Greyburn shook his head.

"Now, more than ever," he said. "I am growing worse every day. Because, even when I know how bad is my course I cannot turn from it. With my eyes wide open I am walking straight on toward the yawning chasm."

"But you *will* stop," she said. "With your own strength of will ; and with my help—and God's !"

"Hear me to the end," he said, "and then you will see whether even you will predict a better life for me."

"I took the thousand dollars which I got from that man, and put it carefully away. I began to see that I must look out for myself. I had a fair education and was an excellent penman. In a few weeks I obtained a good situation. The business of the company which employed me was one of many millions a year. I found that men high in the confidence of the company had banded together to rob it of large sums. A way developed by which I could make money for myself out of this fact, and still run no risk of punishment if detected. I needed a partner with means, and I sought out the man who had taken my old sweetheart. He was unscrupulous, and we soon struck a bargain. Sums undreamed of a few years before fell into my hands, and you will understand that in order to get this money I was allowing my employers to lose a hundred times as much. I could have convicted all the thieves on my evidence and stopped the fraud, but I would not. In fact, the swindling goes on even to-day.

"I told you, Clara, that I did not know the taste of honest bread, but it did not seem to me then that I was doing wrong. I was merely taking advantage of an opportunity. I was not a detective, a spy. What had I to do with prosecuting people? All around me I saw men high in social position doing as I was. It seemed as right as breathing.

"My money came, and with it the desire for freedom. The work at the office tired me. I was on good terms with the officials, and when I gave up my desk I was allowed to name my successor. Through my previous knowledge, and the information which the new clerk gave me from time to time, I kept up my operations. The clerk was not so bright as he might have been, and never dreamed of the importance of the questions which I used to put to him over our coffee. One day a Broadway omnibus ran over and killed him. Then I secured another for his place. A bright, talented young fellow from the country."

"That was my brother Walter?" cried Clara, tremulously. "John was right, then. Oh! Hector, is there no bright spot in this history? Is all as black as the part you have related?"

"Blacker," he replied. "The density of its darkness increases as we come nearer and nearer to this moment."

"But you have had better thoughts," protested the girl. "Your talks to me at Springdale; your letters when you first went home; surely those were genuine."

Greyburn drew a long breath.

"My resolutions have been good enough, but the fates have drawn me on. I am in the hands of a resistless force which allows me no volition. But listen! With plenty of money and my time on my hands, what should I do but seek for pleasure? I had already my third love, a girl I met soon after securing my clerkship. I got a fine house uptown, and took her there. Later I brought home a young creature whom I had met on a trip into the country. Love No. Three rebelled at the entrance of Love No. Four, and there was a pretty noise for a while. Finally Love No. Three left the house suddenly, and I never heard of her or her child afterwards."

"Her child!"

"Yes, her child and mine."

"Oh, Hector, could you see the mother of your child turned out into the world like that! A woman who had loved you and trusted in your honor!"

"I did not know that she was going, and I could not tell where she had gone. I remember being angry at first, and then rather glad. Lena—that was her name—was not the sort of woman I then liked best. She was sweet, trusting, shy—not stylish or showy. She preferred the solitude of our room, when the baby and I were there, to all the world. Her successor gave me little opportunity to think of the lost one, and she soon passed from my mind. I can see this now as you do, and it seems dreadful. For two weeks I have advertised daily in the *Herald* personal columns, offering a reward for information concern-Lena or the child, but have heard nothing ; and I feel sure I never shall."

"The rest is a mere repetition of what I have related. The devil seems to have taken care of my health remarkably well, probably with an eye to his own purposes."

"Don't, Hector, don't!" said Clara, shuddering.

"Well, I won't. If I were to go into details it would last forever. You know better than you did yesterday what sort of a man it is you are to try to love and honor. But good-night. That is all I have to tell you now."

"You know," he said, suddenly, after an hour's pause, "that there is no barrier between us—that I have not climbed in at any attic window this time."

" Hector, please!" she murmured, in tones of entreaty.

He walked the room in silence after that until morning. At seven o'clock he rang for breakfast, which was brought to the room and spread on one of the tables. With difficulty he persuaded Clara to touch it. She had no heart for food or anything else. Walter ! Walter ! was the only theme on which her mind could rest for long. Greyburn did not eat very heartily. The desperate game he was playing did not add to his appetite.

" I am going now," he said, as he rose from his slight repast. " I cannot tell how long I shall be absent, but rest assured I shall return as soon as possible."

" Will my brother be set at liberty to-day ?" asked Clara, raising her tired eyes to his.

" If my efforts can accomplish it," he answered. " And if not to-day, to-morrow."

" Can I see him as soon as he is free ?" she inquired.

" Well—no, hardly. Not just yet. We must see how he takes our new relation. All will come right in time."

Proceeding immediately to the residence of Clarence Perkyns, Esq., Greyburn found that gentleman ready to accompany him to the National Security Bank and to hand over the amount of the wager entrusted to him.

" Do you know, old fellow," said Perkyns, as he grasped his companion's arm, " I couldn't sleep a wink for thinking of you ? After your protestations that night it seems impossible to me that you could have done this. I know that fifty thousand dollars is a snug sum to lose, but really, man of the world as I am, this looks almost wicked."

Greyburn stopped short in his walk and released himself from his companion. He had a look of genuine pain in his countenance and he spoke impressively.

"Perkyns, you have been my friend for years, and I ask you not to say another word. Promise that neither to me nor to others will you make any further reference to this matter, not absolutely necessary."

"I promise certainly," said Mr. Perkyns, and they resumed their walk.

"My tongue is tied now," added Greyburn, "but some time you will understand this better. When you do, you may excuse me or you may not, but you will see the matter in a different light."

At the bank, the check of Mr. Perkyns produced one hundred one thousand dollar bills as soon as presented. Greyburn counted out five of these and offered them to his friend, but they were firmly though politely refused. He then took the entire amount and put it into his pocket, bade his companion adieu and took a carriage for the bank where he made his own deposits. In a few minutes he was closeted with the affable cashier, Mr. Stedman.

"I am ready," said Greyburn, when the door was closed, "to have young Campbell released. You understand the methods. I will see that his counsel applies for a *habeas* and gets him before a judge. You must be ready to acknowledge satisfaction and withdraw your charge."

"Very well," said Mr. Stedman. And with a little further talk in the same direction they separated. Greyburn then wrote the following missive:

CITY, *Aug.* 24, 18—.

WALTER CAMPBELL, ESQ.

DEAR FRIEND : I have succeeded in persuading the officers of the bank that you are not legally guilty in the case they have brought against you. I shall now see that Bird & Bird, the attorneys, apply for a *habeas*.

You must be ready to go at any moment to court, where you will undoubtedly get discharged without further delay.

With best wishes, your friend,
H. G.

Calling a messenger, he dispatched him to Walter's residence. Two hours later, Mr. John Bird came into his office, where Greyburn awaited him, with the news that Walter was free.

"His first words after leaving the court-house were an inquiry for you," said Mr. Bird. "As you instructed me that he was not to see you on any account I gave an evasive answer. The last I saw of him he was in a carriage with a remarkably handsome young woman, going up Broadway."

"Good!" cried Greyburn. "Now write me a letter."

"Write you?" exclaimed the lawyer.

"It is for other eyes," replied Greyburn. "Just follow my dictation."

In a few minutes he had in possession the following:

CITY; *Aug. 24, 18—.*

DEAR MR. GREYBURN :

As you directed, we applied this morning to the superior court for a writ of *habeas corpus* in the case of the State of New York *vs.* Walter Campbell. The defendant was brought as soon as possible before the court, and we secured the dismissal of the court against him. Mr. Campbell was set at liberty and will not hear of the matter again. Our bill for service (one hundred dollars) is enclosed, receipted.

Very truly,
BIRD & BIRD, Atty's.

The client took the letter and hastily withdrew.

CHAPTER XV.

At four o'clock Greyburn knocked at the door of his room at the Hampden. Almost instantly Clara opened it.

"My brother?" she cried.

"Is free," said Greyburn. Then, seeing that she swayed a little under the excitement, he assisted her to an easy chair.

"You will not deceive me," she said. "He is really free?"

"Read," said Greyburn, tossing Mr. Bird's letter to her. She devoured it word by word.

"You are so good!" she cried, smiling through the tears which filled her eyes.

"I?" he cried, starting. "Good? No act of mine should ever be given that appellation. Clara, I am a villain!"

"No, no!" she cried. "I'll not believe it! At heart, Hector, you are a noble and true man."

He gazed at her with passionate longing.

"Must I tell you?" he sighed. "Cannot I let you go on without tearing down even the flimsy fabric of respect which you are trying to raise about me? No, I am resolved. You must hear all."

She looked up in helpless amazement.

"Hector, what is it? Tell me, is not my brother free?"

"Always her brother!" he murmured. "Never me. And never will be."

"Yes, Walter is free," he said, "but that is a slight thing compared with what I have to tell you. Have you the strength to listen to a story, worse—far worse —than anything I detailed to you last night ?"

The girl roused herself and put on a look of determination.

" I will hear anything—everything," she said. " I can and will endure it. Whatever it is, the uncertainty is worse."

" I am not like a prisoner who confesses under the hope of pardon," said he. " You will never forgive me when you know all. But even if it robs me of everything I have hoped and prayed for, I will confess.

"When I first found that I loved you, Clara, I could not understand the feeling. I had thought I loved a hundred times before, but this was not like the sentiments I remembered. I conceived a reverence for you, almost a fear. In your presence I was happy, out of it inconsolably miserable. When you came into my life you made all the rest of it seem hateful. At last I revealed my heart to you. I told you how perfectly unworthy I was of your love, and you, like an angel, counseled me to make myself better. I resolved to do so, but it was a new experience, and though I tried hard I succeeded badly. I gave up my house and companions, but just when I was apparently the most determined to reform, I made the worst step of all. Of that I will tell you later on.

" For two months I wandered over the country, until I could bear it no longer. I *must* see you. I must have an errand sufficiently important to obtain me an audience. I returned to New York and procured the arrest of your brother—Clara ! don't look at me like that ?"

" Go on !" she said, breathlessly. " Walter was not guilty, then ?'

" Yes, he was guilty. Let me have that to extenuate my fault, if it is worth anything. He did forge checks for some three thousand dollars and get the money at my bank, while I was in Springdale, in June. I should not have prosecuted him, however, except as a means of obtaining you. It was the remedy of a wicked and desperate man.

"I got the bank officers to procure his arrest, and arranged it so that he could stay in his own room, guarded by a sheriff. I have kept the affair carefully out of the newspapers, and, so far as Walter is concerned, he goes back to his desk at City Hall no worse for his brief vacation, and perhaps even better for the lesson it gives him."

"And I came here and married you to save him from the net which you yourself had set?" said Clara, her voice trembling.

"Show me some pity!" he replied. "Remember that all there is wrong in this I have freely confessed to you. Had I—could I have—sealed my tongue, you would never have known."

"Hector Greyburn," said Clara, shaking her head sadly, "you are indeed a terrible man. I believe in a merciful God, who overrules all human affairs for our best good. If I did not, it seems as though my reason would fail me. Perhaps Heaven has some great work for us to do and is preparing us for it by a trial of fire."

Greyburn eyed her with the old, passionate longing as she spoke.

"Do you hate me?" he said.

"Hate you, no. In spite of all, you are my husband."

"And if I were not!" he cried. "If by some magic power our union were dissolved—if it could be that we had never been married—would you wed me after this? Would you not thank God for your release."

" What do you mean ?" exclaimed the girl.   " There is something in your words which frightens me."

" Would you like to be freed from the bonds which hold us together ?   Tell me that, before I say more."

" Why do you ask ?" she replied, evasively.

" Because," he said, " a pistol, a rope, a jump from a steamer——"

" Hush !" cried Clara, with horror in her tones. " That would be awful ! Think of rushing in your state into the presence of your Maker !"

" Then you do not wish I were dead ?"

" No ! No !" she cried, making a gesture to stop him.

" But you do wish—be honest with me now—that you were not my wife ?"

" Again I say," she answered, " why do you ask me that ?"

" Because," he said, his face turning the hue of ashes, " you can find release at any moment if you seek it."

" *How ?*"   She said it almost with a shriek.

" By walking out of that door and taking the next train for Springdale."

" But I should still be your wife," she faltered. "Separate living would not sever the tie."

" You do not understand, Clara. You can go when and where you please and I cannot follow you. The ceremony was a sham. The clergyman was a myth. We are not married at all."

She looked then as if in doubt of her own sanity. It was more than she could comprehend.

" It is my last confession," he stammered, " and, as I told you, the worst. Are you glad or sorry ?"

She was too dazed to reply. Her strength seemed hardly greater than an infant's.

" You desire it explained," said Greyburn, seeing the wish in her face. " You came here with me last evening. Your outer garments, your bonnet, were not removed, your gloves are still on your hands. Give me at least this credit, you are not dishonored."

"But why am I here?" she gasped.

"I will tell you all," he said. "A combination of men who had cause to be my friends, led by one whom I had helped to many thousands of dollars, set a trap for my financial ruin. At table with a crowd of men as foolish as myself, I had offered to wager any amount that no one present could name a girl whom I could not betray. After I left you in June I resolved to have a farewell dinner with my old companions and advise them of the fact that they would see me no more. At that dinner I was artfully drawn into making a bet in the way I have described, through appeals to my pride and ideas of honor. When I agreed to make the wager I supposed the sum would be small and the person named some woman unknown to me, and I secretly resolved to forfeit the stakes without a contest. But when my friends proposed fifty thousand dollars as the sum each should deposit, and I saw that there was a plot to swindle me out of the greater part of all I had in the world, the devil in me came to the surface and I determined that they should not succeed.

"I signed the bond and put up the money before I learned the name of the woman I was to ruin. Judge of my horror when I found that the blank space contained your name. But my blood was up. The referee had my money and I determined to get it again. This morning he paid me the amount."

"And my name," cried Clara, indignantly, "my name, which you profess to love so much, has been bandied about among your friends like that of the lowest common creature who walks the streets! Men know that I have passed the night here with you and we unmarried. I will stay to hear no more.

I never wish to see or hear of you again. I did have a regard for you and I pitied you even in the midst of your crimes, but that is ended. For your wickedness toward me, may God forgive you."

She started for the door, but he placed himself before it.

"*Let me pass!*"

"Clara," he said, softly, "listen to me a little longer and then you shall pass if you wish. I will enter no plea for myself, for that would be useless. Now you must think of *yourself.*"

"Myself?" she repeated, vaguely.

"Yes, yourself. If you go from that door, what next? To Springdale? What then? Back to your old life? Impossible! You have left all that behind you. Last night, in the presence of that God in whom you believe, you vowed your life to me. True, the man who asked you those questions had no legal right to marry us, but was not the ceremony binding nevertheless in the sight of Heaven?"

"God will not ask me to carry out a fraud," said Clara. "He will know how honest was my purpose and how basely I was betrayed."

"But think," continued Greyburn. "There are people who know you have been here and with me. More will inevitably learn of it, and when Springdale hears the story you can no longer live happily within its borders. My reputation will be enough to ruin yours wherever our names are coupled together in that way. Clara, it is a very serious thing. It is too late to turn back now. You could not leave me if you would."

She gazed at him for a moment and then recoiled as if stung by a serpent.

"What would you have of me? Must I become the very lowest of human creatures to avoid being thought one? Never!"

"Not at all," he said, in the same soft tones, though with an added sadness. "What I now propose to you is an honorable marriage. I have injured you all I ever can, and I ask leave to make a slight reparation."

"It is some new deceit," said the girl. "I will not trust you."

"I do not blame you," he replied, "but you shall 'make assurance doubly sure' next time. Do you know a single clergyman whom you would trust, who could be sent for?"

"I know one," she replied. "He and my poor papa were old friends."

"Clara, will you marry me? I have bared my heart to you as I never did to another. I love you with all my soul."

"Let me think. Give me a little time for consideration. Whichever way I turn I can see no light. Oh, Hector Greyburn, how much evil one man can accomplish!"

She sat down and cried a little to herself. Greyburn paced the room like a convict waiting to hear whether his doom is to be death or pardon. At last she lifted her head.

He paused before her chair.

"Hector, I *will* marry you. There is no other way. Become as good a man as you are capable of being, and I will learn to honor, perhaps even to love you."

He knelt at her feet, but she raised him up.

"Not to me, Hector, not to *me*. Kneel to *God*, who alone deserves our adoration."

"I kneel to Him when I kneel to you," he said, with profound reverence. "For if ever He makes Himself incarnate it is in such creatures as you are."

She chid him gently.

At eleven o'clock that night a gentleman and lady rode out of the Jersey City station toward the west, in one of the compartments of a Pullman car. The conductor remarked to the porter that they were the strangest couple he had seen for a long time.

"There they sit like they was no relation at all, and as though there was a funeral going on," he remarked. "But I'd bet they're new-married, just the same."

The next morning the papers had this announcement, under the head of "Marriages:"

GREYBURN—CAMPBELL.—26th inst., at the residence of the Rev. Stephen Marsden, in Brooklyn, Hector Greyburn, Esq., of New York city, and Clara, only daughter of the late Rev. Duncan Campbell, of Springdale, Conn.

CHAPTER XVI.

THE appearance of Greyburn's marriage in the morning papers caused a wide sensation. He was known very well, and his escapades had been the theme of conversation at many clubs.

One of the first to have the paragraph called to his attention was Mr. Jacob Mendall. A friend dropped in upon him while still at breakfast and pointed out the announcement. Mr. Mendall was shaken for the moment from his accustomed serenity. He rose hastily, leaving the viands untouched, and summoning a carriage directed the driver to take him with all speed to the residence of Clarence Perkyns, Esq.

"Mr. Perkyns," he began, as soon as that gentleman came into his presence, "have you seen Mr. Greyburn lately? Ah! you have," he added, receiving a bow of assent. "Well, do you know about this paragraph in the morning paper—his marriage with Miss Campbell?"

"With Miss Campbell—Miss Clara Campbell?" responded Perkyns, in undisguised astonishment.

"The same," said Mr. Mendall, as he read with a shaking voice the announcement from the paper which he held in his hand.

"I am much astonished," responded Mr. Perkyns. "This is the first intimation I have had of such an intention on his part."

"But," said Mr. Mendall, coming in haste to the main object of his questionings, "what about the money—the wager, you know—which he made with Middleby? Has he—have you the money. You haven't paid it over?"

"Why, certainly I have," said Mr. Perkyns. "He drew the whole amount yesterday morning, after proving to me that he was entitled to it under the terms of the contract."

"It was this same Miss Campbell who was named !" raved Mendall.

"To be sure. I don't know how you found it out, but you've guessed rightly."

"And he's got the money?"

"Every dollar."

"But it's a swindle, a clear fraud !" cried the banker. "The wager did not provide for a Mrs. Greyburn. It said 'Miss Clara Campbell.' After her marriage she was no longer the party named in the paper. You should have taken pains not to be duped."

"That is between myself and Mr. Middleby," replied Perkyns, bridling. He took up the newspaper. "You will see," he added, "if you look at this, that they were not married till yesterday, the 26th. It was the day before—the night of the 25th—that they passed together with my knowledge. They had rooms at the Hampden."

"Then it was under promise of marriage," said Mendall. It was a cheat, any way you fix it. There should be some honor in a bet made between gentlemen."

"It is my opinion that there was not much *honor* in the whole transaction," said Mr. Perkyns, boldly. "The most honorable thing done yet is this marriage. I wouldn't take part in another such affair for the whole amount of the stakes. Honor, indeed!"

"Do you mean to insult me?" asked Mendall, savagely.

"I fail to understand 'your question," responded Mr. Perkyns. "The only parties to this affair whom I know are Messrs. Hector Greyburn and Otis W. Middleby. What is your interest in it?"

"Perhaps greater than you know," said Mendall, driven out of his senses by the discoveries he was making. "Let me give you one piece of advice, Don't let Walter Campbell know that you are concerned in this. He'd as lief kill you as eat his supper."

"Walter?" ejaculated Mr. Perkyns. "Why, the young woman is no relation of his, is she!"

"Only his sister!" Mendall said, with ill-suppressed fury."

"Surely you jest," said Perkyns, recoiling. "His name was down as a witness."

"Certainly!" raved Mendall. "He didn't know whom we were betting on."

"Whom *we* were betting on!" repeated Perkyns. "It seems to me, Mr. Mendall, that it is *you* who had best look out. I was perfectly innocent in the matter. This is the first time I ever imagined that Walter was related to the party upon whom you and your friend were betting. You knew it all the time, it seems."

"It matters little what I knew or didn't know," snarled Mendall, taking up his hat to depart. "The money is lost, that's the main point." He strolled moodily out of doors and took his carriage for downtown. His next act was to send the following letter:

To OTIS W. MIDDLEBY,
Care Baring Bros., London, Eng:
Don't think of starting home until you hear again from me. Greyburn has got the money from Perkyns and has married and gone away with Miss C. I ex-. pect Walter will be raving and that the deuce will be to pay everywhere. Will send you word as fast as things develop.

In haste,
JACOB MENDALL.

Another man to see the marriage notice early in the day was John Dinsmore. Taking his frugal breakfast at a cheap restaurant in the Bowery his eye fell accidentally upon the paragraph in the newspaper which the waiter handed him. He put down his knife and fork with a noise which attracted the attention of every one in the room and rose from his seat like a madman.

"Whar's that place, the house whar that minister lives?" he shouted to everybody in general, flourishing the newspaper. "For God's sake, gentlemen, some of you show me the way thar!"

The patrons of the place, as well as the waiters and proprietor, shrank away from him. In the intensity of his feeling he had every symptom of being deranged. A policeman was called in and before the blacksmith knew it, the officer's hand was on his shoulder.

"My man, come with me."

Dinsmore looked at him and then at the frightened faces around the room.

"Don't stop me!" he cried. "I fear thar's been

wrong committed. A minute's delay may make it too late. Whar does this Mr. Marsden live? See, in the marriage notices! I'm afeard, sir, thar's been fraud practiced."

The officer looked at the paper.

"That's all right enough," he said. "What are you making such a blessed row about? Greyburn-Campbell. I know the man. Hasn't he got a right to get married if he wants to?"

"But if thar's deception!" cried Dinsmore. "If this item ain't right an' the girl's been deceived! I must go to Mr. Marsden at once and see what he says. If it's a fraud the harm may be prevented. If it's a real marriage, all I say is, God pity her!"

There seemed no reason to stop the man, and the policeman directed him as well as he was able how to find Brooklyn and Mr. Marsden's residence. Arriving there, he learned from the lips of the reverend gentleman himself that the marriage in question was a legal one, and his last hope was dashed to the ground.

Returning to New York, he was walking up from the ferry, when an elderly man accosted him.

"Are you the man who was inquiring the way to Rev. Mr. Marsden's?"

"I am," replied Dinsmore, somewhat astonished. "How did ye know that?"

"An officer who directed you gave me your description. I will tell you something about that matter that will interest you if you will meet me at five o'clock at the Astor House."

"I'll come," said Dinsmore. "Whar shall I find ye?"

"Go to parlor B. I shall be there before you, probably. If not, wait till I come."

When the blacksmith arrived at the Astor House he found Mr. Mendall awaiting him."

"Your name," said Mendall, handing him a chair, "is John Dinsmore."

"The policeman didn't tell ye that," said the black-smith, quickly, "but I don't dispute ye. My name's an honest one, an' I never yet hesitated to own it."

"You know Hector Greyburn," pursued Mr. Mendall. Seeing the look of hate which came into his companion's face he added, "and you do not like him."

The blacksmith looked at Mr. Mendall for a second.

"You're right again, stranger. I don't like him. I never did from the first minute I saw him. Less than ever do I like him this mornin'."

"You also know the girl he has married," said Mendall, "Miss Campbell."

Dinsmore's eyes flashed.

"Wait, now!" said he. "What gives ye the right to pronounce *her* name? Who are ye and what are ye comin' at?"

"Can I trust you never to mention me in connection with what I am going to say?" asked the careful banker. "Swear that, and I will tell you why I asked you to meet me here.'

"I swear," said Dinsmore. "But be careful. The name o' that lady is sacred to me."

"I shall not offend you," said Mendall, "unless it be by speaking unpleasant truths. First, let me ask you another question or two. How long have you known these people?"

"Miss Clara from a baby up. The man fer a year or two."

"Are they legally married?"

"Yes, Mr. Marsden says so."

"Had they not been, what would have been your next course?"

Dinsmore had risen in his impatience and commenced to pace the floor.

"Had he betrayed an' disgraced her, do ye mean?"

he said. "Why, I'd 'a' follered him to the end o' the earth but what I'd 'a' had his heart's blood."

Even Mendall in his revengeful mood quailed a little before the fiery temper of the man.

"I could tell you something, but you are too excited. You would act rashly."

"About Miss Clara?" demanded Dinsmore, stopping short in his walk.

"About Greyburn's treatment of her."

"Tell me!" cried the blacksmith. "I'll be calm as I can. If ye know anythin', tell me."

He seated himself at the opposite side of a table which stood in front of Mendall's chair, and clasped his hands nervously over the marble.

"Hear me, then," said the banker, "but at the first intimation that you are getting excited I shall stop. You need a cool head at this time."

"Go on," said Dinsmore, striving to master his emotion.

"Two months ago," said Mendall, "this man Greyburn met with a party of friends at dinner. Over their wine one of them offered him a bet of a large sum of money that a certain lady could be named, whom Greyburn could not bend to his will within a given time. Greyburn took the wager and the stakes were placed in the hands of a referee. The name of the lady was——"

"No, no!" cried Dinsmore. "Not her! not her!"

"The same."

"Before a crowd o' men! Impossible!"

"Hear me out," said Mendall. "Last Tuesday Greyburn went to the referee and said that he should demand the money the next morning. He proved that he had the lady at the hotel Hampden."

"But they were married!" said Dinsmore, his lips blanching.

"Not at all," replied Mendall. "That was Tuesday. They remained there that night and were not married till twenty-four hours later. To win the bet he must remain with her when she was 'Miss' and not 'Mrs.' Do you see how cunning he was?"

"I see," repeated Dinsmore, like one waking from a hideous nightmare.

"In all the clubs of this city," said Mendall, marking the terrible effect his story was having, "they are discussing what I am telling you. The name of Miss Campbell is a theme for laughter. Her subsequent marriage will not wash out the stain on her fame. Wherever she goes the story will follow her."

"Say no more!" cried Dinsmore, in a passion. "Let me out into the air or I shall stifle!"

"And whence go you?" inquired Mendall.

"First, to see her brother Walter. We'll go together to find this man, an' when we do find him, let him beware."

"I would not go near Walter were I in your place," said Mendall, in a meaning tone.

"Why not?" cried Dinsmore. "Who should revenge a sister if not her brother?"

"Not in this case. He cannot aid you. He made one of the dinner party where the wager was made. His name is signed as one of the witnesses to the compact."

"Walter's name signed to the paper which makes his sister's shame!" cried the blacksmith. "That's too much to believe. Prove it to me if you can!"

"I could prove it easily enough if necessary, but it would take time. What motive could I have to deceive you? It is signed there, I pledge you my word. So you see he is the last person you ought to go to now."

"Then I will hunt for the villain alone," said Dinsmore. "Do you know whar he's gone?"

"He left the Jersey City station on a Pennsylvania

train at eleven last evening with tickets for Cleveland.   Beyond that I know nothing, but you could trace him.   Or, if you are in no hurry, you can wait for a few months, when he will probably return from his bridal trip and boast over the achievement."

" I shall start to-night," said Dinsmore.   "I'm all in a fever.   I can't rest until I'm going toward him. Let him travel whar he likes, I'll find him.   Fur or near, I'll come upon his trail at last."

" Do you need any money for traveling expenses ?"

" Not a penny.   I've enough to go round the globe if need be.   Do you see these hands?   They're not hansum, not the hands of a gentleman, but they've earned many an honest dollar, and I'm willin' to spend every one.   Poor little Clara !   No one can undo the   ong that's done ye, but some one can see that it's avenged."

The last words were spoken more to himself than Mendall.

The eleven o'clock train on Wednesday night bore out of the Jersey City station a newly-made bridegroom.   The eleven o'clock train on Thursday night bore after him a would-be assassin, eager for his death.

———◆———

CHAPTER XVII.

In a little hamlet of northern Georgia, Hector Greyburn and his wife passed those few weeks after marriage usually called the honeymoon.   With the design of keeping their whereabouts from the knowledge of possible pursuers, he had bought tickets for Cleveland, and then left the train at Philadelphia and crossed by a circuitous route into the southern states.

He was without definite plans for the future, but at present he wanted no intrusion, and it seemed very unlikely that any one would trace him to this unfrequented section.

He was not happy. What was the trouble? The dream of his life was realized; the woman he loved was securely in his possession; but nevertheless, a sense of uneasiness penetrated his heart, and he began to question whether the result he had achieved was worth what it had cost to obtain.

Sweet little Clara obeyed his every suggestion without a word. He had respected her scruples in all things, resolving that he would try to win her regard ere he sought to gain her love. But something was lacking everywhere.

"My dear," he said, one morning, as he met her coming from her chamber, "shall we take a walk up the hills yonder? The landlord says the scenery is something remarkable from the summit of the cliff."

In a few minutes she was ready with hat and sunshade to take the arm he offered her.

"Perhaps you would rather not go," he said, pausing, "or would rather wait until another time."

"Just as you please," Clara responded. It was always left to him. She seemed to have no desire nor opinion of her own now.

"Isn't this grand!" he exclaimed, a half hour later, as they stood gazing down the long line of the valley, bathed in the brightness of the morning sun. "Look at the river there in the distance! See the farms with their regular lines of varying color! Is it not worth the climb!

"It is very beautiful," she said, but it sounded like an echo of his own words.

Another day they took a long drive among the hills, stopping for dinner at a quaint old farmhouse filled with antique furniture. Whatever Hector noticed Clara saw too. Whatever he did not see escaped her observation. He tried it over and over and the result was always the same.

"My darling," he said, as they were driving slowly along the homeward road, "you are getting tired of Georgia. I should not have brought you here. The city is a better place for you, where there is some variation in the sights. These hills, valleys, rivers and sunsets tire one after the first few days. Where would you like to go ? Name the place, and, whether it be on this continent or the other, we will hasten there at once."

"I am quite content here," she responded, but her voice did not endorse the assertion.

Greyburn gave a despairing cry.

"As well here as elsewhere, you would say," he said. "I can never make you happy—never ! never !"

Clara looked at him and a sob rose in her throat.

"You are very kind to me," she ventured.

"Because I repress the manifestations of my love," he said. "Because I forget that you are my wife and treat you as if you were my companion merely, my sister. Let me assert my rights, let me even demand a lover's kiss, and you would shrink from me with horror."

"Don't, Hector, don't !" she exclaimed. But he went on :

"To gain you I have ventured everything, and now that I have you, I have not your love. I never can have it. I might have known better. How could a pure, innocent girl love a man whose whole life has been contrary to her convictions of right, one who has gained her by the basest of fabrications ? I will not keep up this sham any longer. We must separate. You to go to some place where you can live as you have always done, and I, Heaven knows where ! to live and die as I began."

The tears flowed down the girl's cheeks as she listened to this declaration, made with such evident earnestness, and her active conscience dictated her answer.

"No, Hector, we cannot separate. We must not think of it. 'Whom God hath joined,' you know. In a few weeks I shall feel better. I confess I have been affected by the strange combination of circumstances which has brought me to this spot, but I shall soon become used to my changed life. Somewhere in the future there must be happiness for us yet."

He threw his arms impulsively around her and was about to imprint a kiss upon her lips when an indefinable something told him that she shrank from the ordeal. He withdrew his clasp and, gathering up the reins, drove at increased speed down the mountain road, his brow darkening more and more as they proceeded. Clara, who knew all that was passing in his mind, felt herself powerless to say anything to relieve him. Within a mile of their destination he checked the horse suddenly and spoke again :

"I have decided. There is no help for it. I realize all that you would say. You feel that you have a duty to perform toward me. I release you from it. You think that you ought to try and save me from evil courses. Had you loved me with all your heart and soul you might have done even that, though I cannot tell. You will never be happy as my wife, and I will not consent to make you more miserable than need be. For the injury I have already done you, forgive me if you can, but in the future we must be strangers to each other."

"No, no!" cried Clara, with a feeling of desolation creeping over her heart. "Not so suddenly. Think of it longer."

"What need," he asked, "when after a fortnight's marriage I cannot even offer you a kiss without your repugnance making itself clearly manifest? It is folly to wait. Separation is the only thing. You can live where you please. I will make over to you any part of my fortune which you desire. It would not do for you to go to Springdale. You must travel to some place where our history will not get abroad. I shall leave here to-morrow. You may go as far with me as you please and proceed onward where you will. The money I can leave subject to your order."

A flush almost of anger mantled Clara Greyburn's cheek.

"Do you imagine," she said, "that I would touch a cent of yours under those circumstances? How would that look? 'Wedded two weeks and then separated with a liberal allowance.' I have earned no rights by my marriage with you, and if you desert me I will take nothing. When you think of me in the future, you may dislike, but you shall at least respect me. You shall not have it to say that I was a fortune hunter. Money! I despise it. My little school, with its ten dollars a week, would have satisfied me forever. Somewhere, away from those who have known me, I can get employment again. But as for your money, never speak of it."

Greyburn looked at his wife with increasing astonishment as she proceeded.

"You do me an injustice," he said, "to suppose that I could ever have an unkind thought of you or doubt the extremest purity of your motives. I can see nothing wrong in my proposal. Unpleasant to you as it may be, you are my wife, and are entitled to a certain share of all that is mine. We are human beings and cannot live on air. You could not even travel north without the means of paying your way, and you might be months in getting such a situation as you desire. You must have money—not mine, but your own—of which I am the legal custodian. Be reasonable, Clara."

The girl shook her head as decidedly as ever. "I could not touch it," she said. "It would seem like a price."

"At least," suggested Greyburn, "you will accept a loan. Put it in that light. You can repay me by sending to my banker in New York whenever you desire. Will you do that?"

"You might buy me a ticket back to Springdale," said Clara, doubtfully. "When I get there I could sell my home and that would give me all I should need. Half of it is Walter's, but I could settle that with him. So much I would be willing to accept until I could repay it, but positively no more."

"Then I will not leave you!" cried Greyburn. "You are not fit to go out into the world alone if you hold such ideas as those. You shall still endure me, and we will see whether a few more weeks of *that* will not induce you to consent to anything. There is something I can do. I can take you back to New York and install you in a house there, and then go and travel for my health for a few years. You are Mrs. Hector Greyburn, whether your husband is at home or away."

"It would be only an excuse," said Clara. "I should feel all the time as if I was eating food to which I had no claim, and I know I could not bear it long. And where would you be? You could not possibly be happy. No, it would never do in the world."

Greyburn took up the reins and drove silently toward his hotel. He said no more till the retiring hour, and then only this: "Good-night, my white angel. Don't let sleep keep away on account of anything I've said. We will talk it over again to-morrow."

The advice he had given his wife he was unable to follow. All attempts at sleep proved futile. At last just as the clocks were striking four, he arose, dressed himself, and went out for a walk up the mountain-side. The cool air invigorated him, and the walk sent the blood quickly through his veins. He climbed up, up, higher than ever before. Just before the sun was ready to rise he became attracted by the silver stream of the river at the base of the hills, and descended toward its banks. A country road ran along the side of the mountain, a hundred feet or so above the river, and Greyburn had to cross this on his journey. He had hardly done so when a man sprang in front of him and barred his progress.

"*Stop!*" cried the apparition.

Greyburn stopped and looked at the man. He was somewhat surprised to see him, but the sentiment did not show itself in his face. The look there would be better described as one of careless indifference.

"I see ye know me," said the man.

"I haven't that honor," responded Greyburn, indifferently.

"Ye lie!" cried the man. "Ye know me well. I saw ye at Springdale that night when ye began this hellish work. What do ye think I'm here fer?"

"I—neither—know, nor—care," said Greyburn, with cool, slow sarcasm. "All I know about you is this, that you are very dirty—and—very impolite."

The man glanced at his hands and seemed to acknowledge the correctness of that part of the description.

"I never *was* a gentleman," he said, with a severity which was meant to be cutting.

"That is evident," agreed Greyburn.

"Neither did I ever ruin an honest man's daughter!" added the other, sharply.

"I should say so," said Greyburn. "They have not yet, I hope, been reduced to such depths as that."

"I can't talk as fast as you," said the man, "but I'll

"Have ye no word to send to yer friends?" *Page 187.*

tell ye somethin' that may interest ye. I've been huntin' fer two weeks fer a man named Hector Greyburn, who's ruined the daughter of one who was my best friend. I've found this Greyburn an' I'm goin' to kill him."

"Indeed! So you add the interesting trade of a murderer to your other occupations," said Greyburn, in the same manner as before. "Let—me—see. I think I *do* recollect you. Your name is—Dinsmore—and you used to be a blacksmith. Yes, that is right. Well, does your new trade pay better than the old?"

"I don't kill fer *money*," said the man, doggedly.

"Really? What else could make a reason in so dull a head as yours? A man who has been content all his life to handle sooty iron and blow a crazy pair of bellows. You shod a horse very well, too. Perhaps you will not succeed so ably at your new profession."

"I'll leave that to you," said Dinsmore, "as you will be my first victim."

"Your first?" said Greyburn, with a mock gesture of horror. "Let me beg you to go and kill a few others for practice. I should hate to be experimented upon by a novice. When you are as expert at murdering as you were at horseshoeing you may command me, but not sooner. I decidedly object to being killed by an amateur."

"Ye are welcome to yer wit," said the blacksmith, "as it will be so short a time that ye can use it. Is thar anythin' ye wish to do or say before I finish ye?"

"There are several things," said Greyburn, "and they will all take time. Could you call around, say—a week from to-day. By that time I think I could be quite ready."

"Have ye no word to send to yer friends in New York?" queried Dinsmore, with flashing eyes, ignoring the levity of the last answer. "None to yer friend Mendall, yer dear friend Mendall, who offered to pay my expenses here? Nothin' at all to Mendall?"

"Nothing," said Greyburn, coolly. "Except—that I have his money."

"Or to Walter Campbell?'

"Only—that I have his sister."

"Do ye dare," cried Dinsmore, "with yer foot on the edge o' the grave, talk lightly o' Clara Campbell?"

"Clara Greyburn, if you please," responded the other, imperturbably. "It is as well to be correct."

"How she must hate ye!" mused the blacksmith, gazing at Greyburn with intense loathing. "But I lose time. I came here to kill ye, an' I'm goin' to do it. I know this ground pretty well. I've ben all over it. There isn't a house within the sound o' pistol shot. No teams are likely to pass at this hour. When yer dead I'll throw yer body into the river down thar. I warn ye I'm not triflin'. I'll give ye two minutes more."

Dinsmore produced a large navy revolver and proceeded to examine the cartridges.

"That's a pretty thing you have there," said Greyburn. "Let me look at it." He reached out his hand as if he really expected the weapon would be given him for inspection.

"Back!" cried the blacksmith, "or ye'll die even sooner than the time I gave ye!"

"How much time is there left?" asked Greyburn, standing with his hands in the pockets of his sacque coat. "Play fair now, fellow. Don't cheat me on the time."

"You have one minute more," said Dinsmore. "In sixty seconds you will be a dead man."

"In *fifty* seconds, more likely," corrected Greyburn. "And do you really mean to shoot me?"

"As true as thar's a God in heaven!" said the blacksmith, raising his weapon.

There was a loud report and a man lay writhing on the sod, while flakes of blood discolored the green grass. It was not Hector Greyburn.

"I hope the scamp is not killed," he said, as he turned with a shudder from the sight of the sanguinary leaves. "What a cold-blooded villain he must be! I suppose I ought to go to the hotel and get assistance to take him there. That wasn't a bad shot to be made from a coat pocket."

He walked around the prostrate form. Dinsmore, who was still conscious, turned slightly, and a new effusion of the life fluid gushed forth. Greyburn took several steps backward and went over the edge of the cliff.

The first fall was only eight or ten feet, but his forehead struck a jagged stone and he knew no more. His body rolled down the sides of the mountain, striking here and there, until it reached the river, when the swollen stream picked it up and hurried it upon its bosom toward the sea.

CHAPTER XVIII.

SEVERAL hours later than the events just narrated, a teamster came along the road leading to Johnsbury, and his horses shied from a creature who lay on the grass by the roadside and feebly waved a handkerchief stained with blood. The teamster's name was Jones. He stopped his animals and went to look at the object which had attracted their attention.

"What's hurt ye, my man?" he asked, after taking

a scrutinizing look at the blacksmith. "Accidentally shot, hey?" he added, picking up the revolver which lay partially hidden in the leaves. "Is it very bad? Can't ye get up? Why don't ye speak?"

Dinsmore shook his head with a feeble motion, which showed that even that exertion cost him a painful effort, at the same time revealing to his questioner, by removing his hand, a bullet mark in the side of his throat, from which blood was slowly oozing.

"Can't speak, hey?" said the teamster. "Wall, what you want is a doctor, that's sartin. I'll take ye back to Chatham Corners, whar old Doc. Robinson 'll fix ye up. Let me cotch holt o' ye an' I'll git ye inter the waggin."

He was suiting the action to the word when Dinsmore made a movement to dissuade him. He pointed toward Chatham Corners and shook his head a little. Then he pointed in the opposite direction.

"Don't want ter go ter the Corners?" queried Jones, interpreting the signs aright. "But ye'll have ter. Johnsb'ry's ten miles at least, an' Chatham ain't *one*. That 'ere bullet-hole wants tendin' ter, an' mighty quick, if I'm ter judge by the paralyzin' it's done a'ready."

Dinsmore made a motion to get at his pocket, but failed. His right arm was well-nigh useless, and he could not reach the place with his left hand. The teamster saw that something was wanted and lent his assistance. A common pocket knife was disclosed, which did not prove to be the article sought. Next came a worn purse, and this Dinsmore opened. Taking fifty dollars in bills from it, he showed them to the teamster, and pointed again toward Johnsbury.

"Ye want me ter take ye to Johnsb'ry an' not ter the Corners, do ye, an' ye'll give me this 'ere money ef I'll do it?"

The blacksmith gave unmistakable assent.

"Wall, I sha'n't!" replied Jones, dryly. "I might have yer death on my hands. No knowin' but they'd accuse me o' killin' ye ef I brought ye into Johnsb'ry dead. No, it's no use, I tell ye," he continued, as Dinsmore took out bill after bill and frantically shoved them toward him to increase the bribe. "I can't do it. I've wasted time enough a'ready argying. Here! put that well arm aroun' my neck, an' I'll h'ist ye inter the waggin."

Dinsmore refused point-blank to render any such assistance and obstinately stretched himself out on the ground as if determined not to be moved. Jones looked at him in some astonishment and presently his temper began to rise.

"By gosh! yer a goin' ter the Corners with me ef I have ter pry ye inter the team with a cart-stake. A man's no bus'ness ter kill hisself jest out of a notion that he prefers a Johnsb'ry doctor to old Cy. Robinson. I'll git the team aroun' here whar it's not so far to lug ye an' I'll have ye aboard as sure's my name's Jones."

The teamster turned at the word and went back to his horses. In a minute he was backing them down to where Dinsmore lay, when he became aware that the blacksmith had moved from his former position. Only a few feet intervened between the road and the precipice, and when Jones caught sight of the wounded man he was making desperate efforts to reach the edge. Hastily letting go of his horses, the teamster sprang to where Dinsmore was and laid a heavy hand upon his clothing. Weak and half-paralyzed, the blacksmith turned savagely and tried to insert his teeth in the friendly hand, at the same time making a violent struggle to precipitate himself over the edge of the cliff. The surprised but now aroused teamster caught the man by his clothing and, in spite of his resistance, placed him by main force upon the bottom of the wagon.

"What the devil's up now?" he said, panting for breath after this extraordinary exertion. "Ain't ye hurt enough yit? Is it suicide yer been tryin' with the pistol?"

Dinsmore caught eagerly at the idea and made signs in the affirmative.

"Why the blazes didn't ye take another shot out o' this navy, then?" asked the teamster, taking up the pistol. "Ef yer wanted ter die ye had chance enough before I come along. Ye could a ben firin' this thing off instid o' wavin' that handkerchief. Durn me!" he continued, after a more careful inspection of the weapon, "not one o' these ca'tridges has been touched off. Say, look a here, thar's some monkeyin' ter this. Ye didn't shoot yerself. Now, who did?"

Dinsmore lay back in the wagon with a moan. He had not strength enough nor sufficient resources in the sign language to reply to this new suspicion. He waved his hand feebly toward Chatham Corners, as if to express his wish to go even there rather than endure a longer cross-examination.

"By gum!" said Jones, as he revolved the matter over in his mind, "I'd like ter understand this thing a little afore I leave here. Fust, I'll look out fer this chickin so't he won't throw hisself out o' the waggin an' break his neck, an' then I'll gaze 'round." In spite of Dinsmore's remonstrances, which took the form mainly of expressions of severe pain, Jones wound tightly around his body a long rope which lay under the seat, securing the ends to rings on the side of the wagon-body. "Ye won't die fer a minute," he soliloquized, "an I'm dumned ef I'm going back ter the Corners until I can give some sort of a notion what's ben goin' on here."

The teamster walked up and down the road, sharply inspecting each object.

"It don't look like a fight," he said, aloud. "The only dents on the grass are whar this feller lay. Prob'ly the chap what shot him wasn't very close. He must a seen him, o' course, or he wouldn't a had his own shooter out. But he claimed that he done it hisself. That's what bothers me. He don't want the other feller troubled, that's sure. Now, why didn't he want ter go ter the Corners? Could it a ben anybody thar? P'raps he thinks they're waitin' ter finish him. Thar ye are agin ; fer he sartinly tried ter finish hisself over that cliff. Wall, I'm dumfisticated ! It's a mighty pecooliar case."

While speaking of the cliff, Jones walked to the edge of it and looked over. Something attracted his attention and he ran down the road a little farther to find a place where he could descend the side of the declivity. Succeeding in this, he was but a moment more in reaching the object which he had discovered. It was a gentleman's stiff hat. The brim was broken in, and the lining torn on one side. He picked it up and examined it with some excitement. Looking a little further, he found a piece of blue cloth, several inches square, clinging to some thorny bushes, and a button such as is used on gentlemen's coats. A diligent search, clear to the water's edge, revealed a few shreds of the same sort of cloth, caught here and there in the underbush, and marks all along, showing that a heavy body had rolled rapidly down the mountain into the river. Jones looked at the swollen torrent, rushing in all its fullness over its rocky bed, and turned to retrace his steps.

"Prob'ly somebody's found the body—what's left of it—som'ers down stream," he mused. "Thar's no use in my botherin' about that."

Dinsmore looked anxiously into the teamster's face as he mounted the wagon and took up his reins. Then he made one more effort to get him to turn about and go away from the Corners, but without avail.

" No, siree !" said Jones, giving a decided shake to his head. " Thar's ben death thar, mister, an' murder, fer all I know, an' I hope I'm a good citizen an' know my dooty. The fust doctor fer ye an' the fust constable fer the rest is my course, an' the quicker the sooner. So lay as comf'table as ye can an' I'll git along to the Corners."

Jones was a humane man, but he was laboring under increasing excitement, and he drove his horses rather faster than a strict regard for the comfort of his wounded passenger would have dictated. Into his humdrum life had come a novel and interesting feature. He had suddenly risen into a being of great importance in the community. In his keeping was the discovery of a fatal accident, at least, and perhaps even a murder. It would not be just to say that Mr. Jones hoped that anybody had been killed ; but if anybody had been he was not displeased to be the bearer of the first tidings. As he rode along he imagined himself on the witness-stand before a crowded courtroom, reciting in a graphic manner the facts in his possession, while the gaping crowd looked on with wonder. Whether accident or homicide it was at least a great mystery, and he, Mr. Amos Jones, would bear the first news in relation to it.

In the little village of Chatham Corners there was excitement enough that morning before Mr. Jones drove into it with his burden. Greyburn's absence at his usual breakfast time had caused surprise, which did not abate when an hour, and then two hours elapsed, and nothing was heard of him. Clara had communicated her own alarm to the landlady, and within a few minutes every person in the village knew that Greyburn was missing. No one could give an account of him. His extremely early rising had taken place before any one else was stirring.

Jones did not live directly in the village, but on a farm in the outskirts. Otherwise he must have heard the inquiries made before he left home. By ten o'clock Clara had become well-nigh distracted.

"Your brother's all right, miss," said the landlady, for the fiftieth time, in a vain attempt to console her. "He's just taken a walk over the hills and got interested in the scenery. Lord ! strangers always do that. I've known 'em to stay all day climbing over the rocks, looking at stones and flowers. Don't you worry, Miss. He'll be home by dinner time, now you see if he ain't."

"But he never did so before," moaned Clara. ' And—and—you don't understand it, Mrs. Baldwin, but I've reasons to fear for him this morning. I'm afraid—perhaps I ought not to say it—but I'm very much afraid we shall never see him again. He said some things last night which frightened me. Oh ! he should not have gone like that ! It will break my heart !"

The motherly Mrs. Baldwin took the weeping girl in her lap and hushed her against her breast.

"There, dearie, don't ! He'll be all right, depend on it. Supposing he's gone away, it's only to go home, I've no doubt, and he'll write to you when he gets there. It's nothing to cry so hard for, dearie. Don't now ! you'll make me break down, too."

She kissed the girl's wet cheeks, but the tears only came faster and faster.

"Oh, Mrs. Baldwin !" said Clara, raising her woe-begone face, "I must tell you something which you mustn't reveal unless I give you leave. He's not my brother at all. We deceived you."

"Not your brother!" echoed the landlady, shrinking impulsively from the childish form and making a movement to disengage the encircling arms. She had very severe ideas of propriety, had Mrs. Baldwin.

"Oh, it's not what you think!" exclaimed Clara, hastily, while the hot blood flew to her face as she read the landlady's suspicions in her eyes. "He is my husband. Here is the certificate. We've been married three weeks. Oh! do you think I'll ever see him again?"

She burst into renewed sobbing, and the careful landlady inspected the little piece of paper which proclaimed her lodger an honest woman. Satisfied with its contents, she drew a sigh of relief and gave it back to its owner.

"So it's a quarrel between you," she said. "Too bad, too bad! Three weeks ought to go in peace, let what will come after."

"A quarrel?" repeated Clara. "Oh, no! not a quarrel. He loved me with all his heart. It is all my fault, all mine. He never spoke a cross word to me and never would."

"But you have been here more than a fortnight," said the cautious Mrs. Baldwin, "and you have never entered his room nor he yours."

The good landlady had her own notions on several subjects, and they were very pronounced ones.

"I cannot explain any more," said Clara, blushing again, and never ceasing to weep. "I suppose I ought not to have told you that we were married. He might not like it. Do you think he will come back? May he not have met with some accident! I think some of us ought to go and search for him."

She sprang to her feet and caught up her bonnet as she said this. At that moment a domestic opened the door and called for Mrs. Baldwin. Clara passed with her into the dining-room, where stood a rough-looking man with a broken hat in his hand.

"I reckon that ye're the lady I want, after all," he said, addressing Clara. "Yer brother hain't ben seen this mornin', has he?"

"No," cried the girl. "What do you know of him? Speak quickly!"

"Was this his hat?" asked the man, holding out the one in his hand.

Clara took the article with a strange feeling and saw that it was bruised and dented. Even this did not seem to convey any distinct notion to her mind. She dimly wondered how Hector's hat got into this man's possession, but nothing more.

"I think it is his hat," she said, laying it on the table. "I don't know. You've seen him wear it, Mrs. Baldwin. Is it the same?"

"It's his," said the landlady, growing a little paler. "I noticed the name inside. Probably there's no other New York hat at the Corners."

"An' this," said the man, producing a piece of blue cloth. "Did he wear a suit like that?"

"The very same!" cried Mrs. Baldwin. "Yes, and that's one of his buttons, too. Oh, my poor child!"

She turned and clasped Clara in her arms.

"I don't quite understand," stammered the girl, looking from Mrs. Baldwin to the man and back again. "The hat is his, the cloth and the button, but —where's Hector!"

"Miss," said the man, "it's hard to be tellin' these things, but I found that hat on the side of a precipice a mile up from here, an' the button an' cloth down near the foot o' the hill."

"Yes—yes!" she exclamed again, "but where is he —Hector? Did it—was he hurt?"

"I couldn't find him at all," said the man, bluntly.

"Then he is somewhere on the way here," cried

Clara. " I will go at once and meet him. Show me
the road." She started for the door.

" Miss," said the man, " ye don't seem to understand. Thar's a river at the foot o' them cliffs. He
must a rolled down inter it."

" But he can swim !" exclaimed Clara, almost pee-
vishly· " If it was a mile wide he could cross it. We
must look for him. You won't go ? Then I will go
without you !"

" Ye've never seen the place, o' course," pursued
the man.   " He went over the cliffs an' struck on his
head an' then rolled near a hundred feet before he
reached the river. He must a ben stunned long before he got ter the water. The stream thar runs
very fast an' is full o' rocks an' eddies an falls.
Now do you see ?"

It was evident that she did at last.

" You think he's *dead ?*" she screamed.

"⸴I'm afeared so, Miss," he said, nodding his head
compassionately.

She did not swoon, though with instant thought the
good landlady and the open-mouthed kitchen girl
caught her on either side. The event was too stupen-
dous to be met in an ordinary way. She even declined the rocking chair which they offered her, and
after a moment's study declared again that she must
go at once to the place where the things were found.

" He was very strong," she said, "and would survive a hurt which might prove fatal to a weaker man.
He may have reached the shore further down the
river and still be too much injured to get home. Go,
my good man, get help and let us hasten to him. I
will see that all are well paid. He is rich. Lose no
time, I entreat you !"

She laid her hand on the teamster's sleeve, when he
spoke again.

" Thar's a man over here in Dr. Robinson's office

that I'm sartin can tell ye all about it. He's badly hurt hisself, but the doctor says he'll pull through. Ef ye're strong enough ter go anywhere's, ye'd better go thar fust."

John Dinsmore lay on a lounge in the office of the only physician at Chatham Corners. He was listening with deep interest to every word which the doctor was saying to a neighbor, who had been called in to render necessary assistance.

"It's a curious wound," mused the old doctor. "Not necessarily fatal, but likely to make trouble enough. Already it has paralyzed the vocal organs and partially deadened the limbs on the right side. The bullet went clear through, you see. It was a close shave. An eighth of an inch more would have ruptured the jugular, and then—good-bye, John !"

Dinsmore made a quick motion with his left hand and was about to insert his forefinger in the wound when the wily physician sprang upon and stopped him.

"Get me that cord !" he said to his assistant. " I've got to tie him again. He's got the suicidal mania, as sure as fate. Jones told me he tried to throw himself over the cliff. There, he's all right now. See who that is knocking at the door, will you ?"

Dinsmore saw as quickly as did the man who opened the door, that Clara Greyburn was the foremost of the party. The mental agony of the moment was terrible. He would have gladly welcomed death in any form to shut out the sight of this woman whose husband's blood was on his head. True, his hands had not done the deed, but his acts had led up to it, and he was not one to draw fine distinctions. A moment before Greyburn fell over the precipice Dinsmore's finger had pressed the trigger which was to send him to eternity. He was a murderer. He had never for a second doubted his full responsibility for his enemy's death. Nor, indeed, was he sorry it had occurred. Had he been able to escape meeting Clara he would have been content. This was the only thing he dreaded and for which he was unprepared.

His first act after seeing who was entering the office was to turn his face resolutely to the wall in the hope that he might escape detection. But close on the heels of Clara and her party came Squire Jarvis, the town clerk and justice of the peace of Chatham, whom Jones had prudently notified on his way to the hotel, and who brought with him his son to serve as scrivener. A dozen other persons, who had learned the news or some part of it, with that celerity which circulates information through a country village, came flocking to the doctor's office, and soon blocked up the doorway.

" Everybody must get out of here except those who have got testimony to give," was the immediate decision of the Justice. " I'm going to take down the statements, so you'll learn about it when the proper time comes. Go now, all of you."

" Mrs. Baldwin an' her gal ain't got no more business thar'than we uns," protested a cadaverous young man with mouth full of " nigger-head." " Treat everybody alike, I say."

This remark was received with applause by the rest of the crowd, which was partially silenced by the reply of the Justice that Mrs. Baldwin and her domestic were the last persons known to have seen Mr. Greyburn alive.

" Wall, I see him, too," put in he of the hatchet face.

" When ?" demanded the Justice.

" Last night, when he drove into the village."

" Oh, we all saw him then," laughed the Justice. " I did, I'm sure. You'll have to go."

Amid the good-natured raillery which this reply

brought on the would-be witness, the outsiders withdrew and Squire Jarvis arranged the table for his son, giving him orders to record in the most careful manner every word of the testimony which might be given.

Amos Jones' story came first, and he told it with every detail. All listened with deep interest to every word, but none more intently than Clara. Dinsmore lay as still as death, with his face to the wall, and even when he saw how much he had committed himself he made no sign. It was not the punishment by the law that he feared. He only wondered what he should do if she came to recognize him.

The examination of the witness had not proceeded far, when at Clara's earnest request word was sent to the villagers that a liberal reward would be paid for any news of the lost man, and she was gratified to learn that a number of persons had gone with all speed to the scene of the tragedy. As for herself, she could not have gone now. A fascination rooted her to Dr. Robinson's office, where lay the man whose acts showed that he knew her husband's fate.

After Squire Jarvis had extracted all the information which Mr, Jones was capable of giving, he turned to Clara.

"We will hear you next," he said. "Your full name, please ?"

"Clara Campbell Greyburn." At the last word she bowed her head a moment in her hands. It brought a new sense of her possible widowhood.

"Mr. Greyburn was your brother, I believe ?"

"Oh, I don't believe I can testify to-day," said Clara, in piteous tones. "It is so dreadful. I do not, I cannot think he is dead. Why must I go through this ordeal ?"

"Believe me," the Justice responded, with great consideration, "I realize the painful necessity which compels my question. But I am a justice of the peace and it is my imperative duty to learn all the facts. If your brother is alive and well, or has met with nothing but a slight accident, what we are writing down will do him no harm. If worse has befallen him, every word we can learn now is of the utmost importance. Will you proceed?"

"I will try," said Clara, striving to master the trembling in her voice. "What was your question?"

"I had just written down that Mr. Greyburn was her brother," said Mr. Jarvis, Jr.

"That is wrong. I know we gave it out so when we came here, and we meant no harm by it, but in reality he is my husband. Mrs. Baldwin knows. She has seen the certificate."

She produced the document and handed it to the Squire. It produced a genuine sensation in the room, and caused the brow of the Justice to assume a yet graver appearance.

"I see by this that you have been married but three weeks. You must have come directly here from New York after the wedding."

She assented.

"Now tell me, as well as you can, without going into too many details, what was the trouble between you and your husband."

"I cannot," faltered Clara. "If he is living I should never forgive myself. If he is dead"—here she spoke with a gasp and moan—"I will let it die with him. There was no quarrel. He loved me ardently. We parted at ten last night the best of friends. Why do you torture me with these questions?"

"You parted at ten last night?" repeated the Justice. "Where did he go then?'

"To his room, I suppose. I did not see him again."

"He *did* go to his room," interposed Mrs. Baldwin.

" I can testify to that, for I saw him enter it. So did Harriet. He was in there at least until after twelve o'clock, for I should have heard him if he had come out before that time."

" You occupied different rooms, then," said Squire Jarvis. " Will you tell me why ?"

" You are distracting me !" cried Clara. " Of what use can such a question be ? We were only married a little while—and ——"

" Well," said the Justice, looking her full in the eyes.

" It was my wish, that is all. It was my wish and he respected it. He loved me better than I loved him. Poor Hector !"—here she broke into passionate sobbing—" bring him back to me, and I will love him now ! I will never leave him, night or day !"

The swoon had come. They carried her into the house, which adjoined the office, and laid her on the bed, where womanly hands set about her restoration. When she had gone, Dinsmore turned toward the group in the room and motioned violently toward the table. They understood him. A pencil and paper were soon at his disposal and his arm was released from the rope. With infinite pains he wrote with his left hand in cramped and almost undecipherable characters :

" For God's sake, don't go on with this ! I killed the man ! Take me away."

" How did you do it ?" asked Squire Jarvis.
The blacksmith took the pencil again and wrote :

" I killed him, that is enough. In God's name take me to jail ; hang me ; anything !"

" I don't understand this," whispered the Squire to his son. " You noticed how he turned his face away when Mrs. Greyburn was in the room. I want to see if she will recognize him."

When Clara could sit up, they brought her in, supported by Mrs. Baldwin, the doctor's wife and Harriet. The blacksmith suspected their intention and covered his face with his arm. It required the strength of two men to remove it and turn him toward Clara. His eyes were shut, and the loss of blood had made his face ghastly white, but she uttered his name with a cry and fainted again.

"Write down 'John Dinsmore,'" said Squire Jarvis to his son, "and get a carriage ready to take him to the Johnsbury jail."

———————◆———————

CHAPTER XIX.

SEVERAL miles from the thriving county seat known as Johnsbury stood a cabin all by itself on the edge of the wood. No habitation was visible from its windows. The place was known as " Phillipses." Old Bill Phillips, the owner, bore a hard name in all the country round. Was a hen-roost robbed? it was at Phillipses that they always looked first, and the fact that they never found anything there did not in the least remove the general belief that Bill was the culprit. Did a sack of corn or a live pig disappear? Phillips was the first name mentioned. Rapid River came tumbling down the hills very near his farm. In this stream there were always plenty of trout. The nearest thing to honest work that old Bill had ever been known to do was to angle for these creatures, and his skill at taking them had given him a reputation hardly inferior to that caused by his unlawful pranks. On the morning that Hector Greyburn's body fell into the Rapid's torrent, Phillips happened to be wandering about an eighth of a mile further down the stream, where lay a particularly fine trouting basin. He had just got comfortably to work and was preparing to pull in a good string of the finny tribe, when a different object attracted his attention.

" By the great horn spoon, that ain't no fish !" he exclaimed, laying down his pole. " It's a man, dead ar alive, or I'm a sucker !"

He sprang with extraordinary agility for one of his years upon a heavy boulder which lay directly in the course the body was taking, and made a vigorous effort to get hold of it, but it eluded his grasp and was whirled rapidly down the stream.

" I wonder if the cuss is alive," he exclaimed, springing back to the shore as quickly as he left it. " He don't want to hit that cocoanut of his many times more agin them rocks if there *is* any life in him. I'll try my fishing-pole and see if I can't anchor him that way."

Phillips ran down the stream with the pole in his hands, and soon had the satisfaction of fastening the hook in the clothing of the floating man. With the careful effort of one who had practiced with the rod on almost every kind of fresh-water fish, he gradually drew the body to the shore, and at last caught it vigorously with his hands and drew it upon the land.

Acting upon his first impulse, Phillips turned the man over on his face in the grass and set about the common methods of resuscitation. For ten minutes he worked with all his might to restore life to the still form, but apparently without avail. All at once he stopped suddenly, as though struck by a new idea. He looked anxiously in every direction to front and rear and then, ceasing his work, he stood for a minute in doubt.

" This fellow is well dressed," he was thinking to himself. " Perhaps he's got a pretty pile of money about him. If he has, haven't I a right to it if I can get it? If he's dead, it won't do him no good, and if he's alive, I'm entitled to something for saving him. By Goshen! I'll examine his pockets, any way."

A gold watch and chain were the first articles found. Next, a diamond stud in the shirt bosom was wrenched off. Finally a pocket-book was discovered, and on opening it Phillips found a number of bills, some of large denominations, only slightly dampened by the water. The sight of the money seemed to put a devil into old Bill's heart, for he hastily pocketed his plunder, and, grasping the body by its clothing, started to drag it once more toward the bank of the stream. In this work he was interrupted in a most unexpected manner. A slight, boyish form appeared on the high road adjacent, and a voice called out:

"Stop!"

Phillips was a coward. None other would have robbed a helpless fellow creature and then sought to bury in eternal silence the only voice which could testify against him. He loosened his hold of the body and turned in a startled way towards the boy, who came with all speed to where he was standing.

"What are you trying to do?" said the lad. "Would you kill the man as well as take his money."

Phillips looked with pretended innocence at his childish accuser.

"Who's thinking of killing any one?" he blurted out. "A man's a right to save a body that he finds floating in the river, ain't he? You wouldn't argy in a court of justice that there's law agin' that?"

"No," said the boy, with a determined air, "but there's law against robbing a man whether he's alive or dead; and there's a thing they call humanity, which teaches us to save a human life when we can."

Old Bill stood on the defensive.

"Who pulled this 'ere body out of the Rapid? Tell me that!"

"You, I suppose, if you say so," replied the boy. "But that gives you no right to put it back again, as you were going to do when I stopped you."

"Going—to—put—it—back!" repeated Phillips, as if horror-stricken at the idea. "You ought not to say that, young fellow. I was only going to get him nearer to the edge of the drink so I could wet his head. That's all I was ever dreaming of, 'pon my word, now."

The boy could not help smiling a little. "His head needs wetting, I should think," he said, passing the soaked hair through his hand. "That's a pretty poor story. What he needs is liquor of some kind. Give me that flask in your pocket and I'll turn some down his throat."

Phillips handed the boy a flask, which happened to be nearly full, but he had no sooner done so than he began to recover a little of his courage, and reached for it again.

"By cripes, boy! I've got a word to say about this matter. You ain't going to fetch this fellow to, and then help him to cheat me out of my honest share of what I have found on him. I don't want no trouble with you, but there's got to be an understanding before we go any further."

"Oh, there has, has there?" said the boy. "Well, I'm telling you that everything will have to be done to save this man's life before anything else. Take hold and help me do that, and then you may reward yourself out of that pocket-book, if you are mean enough to take it in that way."

The old man looked at the lad with an undecided air.

"How do I know you'll do the right thing if I take you at your word?" he asked.

" For Heaven's sake, have some confidence in what I tell you," said the lad. "You know what to do, for I saw you at work before. Hold on ! here is a bullet-hole in his coat. Perhaps he was shot before he got into the water. No, the hole was made by this pistol, which must have been discharged accidentally. Come, will you help me, or shall I go for other assistance ?"

Phillips glanced hastily up and down the stream and back toward the woods. His look was enough to make the boy rise to his feet and grasp the revolver which he had taken.

"None of that ! I've made a fair proposition to you. Now if you don't go to work and help me save this man, there'll be trouble."

Bill saw that he was foiled and at once reassumed his mild manner.

"Sartinly, I'll do anything that's reasonable," he said, beginning to rub the hands of the drowned man. "You'll do what's right, I'm sure. I'll trust you. Hand me the brandy."

He poured a generous quantity down the throat, and for several minutes proceeded to use every endeavor to bring motion into the still form. Just as he was on the point of declaring that there was no use in trying longer, a faint groan brought a bright light into the eyes of the younger of the workers and seemed not to displease even the elder.

" He's coming round," said Phillips, "but this ain't no place to get him clear out of this stupor. There's a little shanty not far off where the fishermen camp sometimes, and if we could get him there and get a fire going, he'd soon be all right. Do you suppose you could bear a hand if I can carry the heft of him ?"

Overjoyed at the proposal, the boy gathered up the articles which had been strewn upon the grass, and lent his slight assistance toward raising the body from the ground. It was a severe tax on his strength, but he bore his part of the burden without complaint. Every forty or fifty steps they halted for a moment's rest. Phillips took every opportunity to reiterate his expressions of confidence in his young companion, and to declare his belief that he would never see an honest man the worse off for trying to save a fellow-creature.

"If I hadn't fished him out, he'd been dead sure before this," he would say. "He wouldn't be any kind of a man to grudge me a little spare change, would he? And you wouldn't be the one to encourage such an idea, I can tell that by the looks of you."

They reached the cabin at last, and stripping off the drenched clothing laid the body on a couch. With the aid of hot water and a lot of old towels which they found, they soon witnessed a marked improvement in the condition of their patient. Rubbing with hot cloths and an internal dose of hot brandy and water did wonders. Phillips seemed to have entirely given up his first ideas and devoted himself assiduously to the work before him. The boy arranged the wet clothing by the stove, where it would dry and then sat down exhausted.

"I can't see as he's got any real hard clip except this one on his forehead," said Phillips, after making a careful inspection. "He's scratched and bruised enough, but that's the only jinooine winder. He'll never look so pretty as he used to in the face, if I'm any guesser. That cut goes slantingly clear across the forehead."

The injured man turned his head and muttered something unintelligible.

"What he ought to have is a doctor, I suppose," said Phillips. "I don't see how it's to be managed, though. It won't do for me to knock all my own intcrests in the head. And yet, the cuss is coming round so comfortable that I really hate to see him fall back now."

The boy sitting by the fire was very busy thinking. Presently he said :

"Let me see that pocket-book."

"You'll do the fair thing now," whined Phillips, handing it over with evident reluctance. "I've dealt square with you and you must do the same with me."

"I will keep my word," replied the boy. He proceeded to count the money and was evidently surprised at the large amount.

"There is six thousand dollars here," he said.

"I knew there wasn't far from that."

"How much do *you* want ?"

"How much ?" repeated the old man.

"Yes.   Don't be unreasonable. I want to treat you fairly, but remember there are two of us to share in this thing.   I've got rights here as well as you."

The old man looked at the lad in a dazed way.

"You want part for yourself !" he gasped.

"Why not ?"

"I—I thought ——" began Phillips.

"Yes, I know what you thought," replied the boy. "Because I wasn't willing to have him killed, you thought I wouldn't take anything for my trouble in saving him."

"Well," said the old man, after a pause, "you ought to have something. What do you say ?"

"There's still another one to share," said the boy.

"Who ? What do you mean ?" cried Phillips, looking thoroughly scared.

The lad pointed to the man on the bed.

"*Him.* You wouldn't leave him wounded and sick like that without a penny, would you ? He must be got away from here and nursed back to health, so that he can rejoin his friends. That will cost money. Come, partner, we must leave him his share. If he can't speak, we will speak for him."

This idea was too strange for Phillips to accept immediately.

"If we leave any money on him, the next man who comes along will steal it," he said, finally. "So what's the use? We'd better divide it, half and half. I say, now, you won't kick at that? I'll give up half to you. I swear I hadn't ought to be asked to do any better."

The boy reflected for a moment.

"The watch, chain and diamond. Throw those in for me and the man and we will accept your proposition. Only there is one thing more : you must help us to get away from here. I shall want food and medicine suitable, for him during the day and a conveyance to take us to some railroad station to-night. The sooner we put a few miles between us and this spot the better for me—the better for you. I shall not leave the man until he is able to go alone, or until his friends find him."

"Do you live in Johnsbury ?"

"No, nor anywhere else. It makes no difference where I go only so that I get away from here."

"It's a curious way of doing it," said the old man. "Why not skip out with your share of the stuff and send word in some way to the sheriff at Johnsbury where he can find the man ?"

"I've taken a fancy to him," said the lad, "and I won't leave him until he is much better, which I feel sure will take weeks of time. And, of course, I don't want to be found around here."

"Blessed if I can see why not ! You could get the whole credit of saving him."

"Oh, yes ! certainly," said the boy. "You are a calculator ! And when the police said, ' You carried this man here from the shore of the river all alone, we suppose ?' and when he told them there was three thousand dollars missing, I should be able to explain everything, of course !"

Phillips surveyed the boy with admiration.

"You're a keen one and you've got the right idea of it. I can get anything you want for him over here at a little settlement, and a carriage after dark is as easy as winking. The place for you to take the cars is about fifteen miles from here at a flag station. How will you explain things to the conductor, though ?"

"Can you get me an ounce of laudanum ?"

"To be sure."

" I'll give him small doses of that if I see he's becoming too clear in his mind. When we get to the cars I will wrap his head up and pass him for my sick brother. If he becomes too troublesome and is able to get along I can leave the train."

"That is first rate," said Phillips, delighted. "Only that laudanum, ain't you afraid to handle that ? It don't take much to kill a man, if I understand it right."

" I know just how much to give him," replied the lad. I wasn't two years in a doctor's office for nothing. You hurry and get that and the other things I've written for on this paper, and get back as soon as you can."

Phillips took the paper and left the cabin. It had come to be quite natural to obey now. The strong mind of the child had no difficulty in dominating the weaker mind of the man. The course which he took led him for a short distance up the bank of Rapid river, and he was just in time to meet the exploring party which had come down from Chatham Corners. There were a dozen men of them, all more or less excited. Seeing him come from the direction in which they were going they sprang toward him and began

to ply him with questions, for which he was well prepared.

"I did see something down the river a piece," he
said, in response to their inquiries, "and I thought at
the time it looked curious."

"How far down?" cried the crowd in one breath.

"How fur?" repeated the old man with deliberation. "Well, I couldn't just say exactly but perhaps
a couple of miles. Maybe three. It was near an hour
ago, anyhow, and I have been walking along at a
pretty even jog."

This intelligence fell like a wet blanket on the seek-
ers for reward. All but two or three concluded to
give up the search and return home, believing that
the body must have been found already by some one.
Those who went on were the youngest of the party,
who kept up the search for the novelty of it, though
without any real expectation of anything more than
getting the first news of the recovery. Phillips
chuckled to himself at the sensation he had created
and went his way.

Just after dusk that night a livery stable keeper of
Johnsbury, who bore not too good a reputation among
his townsmen, was accosted in his yard by a fellow
whose face was muffled in a heavy comforter and
whose voice was evidently disguised for the occasion.
The result of a brief conversation was that twenty
dollars was promised for a night's work, where no
questions would be asked. The stable keeper soon
after drove a hack with one passenger up the road
leading toward Chatham Corners. In an hour he
turned off into an unfrequented by-way and finally
stopped near a small cabin, where the passenger
alighted. It was our new acquaintance, Mr. William
Phillips.

"How is he?" was his first question, after entering

the house and seeing that his young friend was all ready to depart.

"Sleeping quietly," was the reply. "He will ride like a baby. Have you got plenty of pillows?"

"Everything you ordered."

"All right. Get your driver to help us put him into the carriage. After that we must obliterate all traces of having been here, and make sure there is nothing left to track us by."

The midnight train was signalled at Forest Hollow, and a sick man and his brother were given a section in the sleeper. Before this, however, three thousand dollars had been paid to Mr. Phillips, and that gentleman had expressed his unbounded regard for, and appreciation of the lad who had saved him that day from committing a cowardly and brutal murder.

The next morning, when the train reached Macon, assistance was procured to remove the sick man to a small hotel, where he was soon occupying a bed, and his hurt was being examined critically by Dr. Rerdell, the ablest physician of the place.

"You say that he struck his head against the platform on his way to the train?" said the doctor. "It is a serious injury, and though his life is in no immediate danger, grave complications may arise. You had better let me get you a good male nurse, as he needs constant attention. He ought to recover enough during the day to speak. I expect, however, that his first impressions will be of a wandering character, and shall not be surprised if he is unreasonable or violent. The case is peculiar. He has met with a great shock, greater even than I can ascribe to this injury on the head. But don't be alarmed; we'll have him all right in time."

The male nurse came at noon and proved himself an adept at his business. The boy took the opportunity to get a breath of fresh air out of doors. At five o'clock he returned and sat by the bedside while the nurse went to supper. A few minutes later the man in the bed opened his eyes, and smiling very pleasantly into the boy's face, said in a natural voice :

" What is your name ?"

" Charlie Leslie, sir. And yours ?"

" I don't know," said the sick man, with a broader smile, which almost became a laugh. He paused a minute. " I think my name is Bird & Bird, but I'm not sure. If it is, I'm a lawyer, and my office is at the Astor House. Ha ! ha !"

When the boy had summoned the nurse, the sick man was asleep again, and lay as quietly as though he were in perfect health.

CHAPTER XX.

HECTOR GREYBURN had a wonderful constitution. Few men would have survived the injuries which he sustained. That even he did it seems little short of miraculous. In falling over the edge of the cliff he struck first upon his shoulders and side, and the wound in his forehead was caused by a rebound which threw him against a sharp, projecting rock. He was unconscious before he realized that he had fallen. His roll down the hill bruised and scratched him, but did him no serious injury. The splash in the cold water of Rapid River, instead of adding to his hurt, really did much at first to aid his recovery. The coolness of the water tempered the fever which would otherwise have filled his veins. The rush of the stream was so great that he was swept forward too rapidly to have his breathing organs much endangered. Had he been rescued within a hundred yards of the place where he fell, the amount of water which he had inhaled would have hurt him but little. Every yard after that lessened his chances of recovery, and, had he remained much longer at the mercy of the torrent, our story would have ended at this point.

Dr. Rerdell knew, with the intuition of a skilled surgeon, that something more than the cut on the forehead must have occurred to cause the condition in which he found his patient, but as he had no reason to doubt that the statement of young Leslie embraced all *he* knew about the matter, the good doctor kept his suspicions to himself. He visited the sick man twice every day and held subdued talks with the nurse, whose name was Thompson, and who proved himself a very valuable assistant. Thompson was one of those men to whom sleep and rest are superfluities. He remained the whole of each afternoon and night with his patient, and only relinquished his post for a few hours in the morning, when Charlie took his place. Even then the nurse was in an adjoining room, where he could be called at a moment's notice if necessary.

Charlie Leslie was a remarkable youth, as his conduct in this affair would of itself abundantly prove. He was a slender little fellow, of a pale and striking countenance, and might be taken to be anywhere between twelve and fourteen years of age. When he sat at rest by Greyburn's bedside he hardly looked more than the former figure, while the intelligence which he showed in his contact with Phillips and in his dealings with the doctor and the hotel people, seemed fully commensurate with the supposition that he had even passed the latter. His perfect self-possession and the easy way in which he assumed the duties of his position were the subject of admiring criticisms on the part of all who had occasion to note them. He had taken the money left after settling

with Phillips and secreted it about his person. When
necessary to change a large bill he would go to some
banking-house to do it, rather than excite comment at
the hotel. He insisted on settling daily for everything, and could not be turned from his purpose, giving as a reason that he might have to leave at any
moment upon the receipt of expected news.

Within a day or two of his arrival he found the following in one of the Macon papers:

PROBABLE MURDER.—THE GUILTY PARTY ARRESTED.

JOHNSBURY, Sept. 22.—Last Friday a resident of
Chatham found a badly wounded man on the roadside
leading along the Chatham Cliffs. A bullet had passed
through his throat, paralyzing the vocal organs and
rendering him otherwise helpless. He was brought
to Chatham Corners. Subsequent developments
showed that a gentleman who was visiting at the Corners has disappeared, and the wounded man has made
a written confession of murdering the other. How he
received his own wound is a mystery, as he cannot
talk and refuses to explain by writing. Vigorous
search has not resulted in discovering the body, which
was probably swept out to sea. The arrested man is
named Dinsmore. Both he and his victim came from
somewhere in the Northern States, and are not known
hereabouts. The affair has created quite an excitement in this usually quiet locality. The murderer can
survive his own wound but a few days.

Charlie read this paragraph with a good deal of
interest, as it was a partial clue to what he sought.
He could not doubt that the man whom he had rescued
was the one referred to. The place, the time, and the
tell-tale bullet-hole in the pocket, all pointed to one
conclusion.

"Probably the other one struck this man with some
heavy weapon and threw him over the cliffs," he said

to himself. "Then, when the body fell, the hammer of the revolver struck something and sent a bullet through the murderer's throat. It was a marvellous but just retribution. With such a wound he will never live long enough for a trial." ̤

The next morning, when Thompson was out of the room, Charlie again had the pleasure of seeing the light of intelligence beam into the eyes of the sick man. Again he asked his name, and on being told, gratified his questioner by answering : "Oh, yes, you told me that before." In response to an inquiry regarding his own name, the sick man hesitated a little, knitting his brows as if in puzzled thought.

" I'm not sure," he said, presently. "It couldn't be John Dinsmore, could it ? If it is, I am a blacksmith and I live at Springdale."

The lad caught eagerly at this answer.

" And if your name is Dinsmore, you threw a man over the cliff at Chatham last week. Is it not so ?"

" No," said the sick man, promptly. "I did not throw him. He fell. He shot me first with his revolver. That is, if my name is Dinsmore, which I hardly believe. I say, what *is* my name ? You ought to know."

He looked eagerly at the lad.

" Think again," entreated Charlie. You were hurt, cut, nearly drowned. Where did you live ? What did they call you there ? You *must* remember."

He waited with impatience for a reply.

" It's strange I *can't*," said Greyburn. Could it be Jacob Mendall ? Am I a banker with an office on Wall street ? I don't believe I am, and yet every name I can think of sounds just as unreasonable. If I could get up and go out of doors I could find plenty of people who know me. Let me ride down to City Hall and I can tell you very soon."

" What City Hall ?" asked Leslie.

"Why, down-town, of course.   Near the Astor House.   Don't you know where City Hall is?"

"You are very much mistaken," said the lad. "We are in Georgia.   Now let me tell you your name. You are Henry M. Leslie.   I am your brother Charlie."

"Henry M. Leslie?" repeated the sick man, with a vacant stare.   "Are you sure?"

"Quite," said Charlie.

"And you are my brother?"

"Yes."

Greyburn lay quiet for several minutes.   "You are quite certain that my name is Leslie?" he said.

"Positive," said Charlie.   "Do not forget it again. The doctor will ask you when he comes and will consider it a good sign if you answer rightly.   I am very anxious that he should think you are recovering, as I want to get you out of doors."

"Whose house is this?" said the sick man, looking about the chamber.

"It is a hotel.   You were hurt as we were traveling."

Tired out with the long conversation, Greyburn relapsed into silence.   When the doctor came in the afternoon, Charlie said :

"My brother is gaining fast.   He knows his name to-day."

"What is your name?" asked Dr. Rerdell, taking his patient by the hand and applying his fingers to his wrist.

"Henry M. Leslie," was the reply.

"What makes you think so?" asked the cautious man of medicine.

"He told me," said Greyburn, pointing to the boy.

"You did not remember it youself?"

"No."

"But you remember it now?" said Charlie.   "There is no mistake?"

"Y-e-s," said the sick man, rather faintly. "I—re-member—it—now."

The doctor shook his head a little and wrote some orders for Thompson. When the medical man left the room Charlie went with him.

"What do you think?" asked the boy, when they were out of sight of their patient.

"He has not gained as much as you believe, I am sorry to say," said Dr. Rerdell. "Indeed, I am more discouraged than I have hitherto been. It is evident that he remembers nothing. He takes your word that his name is Leslie, as he would if you told him it was Jenkins or Williamson. That shows a bad condition of the brain, which it may take a long time to remedy. Physically, he is coming around fast. Within a week he can probably ride out with safety. But mentally his gain is slow. It may take a long time before he is wholly rational."

Before a week had elapsed they took Greyburn out in a carriage and drove into the suburbs. The ride invigorated him so much that they had difficulty in keeping him from getting out to pick some flowers which he saw by the road-side. In the evening he was not easily persuaded that he ought to retire early. After that, they allowed him to be dressed at breakfast time, and to sit up until nine or ten at night. He began to eat his meals with relish, and to a stranger he bore few traces of his severe illness, other than a long, red gash on his forehead and the bruises and discolorations on his face. At first he wore a bandage about his head, but as the wound was not one which required stitches, this was soon removed. Thompson was still retained, as it was felt that Greyburn should never be left alone, but he came and went about as he pleased. He did not seem to desire to go far from the hotel, except when riding, and paid very little attention to what he saw.

Among the articles which Charlie had found in Greyburn's pockets was a photograph of himself, taken within a few months. The boy had given it a hasty glance and then, not thinking that it was the likeness of any person he had ever seen, had laid it away again. One day, after Greyburn's partial recovery, he bethought himself of this picture. They were alone at the time. Charlie never tried these experiments before third parties. He handed him the photograph and waited to try the effect.

"Very good, don't you think so?" said Greyburn, after inspecting it.

"Who is it?" said Charlie.

"That's an odd question. Myself, to be sure."

"You don't mean that, do you?" said Charlie, trying to fix his attention again. "Think a little, can't you tell whose face that is?"

Greyburn surveyed it once more with a critical eye.

"If that is not a picture of me," he said, "then I don't know anything."

"Look in the mirror," said Charlie, turning toward a pier-glass which stood in the room. "If that person in the photograph is you, who is this man reflected in the glass?"

"I don't know that man," said Greyburn, after a long look, "but this one in the photograph is I. Why, it's clear enough. There's no doubt about it." He walked away as if bored with a discussion which seemed useless. The lad compared him carefully with the photograph, as he sat at the window, looking out upon the street.

"He may be right," he mused. "Those hurts and the ordeal through which he has gone have doubtless changed him much. There is a resemblance to his mouth here, and the chin is much the same, but his own mother wouldn't recognize him. What a mystery this is!"

One day when they were alone, Greyburn broke out suddenly :

"I don't want to dispute you, Charlie, for I like you very much, but I'm sure my name is not Leslie. I can think of many things which convince me you are wrong, and some day I shall be able to tell all about it. What I wish to say to you now is, don't desert me. I have a feeling that you are liable to leave me suddenly, and it keeps me from sleeping well at night. I should be lost without you. If my head ever gets clear again it will be by your aid. Don't leave me, will you ?"

"Certainly I will not," said the lad.

" I have an idea," pursued Greyburn, slowly, " that I have lost a lot of friends. I seem to have had them, and all at once something swept them away. I've got money too, somewhere, plenty of it. Stay with me and you shall lose nothing."

The boy promised once more that he would not leave him, and after that Greyburn seemed much easier in his mind. One day he asked :

" Have you any father or mother ?"

" Neither."

" Brother or sister ?"

" No one in the wide world," the boy confessed, unguardedly, with a trace of sadness in his tone.

" Nor I," said Greyburn. " Why, then, should we ever separate ? Why should we not always be brothers ?"

After that Greyburn's progress toward health was so rapid that Dr. Rerdell acknowledged that further delay in proceeding on their journey was needless.

" I would like to follow this case to its fulfillment," he said to Charlie, " but that is no reason why you should stay here all winter. If your brother is used to the Northern climate he will be better off there than here. Get the best physician you can, wherever you go, and I think you may hope for the best results."

Within a week Charlie and his friend were booked at a little hotel in the outskirts of the metropolis as "Henry M. and Charles Leslie." The careful Thompson had been brought along. Charlie had several ideas in his mind which he wanted an opportunity to work out, so he left Greyburn in charge of Thompson one day and took a train for the city. He had been there before. In a short time he stood on the steps of the Astor House buildings, conning the directory of offices at the doorway.

"That's all right at least," he said, comparing one of the addresses with a memorandum in his hand. "Bird & Bird, attorneys." He ascended the stairs rather timidly, and knocked so faintly at the lawyer's door that he had to knock again before he heard the answering summons to enter.

"Is this the office of Bird & Bird?" he inquired.

"*Of* course," said an over smart boy of about his own age, who happened to be the only tenant at the moment. "Can't you read?"

"Will they be in to-day?" pursued Charlie, too flustered to mind the sarcasm.

"*To* be sure," said the office boy. "At least, Mr. John will. Mr. Jason is trying a case in court, and whether he'll get through or not is more than I can tell."

"Are there any other persons here of the name of Bird?" Charlie found courage to inquire further.

"Not a Bird!" replied the office boy, jocularly. "Not another feathered biped! Not a songster in the cage but just those two! And a pretty pair they are! Owls, both of 'em! Hawks, sometimes! You may tell 'em, if you like. I've given my notice to quit Saturday, so *I* don't care."

Charlie went down the stairs slowly and stopped a moment at the base. A man with a red cap, evidently a messenger, passed him and awoke a new train of thought.

"Here!" he called to the man. "You're a messenger, aren't you?"

"You're right there," said he of the cap, good-naturedly.

"Could you make a few inquiries for me about town and bring an answer to this hotel?" asked Charlie, handing the man a card as he spoke.

"That's out of the city," said the man, "but I suppose I can arrange it if you'll pay for the trouble. I can do your errands this afternoon and ride out to see you in the evening."

"Let me see. Perhaps there is no need of that. The places are not very far from here. You could do all I wish and get back in an hour. I will meet you, say at three o'clock."

"All right," said the messenger. "What is to be done?"

"Take these names and addresses, go to each place described and find out if the man named is there, or if they know where he is. Evade questioners the best way you can. Here is a dollar in advance. If the job is worth more I will pay the rest when you return. Don't let it be known who sent you. If I wanted to be seen in the matter I should go myself."

Charlie walked over to a neighboring restaurant and got his dinner. He had some time to wait, and amused himself with the daily papers until three o'clock, when he returned to the Astor House offices. The messenger came, punctual to the minute.

"I found them all," he said, drawing out his memorandum book.

" Jacob Mendall, banker, Wall street, was in his office this morning, but has gone for the day. The clerks say he seldom returns after twelve o'clock.

" Clarence Perkyns was at the Metropolitan Club, so the porter informed me when I rang. He offered to call him, but I said I only wished to know, and hurried off.

" Harris R. Stedman is cashier of the bank I went to."

Charlie returned to Greyburn with all the information he had expected to get, and indeed rather more ; for he had had his doubts whether the names given him at various times were not entirely fictitious. It was now evident that his patient knew these people, and undoubtedly they knew him also. How to bring about the desired result without compromising himself was getting to be a serious question for Charlie.

The motives of the lad had been pure from the first. Had he not agreed to let Bill Phillips have a large part of the money found on Greyburn's body it is possible that neither he nor his friend would have been alive now. The old man was desperate, and would certainly either have killed the boy or been killed by him, neither event the most desirable that could be imagined. To keep faith with Phillips—a thing which the boy believed on his conscience he must do—it was necessary to remove Grayburn from the vicinity and to hide the fact of his being alive, at least for the moment, from every one at Johnsbury or Chatham. Each day the complications deepened. The money left was being spent rather lavishly, and the time when it would all be gone could not be far off. When the sick man's friends should appear upon the scene they would most likely demand an account of the missing funds. Whichever way Charlie turned things did not look very promising.

The day after he went into the city, Charlie took

out the photograph again and compared it with Grey-burn's face. It would never pass for a likeness, and yet there was something in it which convinced the lad that his friend's story might be true. All at once he noticed the name " Sarony" in bold letters on the bottom of the card, and sprang to his feet with an exclamation.

"What a fool I've been !" he said aloud, "hunting for these Mendalls and Stedmans and afraid to go near the police for facts, when I can learn from this photograph just what I seek. Sarony is in Union Square, and he can tell the name of every picture he ever made by consulting the negative. My search will soon be over now."

With a gay air he donned his hat and coat. Grey-burn sat idly in his easy chair, with his head resting on his hand. He looked up when he saw Charlie, and extended his hand with a smile.

"You'll not be gone long," he said. "I'm sure I'll be able to tell who I am to-morrow. I sit here and think, and think, and just as I am going to speak my name it eludes me. Don't stay any longer than you can help, Charlie. What should I ever do without you ?"

Mr. Sarony took the picture in his hand, when the lad presented it, and looked from it to Charlie with open-eyed wonder.

"What is this, do you say ?" he exclaimed. "I guess you haven't been around very much lately when you ask that question. Every police office in the country has a copy of that photograph. Why, it is that fellow who was killed out there in that Southern place—I never *can* remember names ——"

"Georgia ?" suggested the young lady at the counter.

"That's it," said Mr. Sarony. "And his name was —why, of course—Lord ! I shall forget my own name next—Greyburn. Why, of course—Hector Greyburn."

The boy looked up into Sarony's face, and the photographer saw that he was very pale. He had found a clue at last.

"Are you sure?" he asked, in tones scarcely audible.

"Positive," said Sarony, turning away. "If you don't believe me ask any one you meet in the street. Everybody knows that picture now."

The next morning, when Mr. Jason Bird came to his office, he found that a package had been left there for him. In it were bank bills aggregating a little over nineteen hundred dollars, and a note which made him open his eyes very wide. He remarked to his office boy that he might not be back during the day, and took a hasty departure. Arriving at the hotel where Greyburn was staying, he asked to be shown to the room where he was. Thompson answered his knock at the door.

"Can I see Mr. Henry M. Leslie?"

"Certainly; walk in," said Thompson, looking at the lawyer with some surprise. He was their first visitor.

Greyburn rose at the sound of his new name and came forward to shake hands with the lawyer. As he did so a light seemed to dawn upon him. Before speaking to Mr. Bird he asked Thompson to leave them alone, and the nurse somewhat doubtfully complied.

"You know me, I see," said the attorney.

"You are Mr. Jason Bird, of Bird & Bird, lawyers, Astor House offices," replied Greyburn, promptly.

"And who are you?"

"I am Hector Greyburn."

Both men laughed heartily.

"Well, what have you been up to?" said the lawyer, taking a chair. "Falling off of precipices and that sort of thing, eh?"

"I don't know," said Greyburn. "I haven't the slightest idea of anything, except that we are here in this room and that I have recovered my senses after days of aberration. I owe much to a young boy who has been with me and seen that a doctor, nurse and every other necessity was provided. He went off last night and has not yet returned. His name is Charlie—Charlie Leslie. Really, I owe him everything."

It was several days afterward that Mr. Jason Bird showed Greyburn the note which he got with that package. It contained a good deal of interesting matter, but nothing which compensated for the closing lines:

"You will tell Mr. Greyburn that I shall go far away and never see him again. He probably will not care enough about it to search for me, but if he should it will be useless. Under no circumstances can I ever return to him."

<hr>

CHAPTER XXI.

WHEN Clara recovered sufficiently to be told that Dinsmore had confessed to murdering her husband, she was plunged into the deepest melancholy. Bitterly she reproached herself with being the real cause of Hector's death, for had she been in a wife's true place, he would not have sallied forth alone on that fatal morning. The long train of his plot against her was forgotten. She remembered only the last three weeks of his life, and the horror of his death.

The blacksmith was securely under lock and key at Johnsbury. Every effort to get further particulars of the tragedy had been fruitless. The grand jury brought in an indictment against him, and a rising young lawyer of the county, Mr. Darby Spencer, was assigned as his counsel. Mr. Spencer labored with all his might to get something from his client which he could use in his defense, but Dinsmore continued obstinate. The most that he could be got to say, in his cramped chirography, was that the sooner they hanged him the better he should like it, and that, if Mr. Spencer really wanted to act the part of a friend, he could best show it by making the proceedings preliminary to that end as brief as possible.

Taking warning by the statements of Dr. Robinson, the prison officials kept a constant watch to prevent Dinsmore from committing suicide. Since he had heard Clara declare her love for Greyburn, life had become utterly insupportable. He tried to bribe each keeper, offering to exchange orders on several savings banks in Connecticut, or a deed of some real property he owned in Springdale, for a weapon of any kind and five minutes relief from surveillance. After exhausting all his efforts in making these proposals intelligible, he received the refusals savagely, and declined for days to communicate with any one. It was with difficulty that they made him eat his food. Had they not used actual force at one time, his soul would have left his body by the certain road of starvation.

Mr. Darby Spencer did not get much to encourage him in the neighborhood of Johnsbury. One day he took a drive to Chatham Corners, and found Mrs.

Greyburn. She had been, with due care, bound over in a formal manner to appear as a witness at the coming trial, and would have found escape from the vicinity hazardous, if not impossible, even had she desired to attempt it, which in fact she did not. The world was all alike to her in her widowhood. The quietness of the Corners was no objection to one who had passed the whole of her life in the country. Here she had seen Greyburn last, and here she expected to hear the first news of him, if news ever came. Mrs. Baldwin seemed very like a mother since her misfortune, and Clara would have shrunk from new scenes and people so soon.

Mr. Spencer revealed the nature of his errand with rare tact. He was pleased to find that while the mention of her husband's assailant brought a flood of tears, it brought with them no sign of vindictiveness. Little by little he drew from her what she knew of Dinsmore, and what she had reason to suppose had actuated him in the deed he had committed.

"You would call it jealousy, I presume," he said.

'Perhaps that would express it," replied Clara, " and yet not in the usual sense. John was a man when I was a child, and he always seemed to like me better than he did any one else. When Mr. Greyburn first came to Springdale, John took an aversion to him. We had several talks in which John expressed himself strongly. One night, when Mr. Greyburn called to see me, John waited outside and they had trouble. He seemed to feel that he was my protector, and was always fearful lest I should come to some harm."

"You had no idea that he would come here?" said Mr. Spencer.

"None in the world. Mr. Greyburn and I were married very hastily and privately, for—for various reasons—and no one was told where we were going. Indeed, I am sure my husband made special efforts that our destination should not be known. The fact that John traced us shows how determined he was to find him."

"Is it not probable," suggested the lawyer, "that Mr. Dinsmore had no definite purpose of harming your husband, and that a hasty quarrel sprang up between them when they met?"

Clara shook her head.

"I would like to believe all the good I can of John, but that does not seem possible. He never hunted out our hiding place with a good motive. Besides, he used to be the most peaceful man in the world, and here he was armed with a heavy pistol. No, no! He came from New York to kill Hector, and succeeded only too well in his object."

"Your husband had a pistol, also. Was he in the habit of carrying such a weapon?"

"I did not know that he was," said Clara. "In fact, I know almost nothing about his habits in such things. He would not have told me for fear that I should be alarmed. It is a terrible mystery, and the more I study the less I can fathom it."

"You know the law," said Mr. Spencer, gravely. "You know the penalty of homicide. This man, you tell me, was the friend of your childhood. It is evident that he entertained a deeper feeling for you than friendship when you became a woman. No, do not protest. There is no doubt that he was your unaccepted and hopeless lover. When he found that you had wedded another his sense of the injury was so strong that it overbore his natural qualities. He came here in order to be where he could see you, and meeting your husband, there was an altercation. One was killed instantly, the other reserved for lingering agony. Mrs. Greyburn, do you wish John Dinsmore hanged?"

"Oh, no!" cried Clara. "His punishment already

is terrible. I hope no more blood will be shed in this unhappy affair. I will do all I can to aid you in saving his life. Would that you might also give me back my husband !"

The lawyer waited respectfully until the outburst of grief which followed this remark had abated, and then said :

"The best help you can give me is to go at once to the jail and see Dinsmore. I know it will be hard," he added, as he saw her instinctive aversion to the proposal, " but it may be the means of saving his neck from the rope. If he can only be got into a frame of mind where he wishes to be saved, it will be worth everything. As long as he insists that he had rather be executed it is not easy to do much for him."

Clara agreed, though with some inward struggles, to be at Mr. Spencer's office the next morning at eleven o'clock, and at the hour she alighted from a carriage at his door, in company with Mrs. Baldwin. They all walked over to the jail and were soon ushered into Dinsmore's cell. He was totally unprepared for their coming, and when he saw Clara he gave a cry of agony and resolutely turned his face away.

"John," she said, as soon as she could command her trembling voice, and acting as by previous instruction, " I am very sorry to see you here. We did not think in those happy days at Springdale that we should ever meet like this."

She paused to get strength, for her voice had trembled violently on the last words. The prisoner turned still more away, but the lawyer could see from where he stood that the muscles of his face stood out like whipcords and that the perspiration was standing in beads.

"You have been badly hurt, John," continued Clara, after a pause, "and I know whose hand inflicted the injury. I am very sorry for you." Then she gave up all attempt at coherence and broke out wildly and passionately, "Oh, John! John! Why did you kill him? What had he done to you? What had *I* done to make you take the dearest thing out of my life?"

The prisoner turned his white face toward the group. In every eye but his there were glistening drops. He looked more like a corpse than a living creature, and he showed that each motion caused him a painful effort. In the sign-language, which was now his only resource, he asked for pencil and paper. After it was given him, he waited for some time before using it, as if the flood of his emotions was too great to permit him to proceed. Mrs. Baldwin took Clara in her lap and laid her head on her motherly shoulder. The jailer and one attendant stood near. Mr. Spencer waited anxiously for the expected communication. Slowly and painfully it came:

"I must tell the truth. The God he had never honored took Hector Greyburn's life."

"I believe every word of it," said the lawyer, encouragingly. "Tell me now why you stated differently to Squire Jarvis."

The prisoner wrote again:

"I was desperate."

"Perfectly reasonable," said the lawyer. "You were much excited and under great physical pain. But how *did* Greyburn perish? Tell me in brief now and we will get the fuller particulars later."

The prisoner wrote:

"He shot me, near the edge of the cliff. He stepped backward, slipped and fell. He rolled into the river."

Dinsmore watched with an eager eye the effect of

these revelations upon Clara. When Mr. Spencer read the last one aloud she exclaimed :

" Why should Hector have shot you, unless you first assaulted him ?"

Dinsmore wrote once more :

" We were both armed. He fired from his pocket. We had had words."

" You had best go now," said Mr. Spencer in a low tone to Clara, after he had read the last effort. " I have the clue and believe I can save him. His own confession is the only evidence against him."

After the others had gone, Mr. Spencer addressed Dinsmore :

" This Greyburn was a scoundrel."

The prisoner assented unmistakably.

" You pursued him because you knew he had taken an unfair advantage."

Again the prisoner assented.

"When you met you were both armed. He fired a cowardly shot from his pocket, and the judgment of Heaven took him to his account."

Dinsmore pantomimically corroborated the description.

" You don't propose to allow them to hang you for a thing like this ?" said the lawyer. " You've been a little desperate, but you're all over that. I'm going to get you out of this scrape and I must have your aid."

The blacksmith looked undecided.

" I want you to take this pencil and paper and write down, slowly and carefully, all that you can remember in relation to this affair. Give me dates, places, names of persons, everything which I can use. The fact is, there is no evidence against you yet at all. They can't even prove that the man is dead, as no

one has seen the body. Be a man, Dinsmore ! You
are good for many a year of life yet. Don't let them
down you on this lay, whatever you do !"

The blacksmith seemed at last to agree with the
lawyer's words. He caught up his pencil and wrote :

'I will do as you say. Come to-morrow."

At the January term of the Supreme Court the
trial took place. The court-room was crowded. The
evidence for the prosecution was put in with great
care. It was shown to the jury that the accused had
for a long time held a grudge against Greyburn. His
actions at the time Jones discovered him were detailed
at length. His written confessions, in which he
acknowledged the crime and expressed his willingness
to be hanged for it, were not forgotten. His subsequent affidavits, carefully drawn and sworn to, could
not have the weight of his admissions before seeing
counsel. The jailers told how he had tried to commit
suicide. Everything which pointed to his guilt was
spread before the court. To meet this Mr. Spencer
had to rely upon the fact that his opponents could
really prove nothing more than that a man had disappeared, and that a hat, some cloth and a button,
which looked like his, had been found.

The trial lasted several days. An end of the evidence was reached at last, and Mr. Spencer began his
plea for the defense.

" Your honor and gentlemen," he said, " we have
here one of the most extraordinary cases ever brought
before a jury in this or any other country. On a
certain day of last September a man was found
grievously wounded about a mile westerly from
Chatham. A bullet had passed through his throat in
such a locality that, we have the word of medical
men of repute, had it varied its course by a quarter
of an inch, this trial would have been rendered a

superfluity.   This man, so wounded, was found by
a passer-by and conveyed to the village of Chatham
Corners.   So severe were his injuries that he could
not move without assistance, and could not, nor can he
to-day, speak a single intelligible word.   In that
state, one we must all agree of such a nature as to
call for the sincerest pity of every creature worthy
the name of human, he was within two hours clapped
into a vehicle and taken post-haste to this town,
where the iron doors of the county jail received him.
Let us see on what pretense.

"The person who found this wounded body found
also—as he tells us, and I don't dispute him—a hat, a
piece of cloth and a button.   He found indentations
in the side of the mountain, which might have been
made by the rolling over it of a heavy substance.   On
reaching Chatham the discoverer of these wonderful
objects heard that a person that had been boarding at
the hotel there was missing.   He found also that he
was said to have worn a hat, a suit and buttons cor-
responding to those discovered.   The wife of the
missing man, with other people, went to the office of
the local physician, where this poor, helpless creature
lay, and under the guidance of a justice of the peace,
they proceeded to hold a court of inquest.   When the
wife came to testify, she was so affected as to swoon
away, and while they were restoring her, they allege
that a confession of murder was extracted from my
client.

"You have seen the documents, and I do not dispute that they were written by the defendant.   They
are produced as damming pieces of evidence, and will
be dilated upon with great emphasis when my
brother, the Attorney-General, gets the floor.   In
order to save his valuable time we admit them to be
genuine.   And we shall show you exactly how they
came to be written, and how perfectly consistent they

are with the entire innocence of the prisoner at the bar."

Mr. Spencer went on to give the history of the acquaintance which grew up between Clara and Walter Campbell and Hector Greyburn. He represented the latter as a prince of villains, bent on the destruction of both sister and brother. He sketched their connection down through its varied stages, until the infamy was completed at the Hotel Hampden. Then he spoke of Dinsmore, the honest, hard-working mechanic, the friend of their childhood, giving up his business and going from place to place to watch over the orphans of his old friend. At last he met the man who had ruined their peace, and received in his own throat the bullet, more kindly than the deceptive tongue and the seductive glance. But at the moment of Greyburn's triumph, the All-Seeing Eye was upon him, and he fell over the rocks and sands into the river below. If he was alive, God only could tell, but if dead, he passed at that moment of his life when all his sins clustered most thickly around his head.

"They took the body of John Dinsmore, himself nearly dead," said Mr. Spencer, in conclusion, "and brought it to Chatham. What do you suppose passed in the mind of the stricken man in that hour? The woman for whom he lay writhing in agony was sure to misconstrue his devotion, and though innocent as a babe in its cradle, dark suspicion would point its finger at him. What had he to live for? They handed him the paper and he wrote, ' I did it ! take me away, hang me, anything !' Gentlemen, this is not evidence. Put yourself in his place ; half insane from mental and physical pain ; dreading to face the tearful countenance of a woman wildly loved and woefully lost. My client is innocent. They have not attempted to prove that he killed this Greyburn, they have not proved that the man is dead, but I mistake a Georgia

jury if it would not say, even if the body of this missing man lay before it, that his fate was just. We dispute the killing, we question the death ; but if you can
say on your oaths as men and jurors that this maimed
and crippled creature took the life of the man who so
wronged him and his, I pray you consider well before
you make such an act into a capital offense."

The Attorney-General was about to begin his reply,
when a slight, pale-faced boy, who had just edged his
way, as only a boy can, through the crowd, cried out :

"Let me testify ! I know all about it. The man
is not dead. He is in New York city. I left him
there a week ago."

The excitement which this created in the court-
room can be imagined. The lad was taken to the
clerk's desk and sworn, even the Attorney-General
being too much taken aback to ask for delay.

The boy said : "My name is Charlie Leslie. Last
September I was walking one day from Medway to
Johnsbury. It was early in the morning. About a
mile from Chatham, which I had passed through, I
heard a noise down by the river, and on going closer
I saw a man bending over what appeared to be a
dead body. In the man's hands were papers and
money. As I watched him I saw him look up and
down the stream, and then begin to drag the body
toward the river. Being alone, I hesitated for a moment, and then called out 'Stop !' and ran toward
him.

" He ceased his work and began to excuse himself.
I prevailed on him to help me save the life in that
body instead of destroying it. We carried it to a cabin
in the woods near by. At night we got a carriage
and took the man to the station at Forest Hollow.
From thence I took him myself to Macon, where we
remained for some weeks at a hotel. Dr. Rerdell
attended him and found him so much injured that he

could not remember his own name. He spoke of parties in New York city and I took him there, where he was proved to be Hector Greyburn."

Leslie spoke with great rapidity and with considerable excitement. His words produced a profound impression in the court-room, and when the Attorney-General began to cross-question him a murmur ran through the audience.

" You have your story well learned," said the lawyer, " but I fear it will be regarded as rather improbable."

" Do you think I would lie ?" demanded the lad, hotly.

" Oh, no !" responded the lawyer, " nobody ever lies in court, but I shall have to ask you a few questions. If what you say is true, it saves a life. If it is untrue, it will send you to prison and do this man in the dock no good. Now, who are you ?"

"Charlie Leslie," said the boy again.

" You told us that before. What I ask is, *Who* are you ? Where do you live ? Who are your parents ?"

The child did not quail before the glowering eye of the distinguished advocate.

" I will not answer you," he said, boldly. " You have no right to ask me personal questions."

" We'll see about that," said the Attorney-General, while the excitement in the room rose to fever heat. " Do you know what they call contempt of court ? Refusing to answer a question is contempt of court, and you can be sent to prison for it."

" I was not brought here," replied the boy, defiantly. " I cannot be made to talk about myself. I came of my own accord, to save an innocent life."

A murmur of applause ran around the room. The Attorney-General turned to the presiding justice :

"I appeal to your honor. Shall he answer me or shall he not ?"

The judge, a kindly old man, with white hair and benignant features, turned to the boy and said, in the most winning tones :

"Surely, my lad, you can tell the gentleman where you live and who your parents are. We shall get along much faster in that way."

"Let him ask me about this case," responded the boy, in a mollified tone, and I will answer him. I'm not on trial, and my own affairs are nothing to him."

"Perhaps you had better cross-question him on the evidence he has given," said the judge. "He is evidently unused to these proceedings."

The lawyer did not look satisfied, but he turned again to the youthful witness.

"You say that this adventure of yours began in September last ?"

"Yes, sir."

"You were going from Medway to Johnsbury ?"

"I was."

"Were you familiar with this part of the country ?"

"Not at all."

"Where had you stayed the night before ?"

"At a house in Medway."

"Whose house ?"

"I do not recall the name."

The lawyer did not press the point, but looked knowingly at the jury.

"What was the name of the man whom you first saw with the body near the river side ?"

"I cannot answer."

"Have you seen him since you left on the train for Macon ?"

"No, sir."

"I want to know his name."

"I will not tell you."

"*Will* not?" said the lawyer.

"*Will* not," repeated the witness.

"Why?"

"Because I am under a pledge not to reveal his identity."

The lawyer did not press the question further, but he gave the jury to understand by his manner that he considered the whole of the lad's testimony untrue and consequently valueless.

"You say that you persuaded this man to forego his intention of robbing that body and committing it to the water. How did you 'persuade' him?"

"With a revolver," said the lad, quickly.

"Ah! my young man! So you carry weapons, do you?"

"I do not. I took that one from the pocket of Mr. Greyburn."

"Was it loaded?"

"It had five cartridges not used and one which had been exploded."

"One fired, eh?"

"Yes, sir, and a hole in his coat pocket showed where the shot went through."

"And you took that revolver, you mean to tell us, and 'persuaded' that man to help you carry the body to a cabin in the woods. How did you know that there was any cabin there?"

"The man told me."

"You 'persuaded' him to tell you that there was a cabin in the woods, did you?"

The boy looked appealingly at the judge, but he saw that he was expected to answer.

"I will tell you one thing more," he said. "There was a good deal of money in Mr. Greyburn's pocket. I agreed to give half of it to the man if he would help me restore him."

"*You* agreed?" said the lawyer. "What right had *you* to the money?"

"I took it," said the boy, growing restive again. "I had to give part of it back to save Mr. Greyburn's life and perhaps my own. There was no help near, and it was not a time to demur."

"So we are to understand," said the lawyer, "that you divided between yourself and some one else a large sum of money found on the person of a drowning man."

"Precisely."

"You confess, then, that you are a thief?"

The question was sufficiently brutal. The judge expostulated, and the audience could hardly be kept within bounds.

"I won't say another word to you!" cried Leslie, as soon as he could be heard.

"Take him. He's your witness," said the Attorney-General, turning to Mr. Spencer. "And look out that he don't bite you."

"My boy," said Mr. Spencer, in a mild tone, "I appear here for Mr. Dinsmore, and I believe every word that you have said. There are one or two things which I would like to have you answer, and I will put the questions. If you think they are improper, you will say so, and we shall proceed on good terms. Now, when and where did you last see Mr. Hector Greyburn?"

"In the outskirts of New York city, at the Hotel Lincoln, a week ago."

"How do you know that the man whom you saw there was Mr. Greyburn?"

'I found a photograph in his pocket and carried it to the artist who made it. He instantly told me that I had the picture of this missing man. I carried a note to Mr. Bird, a lawyer in the Astor House building and a friend of Mr. Greyburn, telling him where to find him, and then I left the city."

"What did you do with the picture?" asked Mr. Spencer.

The lad hesitated a minute and then, seeing the incredulous smile of the Attorney-General, he said:

"I have it in my pocket."

"May I see it?"

Leslie produced the photograph, and it was passed to several persons present from Chatham, including Mr. Justice Jarvis. Their demeanor showed that it was a likeness of the man supposed to have been murdered.

Mr. Spencer addressed the court:

"Your honor, I think I am justified in asking, even at this stage of the trial, for a stay of proceedings. This lad's story is, I admit, remarkable, but he has told it in a frank and open manner, and its truth or falsity can easily be demonstrated in a few days' time. We can summon Dr. Rerdell of Macon, whom we all know by reputation, and affidavits from New York are easily procured."

The Attorney-General replied:

"May it please the court—I am not surprised to see my brother grasp even at such a flimsy straw as this one. Were I in as desperate a position as he, I might be tempted to do it myself. Look at the case a minute. We have in this dock a self-acknowledged murderer. Twice he has written his guilt with his own hand. We have also other testimony tending to substantiate his confession beyond a doubt. At the last moment this boy comes in with his Arabian Nights' tale of rescuing a drowning man, compelling another, by the use of a revolver, to aid him, constituting himself the guardian and protector of the rescued individual, and at last discovering him to be the long lost Greyburn! To me the story is unutterably silly. I trust your honor will allow this trial to finish this afternoon, and if this sort of stuff is worth anything the Governor can set the verdict aside. I also ask you to commit this boy without bail as a witness to await the pleasure of His Excéllency. I intend to proceed against him for perjury at the proper time."

The judge was about to speak, when Mr. Spencer rose once more. By his side stood a man with a long red mark across his forehead, who had just entered the court-room.

"Another witness, your honor."

"I object!" sharply responded the Attorney-General. "This farce has gone on long enough. Will your honor let the case proceed? I am ready to make my argument."

"Who is the witness?" asked the judge.

"*Hector Greyburn!*"

The man stepped forward.

CHAPTER XXII.

In the bustle and confusion which followed the acquittal of Dinsmore, Charlie Leslie wandered almost unnoticed from the court-house, and took a road leading out of Johnsbury into the country. Greyburn missed him within a few minutes, and had some difficulty in discovering the direction he had taken, but learned it at last from a man who had encountered him on the outskirts of the town. He repaired with great haste to the nearest livery stable, secured a carriage and driver, and bade the man follow the boy with all possible speed. They descried him when they had gone about a mile. He saw them at the same time, and turned abruptly into the woods as if to escape their notice. The driver touched his horse with the whip in obedience to orders and drew up at the place where the lad had vanished. Greyburn sprang from the carriage and plunged into the wood, and in another moment found the object of his search. The child was sitting, or rather, half lying, on the ground at the foot of a tree, and it required but the most hasty glance to see that he was suffering physical pain.

"Charlie, my boy," cried Greyburn, sinking on one knee beside him, "you are suffering. What is it? Tell me."

The boy uttered a faint groan and managed to get upon his feet. He took several steps and then sank again upon the grass.

"Let me put you in my carriage," said Greyburn. "I can easily carry you, and you are too weak to walk."

"Don't touch me!" exclaimed the child, shrinking away. "You have no right. Why do you follow me?"

"Do you wish to die here without help?" asked Greyburn. And the boy answered, in a whisper:

"Yes."

"But I cannot let you!" cried the other. "When I was badly hurt you saved my life. It would be a poor return were I to leave you in this condition."

"*You'd care!*" No words can express the irony of this remark or the look which accompanied it.

"Certainly I should care, and very much. I have become greatly attached to you and feel that I owe you more than I can ever repay. I have no friend left but you, and now you would desert me."

The lad looked incredulously at the face which bent above him.

"The pretty lady whom you call your wife—are you going to leave her?"

"She does not love me," said Greyburn, choking down a rising in his throat. "I am not good enough for her. She is an angel, I a poor ordinary mortal."

There was no mistaking that he meant what he said. The boy eyed him narrowly and seemed to relent a little.

"What relation shall we bear to each other if I go with you?" he said.

"Whatever you please," replied the man. "I want you as a companion, a friend."

"Make me a servant and I will go," said the boy. "I will accept nothing else. I will eat no bread which I cannot earn; least of all, yours," he added, in a lower tone.

"If you will have it so, a servant you shall be," said Greyburn. "You may do anything but lie here and perish. Put your arm around my neck so that I can lift you easier!"

But the boy shrank from him again.

"The coachman," he said, pointing through the trees. "He is stronger than you."

"Nonsense. I can lift three like you."

"Before you were hurt, perhaps," persisted the boy, "but not now. You must not try it. Send the man here."

"As you will," replied Greyburn, releasing him. He called for the driver, who soon placed the child in the carriage.

"Now where?" asked the coachman.

"To Forest Hollow," said Greyburn.

"No," corrected the lad, "to the hotel in Johnsbury."

"I do not wish to go back there," said Greyburn. "I hate the place. I wish to get to New York as soon as possible."

"You have not spoken to you wife," said Charlie, in a low tone.

"I will write to her at the station and send back the message by this man."

"And after she has thought you dead for months," said the boy, reproachfully, "would you only send her a formal letter?" He turned to the driver and spoke louder:

"We will go to the Johnsbury Hotel."

Greyburn made no protest. He was looking intently at his companion. Presently he asked: What is it that makes you ill?"

"I have had no food for two days," replied the lad, "and I was a little faint. It is nothing."

"No food!" cried Greyburn. "Driver, hasten your horses. Poor child!"

He spoke the last words very tenderly, but the boy's lip curled in a just visible disdain.

"Don't think that I mind it," he said. "There are worse things than hunger. My last penny was gone; I could not beg and I would not steal. I expected to die."

"Surely you would have asked assistance rather than starve to death?"

"Not I!" said the boy, proudly.

"But you are entitled to some reward from the State for your evidence in the trial."

"Yes," said the lad, with a faint smile. "I came near getting it. A term in the penitentiary. That lawyer offered it to me twice. I know they pay witnesses and I knew I was starving for the want of a few pennies, and yet I wouldn't touch their money. Does that seem strange to you?"

"Very," said Greyburn.

"I thought it would," replied the boy, turning away.

The brisk drive in the air of the early evening invigorated the lad so much that he alighted from the carriage without assistance and walked into the office of the hotel.

"I wish supper prepared as quickly as possible for myself and friend," said Greyburn to the clerk.

"For himself and servant," corrected Charlie.

"He is right," Greyburn assented. "Get one supper of light food suitable for a sick person and the other of anything you have. Serve them in a private room and let me know as soon as they are ready."

Greyburn sat down beside the boy.

"Now, my little servant," he said, gently, "give your master what further orders you have ready."

"Send a messenger to find your wife," said the lad, without seeming to notice the witticism, "and make arrangements to see her before you sleep to-night."

The man looked at the lad for a moment, but he cried, "Oh, go! go! why do you hesitate?" and he went to find a messenger.

"I have sent to her," he said, when he returned to the boy's side. Charlie made no reply.

When supper was ready the boy ate sparingly, not at all like one who had not had food for eight-and-forty hours. Before they finished the messenger returned and stated that Mrs. Greyburn had gone to Chatham immediately after dinner, before the appearance in court of either Charlie or her husband.

"Order two fast horses and a double carriage without delay," said Charlie to the messenger. "We will go at once to Chatham Corners."

When Squire Jarvis broke into Mrs. Baldwin's little private sitting-room, and told her and Clara that Hector had appeared alive in court, there was a pretty flurry for a while. Clara demanded to be told the principal facts in the case over and over again, and gave vent to her joy in spasms of alternate tears and laughter. At last she recollected herself enough to inquire whither he had gone when the court adjourned. The squire could only inform her that he had seen Greyburn drive away on the Forest Hollow road, and that he had probably taken the train which passed there at seven o'clock.

This information fell upon the young wife like a chill. It was evident that her husband had come from New York merely to save Dinsmore's life, and that object being accomplished, had started at once on his return. She grew so ill that Mrs. Baldwin ordered all visitors from the house. She tried to persuade the girl to go to bed and receive medical attendance, but without avail.

"It is not medicine I want," she said, "but Hector. Oh, he is cruel ! Had he but come and shown me that he was alive ! But to go without a word, that is terrible !"

The landlady could not induce her to lie down. She talked incessantly of the wonderful story of his rescue, and declared that she would not be thus deserted, but would take the cars for New York, and compel him to own her. She grew hysterical as time went by, and made Mrs. Baldwin say over and over that he *was* a good man, and a fine-looking man, and she was sure he loved his wife, only there had been so much foolish trouble, bless her heart ! It would soon be all over, so it would, and the sweetest and handsomest couple she had ever seen would be united and happy, just as they ought to be. Yes ! yes ! yes !

About nine o'clock a knock came at the outside door, and the landlady went in person to open it. A boy stood there, while a few steps away waited a carriage drawn by two horses.

"Can I see Mrs. Greyburn ?"

"Well, I don't know," hesitatingly answered the landlady. "She is not very well to-night, and ——"

"I wish to speak about her husband."

Mrs. Baldwin waited no longer, but conducted him to the room where Clara was.

"Mrs. Greyburn?" said the boy, interrogatively.

"Yes," said Clara, all in a tremble. She dreaded to hear any news, lest it should be of an unpleasant nature.

"They have told you—somebody—about your husband being saved, and about a boy who came to court to testify ——"

"Yes! yes!" cried Clara.

"I am that boy."

She caught his hand and covered it with kisses.

"I have something to say," he went on, "and perhaps you would rather we were alone." He looked at the landlady, who at once left the room. Clara stood as she had risen, clinging for support to the back of her rocking chair.

"I asked your husband to-day why he did not go immediately to you and he replied that you did not love him. Is it so?"

"Oh, no? It is not so!" cried Clara. "He should not have said that."

"He also said," the lad continued, "that he had won your hand by fraud and that two men had narrowly escaped death on account of that act. He said that he was unfit to join his life to yours and that he wished to undo what evil he had committed, so far as possible, by giving you a deed of separation, with one half of his property."

The girl clung yet closer to her support.

"He acknowledged all the wrong to be on his side, and hoped you would pardon his sins against you. He feels certain that were you to accept him as your husband your natures are so dissimilar that a rupture must come in time. Are you agreed?"

"No, no!" cried Clara, starting as if from a dream.

"I do not know him." *Page 251.*

"He is my husband. Bring him to me! He shall not make me say the words which will part us."

A shadow fell between the lamp in the hall and the girl who was speaking. The door had been opened. A man whose face was covered with marks and scars, and whose forehead bore one long red gash, disfiguring him forever, stepped inside and extended his hands.

Clara gave a loud scream, which brought the landlady and the maid Harriet into the room. She threw her arms around Mrs. Baldwin's neck and wept convulsively.

"Do you know this man?" asked the lad, pointing to the intruder.

"No!" cried Clara, in extreme terror. "I do not know him! He frightens me! Take him away."

The apparition stood like a statue.

"We will go," said Charlie, in a low voice.

They re-entered the carriage, and the driver looked inquiringly at the boy, who said :

"To the nearest railway station where we can get a train for Macon."

With a snap of the whip, the horses set off at a gallop, and bore them rapidly away.

CHAPTER XXIII.

MENDALL had no sooner sent John Dinsmore on Greyburn's trail than he repented of the act into which his hasty passion had led him. The loss of his wager by what he regarded as a contemptible trick nettled him so severely that for the time he was hardly responsible for his actions. Mendall loved money. He had made a good deal of it in his time, but, like all speculators, he had also had his turns of ill luck, and this was not the only piece of adverse fortune which he had of late experienced. Unfortunate investments in some Arizona mines and a bad twist in Wall street margins made him look forward with particular pleasure to the day when the amount of the wager should be put into his hands, and when he discovered how his late partner had outwitted him, he was beside himself. His meeting with the blacksmith came at the worst time possible for both.

The next morning, when he had time to reflect, he voted himself an ass. Nothing could be done, however, to stop the mischief already set afoot, and his only hope now was to keep Walter from joining in the murderous hunt. To do this he realized that he should have to rely wholly upon Gabrielle. As early as he thought it probable that Walter had left the house he presented himself there and sought his accustomed audience.

Gabrielle was looking her sweetest that morning. She was in one of her happiest moods, and she came at once to where the banker awaited her and threw her plump arms about his neck. With an abruptness very unusual for him he disengaged himself from her embrace, and said :

"Where is Walter ?"

"Gone to City Hall, I suppose. He left here about an hour ago."

"Did any one call to see him yesterday ?"

"No one. Why ?"

"Look at this," said Mendall, handing her a newspaper. Gabrielle's eyes expanded as she read the notice.

"That means trouble," said Mendall, "unless you are manager enough to stop it."

" Why should it ?" asked the girl. " Isn't the marriage all right ?"

" Yes," said Mendall, "now. But there is a long
story to it. Walter will hear it most likely from somebody or other before the day is out, and come rushing home to get packed up and after them. He may
come any minute. If he does, he mustn't see me
here."

Gabrielle disappeared for a few minutes. When
she returned she said, " Williams understands. If he
comes, he won't enter this room until I am ready for
him. Go on ; you interest me."

" As I said," repeated Mendall, " they are married
all straight and right now, but the whole town will
know in a few days that they passed the night *before*
their marriage in a room at the Hampden. Greyburn
had made a bet, you see, of a good deal of money,
that a girl could not be named but what he could get
to pass a night with him, and they named this Campbell girl. He brought her here, they stayed at the
Hampden, he got his wager, married her the next
evening, and they have left for the West, no one
knows where."

" But I understood," said Gabrielle, " that she was
a wonderful pattern of propriety—a perfect Beatrice
Cenci !"

" So everybody supposed, or no one would have bet
fifty thousand dollars on her name," said Mendall,
growing exasperated " Of course he promised her
marriage immediately after, and that made all the
difference in the world. No one imagined that he was
a marrying man, or they never would have wagered
with him."

" How many people know about this ?"

" God knows !" ejaculated the banker. " Not less
than a score and perhaps a thousand. I shouldn't be
surprised to see it in the evening papers. It will take

nerve to tell it to Walter, but some fool will be sure to do it, and then he will come tearing up here swearing blood and vengeance. When he comes, you must be ready for him. Don't let him go on any account. It would be a wild-goose chase at best. Besides, there is another crazy-head gone already, and that is quite enough."

" Who ?"

" Why, that lunatic of a blacksmith who came here that day to see Greyburn—Dinsmore is the name. I met him last night on the road to the Pennsylvania depot, at which he had learned in some way that they had taken passage. He had an idea that he ought to kill somebody to right the wrongs of the family. He will probably get killed himself before he hurts any one else."

" Jacob," said Gabrielle, coyly, " what an interest you take in these people. You must have a good and sympathetic heart."

He tried to laugh, but her humor was not to be mistaken.

" You think so much of Walter, now," she went on. " Quite like a brother, one might say. Your money helped him to this house and its furnishings; yes, and to me, not the least in his sum of delights. Then, fearing that he was getting too much of the sweetness, you have done him the supreme kindness to call up almost every day and appropriate a portion to yourself, just to keep him from getting cloyed ! There is Greyburn, too. They say that when he met you he was as poor as a church mouse and that you helped him to wealth as one might help another to a biscuit. Do you do good just for the sake of the approval of your conscience, Jacob ? Just because virtue is its own reward ?"

The girl laughed merrily.

" Tell me," she went on, smiling up into his face, .

"what you and Walter are up to together. Let me into the secret. You've made lots of money—you and Walter and Greyburn. How do you do it? I want to make a little, too."

"You?" said the broker. "You don't want money. You want jewels and silks and velvets. Money is to you only a medium of exchange for luxuries."

"*Is* it?" mocked the fair creature. "Now, perhaps that is where you are mistaken. Perhaps I like things more substantial than silks and diamonds. Real—estate—for instance. Real—estate—eligibly situated—likely to rise in value. Eh, Jacob?"

The banker was visibly disturbed at the insinuating character of the reply, but he turned it off with a flattering answer.

"You are a witch," he said, "and whatever you want, you are sure to get in time, that's certain. But we must not forget this matter of Walter. Can you manage to keep him here if he's inclined to go?"

"I can keep him easily enough," said Gabrielle, turning the most entrancing contour of her face toward the banker, "but why should I trouble myself? He may go and get killed,' you will say. Well, what then? I shall have *you* left. 'But you may get angry if I don't do as you tell me.' Well, what then? I can open the windows and call to passers in the street. The world is full of men, and I ought surely to find lovers somewhere among them. You are sober, Jacob, but you know it's true. Come, look at me! Am I not handsome enough to get some one to love me?"

She rose and stood with her white morning dress touching him. In her hair were azaleas. Her cheeks had their own pink and whiteness.

"Do you wish Walter and his sister's husband to

get into a fatal quarrel?" protested Mendall. "They have both been lovers of yours. Would you like to have them killed?"

"No," said Gabrielle, with a toss of her head. "I shouldn't like it; but after all, it's their business. Men are always killing somebody, any way. I suppose it's their method of enjoying life. Now, Jacob, what I do say is this: *I* have no object in keeping Walter here. *You* have."

"I understand," he admitted. "What shall I get you, another necklace?"

"I am tired of necklaces," she said. "I want something more substantial. I want real estate. Don't shake your head, for I mean it. I don't want it on the line of the Manhattan Improvement Company, for I don't wish to speculate, but I do want it right here in this street, at this number. Do you see? I want this house we are standing in."

"You are crazy!" said Mendall. "I paid thirty-five thousand dollers in cash for this property."

"It was too cheap," cried the girl. "I want it and I will give you forty thousand dollars."

"In what?" said the astonished banker.

"Partly in cash and partly in my undying love and affection."

"Principally in the latter commodity, I guess," said the banker, smiling in spite of himself.

"To resume, as they say in novels," said the girl. "You want Walter kept here and you want him quieted down. *I* will do it. In exchange you will give me—let's see—you don't want to sell this real estate—well—say five thousand dollars in cash."

"Done!" said Mendall, relieved even by the mention of so large a sum. He had really thought for a moment that the house was going out from under his feet. "How shall I know the result?"

"I will send you word," she said. "Williams will carry a note to your rooms."

"Now for a kiss," said Mendall, "and I will go."

"Only one," said Gabrielle, laughing. "My kisses are like roses at Christmas—they come high, but people must have them. I will make you a present of one to bind our bargain."

She stood on tip-toe and submitted graciously to his embrace. Then he left the house by a side entrance.

When Walter came home she saw at once that he had heard nothing. It required a little more courage than any one had had that day to tell him that his sister's name was on the lips of every man about town, mingled with coarse laughter and vulgar jest. Gabrielle secured him at once for a ride in the Park, and it was quite late when they returned. They dined at a chop-house on the road, where private suppers were served, and met no one whom they knew. When they reached home Gabrielle put on her most bewitching manner and kept Walter from his usual half hour over the evening papers. She made him light his cigar in her boudoir and kept him talking until she knew that the last train out of the city had gone for the night.

"Do you really love me, Walter?" she was saying, as the clock struck twelve.

"How many times must I answer that?" he replied, going to where she stood before the mirror, and clasping his arms about her waist.

"I know you say so," taking out the pins which confined her luxuriant hair, and allowing it to fall around her like a cloud, "but I often think that some more beautiful face will after a while win your love from me."

"There is none more beautiful," he answered. "None in the world. Gabrielle, you are seraphic!"

"So you will tell your next love," pouted the beauty. "'Men are deceivers ever.' You know the verse."

She took up a paper which lay apparently by accident near by. He was lost in contemplation of the loveliness of her shoulders and arms, and neither spoke for a moment. Suddenly she called out:

"Oh, Walter! Who do you think is married?"

"I'm sure I can't guess," he replied, with a smile. "Perhaps the Grand Llama of Thibet."

No, she said, "it's more wonderful than that. It's Hector Greyburn. And, heavens! Why, you must have known all about it."

"Not I!" said Walter. "At least, I only know that he was terribly in love. He told me that last summer."

"You know who he was in love with, then?" said she.

"I haven't the remotest idea."

"You knew he had been to Springdale?"

"Yes," said Walter, looking sorely puzzled, "but not to get acquainted. He only visited at my house."

"Well?" Gabrielle interrupted. A light flashed on the young man instantly.

"It's not a thing to joke about," he cried, a little warmly. "Whom has he married, anyhow?"

"This paper says that she is 'the only daughter of the late Rev. Duncan Campbell, of Springdale.'"

Walter seemed to shrink into the depths of his easy chair. The outburst she looked for did not come yet.

"Shall I show it to you?"

"No," he said, in a hollow voice. "The sight of it would blast my eyes."

"Do you care very much?" she said, creeping softly to him and putting her arms about his neck, "Walter, darling, do you care very much?"

He looked at her as a drunken man might. A struggle was going on within.

"She ought to have told you, dear, but you know how it is in love. She may have feared that you would make trouble, and taken this way in the hope that you would forgive her after a little while."

He did not answer yet.

"Darling," she continued, sitting down in his lap, and laying her face against his, "don't mind it. I hate to have you feel bad. It can't be helped now. There! kiss me, and let us think no more about it."

She was acting upon him like a narcotic.

"Walter, you don't answer me."

He put his arm around her, and drew her closer.

"I'll never speak to her again," he said, at last. "It is a disgrace. I am her only brother. Everybody will find out that she didn't think enough about me to let me know when she got married. To him, too! She'll get enough of it in a few months!"

"It's better they're married than if they had gone away without, isn't it?" said Gabrielle. She was feeling her ground cautiously.

"It's about the same thing when she's married a man like him," said Walter. "How long will he live with her before he strikes a new fancy? In a little while she'll come crying back, and wish she'd consulted *me*. Then it will be *my* turn."

He looked very ugly.

"I would forget them," said Gabrielle, kissing the set lips, and looking her sweetest into the frowning eyes. "They are not worth thinking of. Come, dearest, smile again. You have quite sent a chill over me ; and we were so happy a few minutes ago."

"You are right," said Walter, returning the kisses which she gave him. "We will speak of them no more."

The Greybürn sensation was the usual nine days'

talk at the clubs, and then went its way like others of its class, and made room for something newer. The full details of the affair never got into the possession of very many people. The fact of the wager was known, but the general supposition was that the marriage had in itself won the bet, and many were the compliments showered upon Greyburn's "shrewdness" in carrying off at the same time a heavy wager and a handsome wife. Even this did not reach Walter's ears. He quite forgot the bet made at the dinner. Indeed, his condition on that occasion was such that nothing in relation to it made a lasting impression. Those of his acquaintances who heard the story of his sister's marriage supposed that he had heard it also, and did not care to enter into conversation with him on what must prove a disagreeable subject. It often happens that the person most interested in anything is the last person to hear of it, though it may be the common talk of all around him.

When, a few weeks later, a telegram appeared in the papers, stating that Greyburn had been killed, and that Dinsmore was under arrest for his murder, it produced another sensation in the city, but nothing like the previous one. A murder is not to be compared with an elopement as an item of interest, especially if the parties to the latter are young and handsome, or otherwise distinguished. At Springdale, where they knew Dinsmore well, and his supposed victim slightly, greater excitement prevailed, and many were the theories raised and debated. Walter Campbell heard of this affair, as he had of the other, through Gabrielle, who handed him a paper containing the item, as they were sitting one evening at dinner.

"A pair of fools ; pass me the wine," was his only

comment, and whatever he may have thought, he did not allude to the subject again.

Jacob Mendall was sorry when he heard that one of these men was dead, and the other unlikely to survive, and yet it solved a very annoying problem for him. He wired Mr. Middleby to come home at any time, and went about his business with renewed zeal.

Rev. Arthur Reycroft, Clarence Perkyns, Esq., and others of Greyburn's intimate friends heard of his death with real regret. The former gentleman, especially, moralized on the sins of humanity in general, and Greyburn in particular, and ended by going to call on the fascinating Gabrielle, whom he knew was now located in his friend's former residence.

She received him with open arms—metaphorically ; and would have made the metaphor an actuality had he not retired behind his dignity.

" Mr. Arthur, I am delighted !" were her words of welcome. " There is no man on this whole globe—and that is counting a good many—whom I had rather see than you. Come up to my boudoir. I have ever so much to say to you."

" Your boudoir ?" he repeated, inquiringly. " Your parlor would be better, I think. I am not used to seeing ladies in their boudoirs."

"Now don't be scared," laughed the siren. " It's not my bedroom, if that is what you are afraid of. It is the room where I always receive my friends. Oh, it's a perfectly proper place, or I wouldn't invite *you* into it."

"On that assurance I will go there," said Mr. Reycroft.

After a few words on general topics he said :

" You have noticed, of course, the telegrams in the papers in relation to Mr. Greyburn."

"Yes," she smiled.

"Terrible, isn't it ?"

"Well, y-e-s," she said, hesitating a little. "I suppose so. Still, we must all die, and a sudden death is the easiest."

He looked amazed at the lack of sorrow in her tone and look.

" Do you recollect the first time you saw me ?" he said. Then, seeing that she seemed in doubt, he added : " Here, in this house, in his room, when he sent for you and I asked you so many questions."

"Oh, yes," she said, brightening. " I remember it well."

"You haven't forgotten, have you," he proceeded, " how devotedly you loved Mr. Greyburn then ?"

"No, indeed !" laughed the beauty. " How much we did care for each other ! It was really romantic. How long ago was that ? It seems a century."

" Much less than two years," said Mr. Reycroft, gravely.

"Oh, you are mistaken, surely !" she cried. " It must have been before the war, at least. I was a child then. Now I am an old woman. I've almost reached my twenty-second birthday. See the wrinkles on my forehead." She knitted her fair brows and laughed gaily. " I'm aging fast. Do look at my hair. There must be silver threads in it."

She plunged herself down at his feet and submitted her golden tresses for his inspection. He shook his head, half smilingly, half sadly, and she rose again and took a chair opposite to him.

"Only one man in a thousand would have let me get up without a kiss," she said, with a bewitching pout of her cherry lips. " Oh, don't think that I mind it ! I'm glad there is somebody with such perfect control over their actions. It gives me confidence in the universe. If I was out on a ship, you know, and the passengers were all drinking champagne, I would like to hear that the captain was sober. So with you. Whenever I see how different you are from others, I say, ' Here is a man who is standing on the bridge and keeping a look-out.' Do you understand ? Somebody must do it and it fits you splendidly."

"They have never found his body," said Mr. Reycroft, to bring her back to his original subject.

"Ah !" she said. "I didn't know."

"Which, of course, leads us to hope a little longer that he may be alive. And yet, if he were alive we would be almost sure to get news of him."

"I should think so," she assented. "By the way, this fellow who killed him called here one day. He came into this very room and stood right where you are sitting now."

He moved his chair involuntarily a little away from the spot.

"Why did he come here ?"

"Oh, he would have it that Mr. Greyburn was in the house. He had the impudence to say that as I was here he could not be far off. When he left he was breathing out threatenings and slaughter against Hector if he ever did any harm to Miss Campbell. He seemed to think that marriage was a capital crime. I have always declared it foolish, but I never claimed that we should condemn its votaries to death. I have always thought their punishment severe enough of itself.

She said this with an arch smile and Mr. Reycroft replied :

" I see that you wish to draw me into another dis·cussion. I am ready for you, but you must not look for soft language. In speaking of things I shall call them by their right names."

" I know what you would claim," said the girl. " You would say that it is better to be married three weeks and then be shot dead, than to live as I do under the 'mistaken impression' that I am happy."

"I would say it were better to be shot dead a thousand times than to go on from year to year preparing for an eternity of remorse."

"I heard a minister preach once from this text," said she, slowly :

> " ' He knoweth our frame,
> He remembereth that we are dust.'

Don't you think that our circumstances will have something to do with it when we go to be judged ?"

"Only God can answer that," said Mr. Reycroft, devoutly, seeing that the girl had dropped her bantering tone. "It is for us to live as nearly right as we can, and not allow our weaknesses to master us without a struggle. We must work out our own salvation."

"They say that He is merciful," she answered. "To whom should He show mercy unless it be to those who need it most ?"

"He *is* merciful, truly," said Mr. Reycroft, "but that does not excuse us from presuming on his mercy and devoting a whole lifetime to breaking His laws."

"If you knew my life you would say that He might well consider me a subject of mercy," said Gabrielle, looking steadily at him. "Shall I tell it to you ?"

"If you would like to."

"I was born in the slums of this city," she began. "My father was a longshoreman, when he did anything. My mother did laundry work. She was of good family, she has always told me, but sunk by her marriage to the level of her husband.

"My mother supported us—what support we got. My father was generally drunk. Half a dozen of my little brothers and sisters did my mother bear, and they all died because proper doctors and medicine are not to be had for the poor. I was the last one, and I lived, Heaven knows why! They couldn't kill me. I breathed the fetid air of a garret where, in one room, we were expected to eat, sleep, wash, iron and die. In that garret I was born. I do not see how my mother found time to bear me. She was always at work. Sometimes my father would strike her with his fists, but she never complained. When she left a good home to marry a young loafer she was told that she would have to lie in the bed she made. And she never tried to escape the chains which she had forged for her own limbs.

"The first thing that I remember hearing was that I was pretty. My father was a handsome man in his younger days, and my mother—but then, everybody's mother is beautiful. As soon as I could carry small bundles of laundered goods to the houses of ladies for whom my mother worked, they all remarked how pretty I was. They fondled me and gave me little presents in the way of clothing, which my father stole and pawned whenever he could get at them. I had a taste for dress, and learned to hide things when my father was around, and wear them when he was away. I can remember sitting by my mother and caressing the lace and edgings on the goods she ironed, as if they were living things.

"When I grew older, not only the ladies admired my beauty, but the men. They stopped me on the street and gave me bits of silver in exchange for the kisses I never dreamed of denying. Then my father died, falling in a drunken fit, and my mother, till now exempt from the habit, took to drink to drown the sorrows which beset her. I had to take hold of the irons to get work done when it was promised, and I didn't like it. I was inexperienced, and the ladies

for whom the work was done didn't like it, either.
My mother lay drunk a whole week once, and we got
out of bread. A young student of one of the divinity
colleges—yes, I mean it!—relieved our necessities,
and ——

"But why go on? I soon had good clothing, plenty
of food, and saw my poor old mother relieved of want
and work. Does she know where I get the money,
you would say. Certainly not. I tell her the best
story I can invent and she believes me. In her comfortable little home she blesses me over her bottle of
gin, and is seldom sober long enough to think much
about it. I'm sure I don't want her to think. The
more she drowns her thoughts the better!"

"Mr. Greyburn was not your first lover, then?" said
Mr. Reycroft, as she hesitated.

"My first!" echoed the girl. "No, nor my—oh!
I've lived the whole life. I know the whole story.
To-day the favorite of a governor or a congressman,
and to-morrow soliciting the merchant or the clerk on
their way home at midnight. I could tell you things
which you would discredit, and yet they are true as
Heaven!"

"It is terrible!" said Mr. Reycroft.

"Terrible? Perhaps so. But if this is terrible,
what word will describe the married misery of the
place where I was born? My mother was once as
handsome as I, and better educated. Do you think it
was by deliberate choice that she sank to be a miserable washerwoman, bearing children whom she knew
were more likely to die than live, for a wretch who
repaid her devotion by curses and blows? Poor food,
poor clothing, no comforts, nothing but slavery. That's
marriage! that's the state the preachers would have
us be content in!"

The girl had wrought herself up to a high state of

excitement. She began to pace the floor as she talked.

" You should go and see the place where I lived. I can find it. It was up six flights of rickety stairs. There was no plastering on the walls. The roof leaked. The room was half the time full of steam from the boiler. We lived like hogs. Now, look around you. See this room. Compare it in your mental vision with the other. I wore then nothing but what was given me in charity, and most of that got stolen sooner or later. Many a time, after going a long way and bringing home a little money for my mother's work, my father has taken it away at the street door and we have gone hungry. Come to the pantry in this house. Look at the clothes I wear now. This dress is silk. This basque is velvet. These stones in my ears are diamonds. Why, these boots were twenty dollars a pair. I wear nothing but what is elegant, and I have grown to need them all. Do you think I could go back to my old life ? Not until the butterfly can become a chrysalis again !"

Mr. Reycroft was at a loss how to reply. He had never seen Gabrielle look so magnificent as she did while making this defense.

" You may talk to me of your heavens and your after lives till you are tired," she said. " I am going to live the life I have for all of later possibilities. I must take the world as I find it. Men are the beings in possession. Marry them and they will degrade you until you are the mere slave of their caprice. Refuse to wed and they come to your feet. What could I have done in the life that you call virtuous? The same road that my mother trod was the only one open to me. Do you think I would accept it ? Not for all the heavens ever dreamed of would I live the life she did !"

"All women in your place could not be sure that

they would be treated as well as you have been," ventured Mr. Reycroft, when she paused for breath.

"Let me tell you the truth," said the girl, stopping in her walk. "I never really loved a man yet. I liked my first lover very well, and am grateful for what he did in lifting me out of my degraded surroundings, but that is all. I liked Hector. I like Walter, but I would leave even him to-morrow for another lover without caring for the difference. It is all a matter of expediency with me. Some people have talents which they can turn to account. I have nothing but beauty, and I must use it where it brings the best returns. If I am punished for it there will be others reckoned in the same account, and some who hold their heads much higher in this world than I have ever pretended to hold mine."

When the Rev. Arthur Reycroft took his leave it was without much hope that he had succeeded in converting Gabrielle from the error of her ways.

------◆------

CHAPTER XXIV.

HECTOR GREYBURN established himself with Charlie in an ordinary suite of apartments in a quiet side street of the city. After his strange encounter with his wife at Chatham he grew moody and was very little like his former self. He stayed indoors most of the day and only strayed out after nightfall, when he took long walks which sometimes lasted until nearly daybreak. In these walks Charlie usually accompanied him, though many of them were so severe as to try the boy's slight strength. Sometimes they went up the avenues, away out toward Harlem. Again they crossed the ferries and plunged into the streets of Williamsburg, Brooklyn and Hoboken. Often their walk led in and out among the devious ways of Five Points, Bleecker Street and other old-town localities. They penetrated places where murders have been committed for ten dollars in money or jewelry, but no one thought of disturbing the scarred man, dressed in plain clothes, or the delicate child by his side. This went on for weeks before the idea stole into Greyburn's head that it might not be exactly the sort of life which his young companion craved.

"This must be dull music for you, Charlie," he said, then. "It's not what you expected, is it, staying hived up in this den all day and wandering like a ghoul over the city at night?"

"I am content," said the lad, "that is—for myself. But for you it does not seem right ; you, who are capable of doing so much in the world, if you only would."

"I ?" said Greyburn. "Yes, I've done a good deal in the world already, and it would have been considerably better off if it had never made my acquaintance. Do you know the sort of life I've lived?"

"Yes," replied the boy, "I know. But the future —the great future, rich in possibilities—that is open to you still."

It reminded him unpleasantly of Clara's words. He looked long and earnestly at the little speaker. Then he said :

"Charlie, who taught you all the goodness you know? or did it spring up in you naturally, like the violet in spring? What an oasis you are in this desert-world !"

"My mother taught me to love right and hate wrong," said the boy, "and everything that I have seen elsewhere emphasizes her teaching."

"And she is—"

"Dead—yes," said the lad, dashing a tear from his eyes.

"Your father?" said Greyburn. "Tell me about him. Was he also of the angelic mould, or was he a a man like other men, eating and drinking with publicans and sinners?"

"He was a bad man," said Charlie, quickly, "a *very* bad man, unfit to live on the same planet with my mother. Whatever good there may be in me comes not by inheritance from him."

"At what age were you left an orphan?"

"At nine. My grandfather took me home then for a little while, but we could not agree and I ran away. Next I stayed two years in a doctor's family. Young as I was, he gave me wages besides my board, and when he died suddenly, I had a hundred dollars in my pocket. I came to New York to get employment, and finally went South with a troupe of theatrical people. They stranded in one of the hill towns of Georgia, and I was walking to Macon when I saw you lying on the banks of Rapid River."

"If you had not seen me I should have been 'down among the dead men' now," mused Greyburn. "The fortunate stranding of that theatrical venture enables me to sit here talking with you, instead of accepting an invitation to dine with his Satanic Majesty."

"It does seem providential," responded the lad, "that I should have been there."

"Providence or luck, or whatever it was," replied Greyburn, "it was very convenient. I suppose that man would have thrown me back into the river like a dog-fish after he had stolen my valuables."

"Do you know what became of Dinsmore?" said Charlie, changing the subject.

"I'm sure I don't," said Greyburn. "I haven't

seen a soul that I used to know but Mr. Bird, and I don't think I care to. They wouldn't know me, any way." He turned to the mirror, and added, bitterly : "What an injury that blacksmith did ! Not for all the wealth in the world would I have exchanged the face I used to have for this one. And yet—I can't explain why—I don't feel at all like seeking revenge on him."

"I should think he had been punished enough," said Charlie. "He cannot speak a word, and it is a question if he ever walks alone."

"What is that compared with my injuries ?" responded Greyburn. "Before he met me I had a face ; now I have a mass of scars and disfigurations. They said that I was the handsomest man in New York— look at me now ! Loss of voice ? that's a bagatelle ! Loss of locomotion ? one can ride if he can't walk ! But for a face like mine, what physician knows the remedy !"

"It's not so very bad," said the boy, soothingly. "A cut across the forehead, and another scar or two, that's all. You overrate your disfigurement, Mr. Greyburn."

The man rose with a quick motion and pointed to a handsome vase upon the mantel-piece, from which a small fragment had been broken.

"Look at that Sevres," said he. "It will hold flowers still ; it has lost none of its containing capacity ; but who wants it in their parlor ? A piece of the rim has been broken off, and the value of the article is gone forever. It was a thing of beauty. What is it good for now ? *That !*"

He struck the vase across the center, and it fell on the floor in a hundred pieces.

"If somebody had struck me that way it would have been better," he added. "Only that vase will not reappear somewhere again, and I might."

"Beauty is not everything," ventured the boy.

"No, but when the beauty of a thing is gone, who wants the rest? You saw my first blow. My wife, whose eyes rained tears because I did not fly instantly to her side, shrank from this face. 'Take him away! he frightens me!' I can hear her now. I don't blame her. I *do* look frightful. Unless that mirror lies I would do to scare crows with."

Charlie did not reply. His fund of condolence was exhausted.

"If you had known me," Greyburn went on, "before that September morning when I went tumbling like a beast to my doom, you would understand it better. I had a complexion like a girl's, fair and rosy, not an imperfection in it anywhere. Many are the red lips which have been pressed to mine, many the bright eyes which have wandered lovingly over my countenance, caught in the meshes of its winning smiles. Had my voice failed, I could have borne it ; had my limbs refused their office, that were easily endured ; but to lose that face is not a thing to bear with equanimity, and until to-day I could not even trust myself to speak about it."

"Feminine conquests are denied you by your marriage vow." said Charlie, " and your masculine friends will not mind."

"My marriage vow !" repeated Greyburn. "That is dissolved by all the laws of reason when my wife exclaims that I frighten her and demands to have me taken from her presence. I do not profess to be a saint. No woman with any pretensions to beauty would care for me now, but if no female eye looks brightly into mine it will not be on account of my marriage vow. You cannot understand me, Charlie, and no wonder. You are of the skies, angelic. I am of the earth, earthy."

"You wouldn't wish your wife, separated from you

though she is, or your daughter—if you had one—to entertain your views," ventured the lad.

"That is an old way of begging the question," Greyburn responded. "I shouldn't wish my wife or daughter to scrub floors or sell matches in the streets."

"Death is a kinder fate than dishonor to a woman," said Leslie, loftily.

"It is nonsense to say so," said Greyburn. "I have had my trial with those ideas. When I met Clara I took up the purity business, and it has done enough for me. Had I let it alone I should have been to-day contented in mind, fair in face, rich in friends and comforts. Now I am an outcast, with no friend in the world but you, and so hideous that I have to take the kindly season of the night to make my walks abroad. I've gained this by being virtuous, and, by all that's worth an oath, I'm sick of it !"

"You reason strangely," said the lad. "You have acknowledged to me that you dealt wrongfully with Miss Campbell in order to win a wager, before you were united. *I* should ascribe your fall over the cliffs to the retribution of Heaven."

"What a lot of exploded ideas you carry in that little head of yours !" exclaimed Greyburn. "Do not the best people in the world meet with accidents as well as the worst ? When a boiler blows up or a train is derailed are the good separated from the evil ? I have had love all my life and I can't live without it. What affection will not buy, money will, and I shall have a sharer of my apartments before another week has passed over."

"Not while I stay here," said Charlie, firmly.

"It's no use balking me," said the man. "If I cannot do one thing I shall break out in a new place. Deny me the charms of woman and I will try those of wine, drink in the pleasures of the opium-taster or frequent gambling shops. I shall go to the bad, rely upon it, and shutting off one avenue will only open a thousand others."

The next night, when Greyburn put on his wrappings to sally forth, he said, "I don't want you to come with me to-night, Charlie."

The boy made no reply except to advance toward the door.

"I said," repeated Greyburn, slowly, "that I didn't wish you to go with me to-night."

Without further parley he closed the door behind him and went into the street. It was a rainy, drizzly evening, not one to be chosen for a promenade, but it was all the same to him. Up and down the streets he walked; along the wharves where the vessels lay; among the lanes, where poverty and vice, like twin brothers, stalk hand in hand; past houses whence came the sound of music and dancing, and where the shadows of women and sailors were thrown upon the curtains; past cellars, whence issued staggering drunkards; past all the many colored sides of the great monster which is continually, day and night, sucking the life blood from the body politic.

A noise, the loud voice of a woman in her cups, rose above the other sounds of the street. Greyburn followed with careless steps the crowd which was gathering. An aged creature occupied the sidewalk in front of a block of houses, and was answering in a high key the taunts of several mischievous young men who seemed to take great delight in annoying her.

"Ye're a pack of liars!" hissed the crone. "My daughter's as honest a girl as ever breathed the air of New York. Don't ye tell me she's not. Supposing she does come here in her carriage, what of that? Don't I tell ye that she's housekeeper for a rich gentleman? Why shouldn't she come in his carriage if he's willing?"

"Housekeeper! Oh, yes!" yelled the young fellows, derisively. "That's very good, Mother Delaporte, very good!"

"Ye're fools, all of ye!" screamed the woman, growing frantic. "It's because she's a beauty and your sisters are scraggy and homely that ye're jealous of my daughter. She wouldn't look at such as ye. Ye judge her by your own kin, and she's not made of the same dust as yer dirty mothers and sisters. Do ye hear that! I only wish my Edward was here. He'd fix ye, villains that ye are, to malign an honest girl who's working hard to keep her poor old mother from starving."

"Where's her Edward?" mockingly asked a bystander.

"He died drunk, long ago," replied another. "Old Mother's going like him, I guess."

The hubbub raised an immense crowd in the street, and at last the unvaryingly tardy policeman made his appearance. When he reached the old woman he grasped her in no gentle manner by the arm.

"Here, get into the house, will you! If I hear another word out of you to-night I'll put you into the station!"

"Oh, ye will, will ye!" cried the woman. "Ye'll arrest me and never touch those lying villains who followed me to cry down the name of my dear, good, sweet daughter. Let me alone?" she screamed, as the officer tightened his grip. "Drive this crowd off and leave me in peace. It's them that's making all the trouble."

The old woman caught hold of the fence by which she was standing and clung with all her might to the palings. The officer raised his club and struck her across the fingers; not severely, but yet enough to elicit a howl of pain and rage. The creature struck at him in blind fury and he raised his club again.

This time the blow would have been harder, but his arm did not descend. Greyburn, who had edged near to the scene, caught the policeman's hand. The crowd saw this and raised a shout of joy. An officer in trouble is always a welcome sight to hoodlums.

The policeman's eyes met Greyburn's squarely and the former quailed a little.

"If you think it your duty to arrest this woman I will help you to take her to the station-house, but you shall not strike her."

"Who are you?" demanded the officer.

"I am a citizen of New York."

"I am doing my duty," said the officer, growing bolder as he saw how quiet was Greyburn's demeanor, "and I will not be interfered with. Come, old woman, are you going along or shall I try to club you again?"

The officer raised the club, but Greyburn wrenched it from him with a quick motion. At that instant a carriage which was trying to make its way through the street stopped, hemmed in by the dense assemblage, exactly opposite to the place where Greyburn was. The faces of a young gentleman and lady appeared at the window, and when they found that they could not immediately proceed the gentleman alighted. With that respect for good clothes which comes instinctively to some people, the throng made easy passage for him.

"Say, what's this?" was his exclamation, as he came to the scene of the disturbance.

"This man is assaulting me," said the officer. "If you are a friend of the law, I call on you for assistance."

Greyburn looked at the new comer and staggered back a step.

"Walter!" he said, below his breath,

The young gentleman did not know him, but he did recognize the officer.

"What, Daniels!" he exclaimed, "is it you?"

"Yes, Mr. Campbell," replied the policeman, "and I wish you'd assist me in locking this man up. I was doing my duty here in arresting this woman, when he interfered."

"You'd better let him and the old woman go, both of them," was Walter's advice. "There's no use in having more trouble. You won't make any further disturbance, will you?" he said, soothingly, turning to Mother Delaporte.

"Ah! but they said," she cried again, "that my daughter—my darling, sweet, pure and lovely daughter—wasn't an honest girl. Had they a right to say that, mister? And she the sweetest and the most beautiful girl in New York, and working hard to keep her poor old mother in comfort. Wasn't it a mean thing and a cruel thing to say! Oh, dear! Oh, dear!"

The woman burst into loud lamentations. But in a moment soft young arms were around her neck and peach-like cheeks were nestled close to hers. The young lady in the carriage had left it and knelt in all her silks and velvets in the dirt of the street.

"Mother, darling mother! It is I, Gabrielle. They shall not abuse you. How could they! How could any one in the semblance of a man be so cruel!"

Walter Campbell beheld this singular scene with the utmost astonishment. He looked helplessly at his carriage in a vain hope that *his* Gabrielle might still be there and that this Gabrielle, so like her in dress and tones, might be another. He looked at Daniels; he looked at Greyburn; he looked at the crowd; and there was no hope for him anywhere.

Gabrielle assisted her mother to rise and succeeded

in stilling the complaining voice.   Then she turned to
her lover.

"Will you bring the carriage here so that I can get
her into it ?   She lives but a few blocks away.   The
crowd is so great that we could make little progress
on foot."

She lifted her beautiful eyes, all aglow with the
excitement of the scene, and placed her gloved hand
upon Walter's shoulder.   He drew back as if something poisonous had touched him.

"Who is that woman ?" he demanded, roughly.

"My mother," replied Gabrielle, bridling.

"Then take her and go your way with her !" he
said.   "You can't do it in *my* carriage, though.   Did
you think I would have it used for a thing like that ?"

He looked with loathing upon the object of his
scorn and strode away.

Gabrielle checked a rising exclamation and turned
again to her mother.

"Never mind, mamma dear.   I'll go home with
you.   No one shall speak cross to you while I am
here.   Come, lean on my arm."

The excitement of the last quarter of an hour had
removed all traces of liquor in the old woman's gait,
and she did as she was asked, but the crowd, more
from curiosity than ill humor, hemmed them in so
closely that they could only proceed with slowness.
Greyburn watched them for a few moments and then,
stepping forward, he said to the girl : "I beg your
pardon, but have you far to go ?"

"Only to Barnes court," she replied.   "About ten
minutes' walk from here."

"Shall I get you a carriage ?"

"No, thank you.   There is no stand near here and
it would take too long, I fear.   But if you would be
so kind as to take my mother's other arm, I think we
could get along faster.   Unless," she added, ironically,

"you, like my late escort, are afraid of contamination."

The crowd, seeing that all interest to them in the affair was ended, began to disperse, and when they reached the comparatively quiet shades of Barnes court they were nearly alone.

"Will you come in ?" said Gabrielle, as she opened the door with a key obtained from her mother.

"For a moment ; just to see that all is well," he responded. But, as he put his foot upon the threshold a hand was laid upon his arm. He turned and saw the face of Charlie Leslie.

"You here, Charlie ! Why, boy, this is two miles from our home."

"I know it," said the boy, "and it is time we were both there. Do not enter this house."

"Why not? I must at least go in and take a decent leave of the people here. I have just escorted an old lady home who was in trouble in the street."

"She is in no trouble now," insisted the lad, "and it is very late. *I* am going, and you will not let me go alone."

"Well, give me just a moment, to say good-night, and I will go with you."

"Then I must go in also," said Charlie.

"Certainly. That's all right," said Greyburn. "Come in."

CHAPTER XXV.

THEY went into the house. A gas jet was lighted in a neatly furnished sitting-room, where Gabrielle and her mother awaited their coming. When Greyburn entered, the old lady poured out her thanks for his assistance in saving her from being clubbed to death, as she insisted on putting it. After these thanks had been given over and over again, for some minutes, Gabrielle suggested that her mother ought to retire and get her rest.

"I shall stay over night, mamma dear," she said. "Go right to your room and get to sleep. In the morning I will tell you all the news, as I always do."

After her mother had gone, Gabrielle turned to Greyburn.

"I owe you many thanks, sir, for your kindness to my mother this evening, both in rescuing her from the brutality of that policeman and in assisting us home. In such a dilemma it was a surprise and delight to receive the services of so true a gentleman."

Greyburn hesitated a moment and then said :

"Gabrielle, don't you know who I am ?"

She looked up the least bit startled. Her eyes wandered over his face and she shook her head.

"I thought when you first spoke to me that I had seen you somewhere, but I cannot remember definitely. That is not strange, however. I have known so many people."

"Charlie," said Greyburn, looking at the boy, "you can see now whether I have changed or not. This woman has eaten at my table, sat by my side, lain in my arms. Not for once or twice, but for months. And she does not know that she ever saw me."

"Ah ! now I do," said Gabrielle, rising and offering her hand. "It's Hector."

He took the hand and held it.

"But you did not know me," he said.

"Not at first, truly," said the girl, assuming her most winning manner, " but that is easily accounted for. It is a wonder that I know anything after what I have just passed through. My head has been in a whirl, and how could I have expected to see you in this out of the way place. Now that I am getting calmer, I know you well enough. And I am very, very glad to see you."

"I am not at all changed, of course," he said.

"Oh, I won't say that !" she exclaimed. "You are a little more slender—and you've let your beard grow—and—and—you must excuse me for saying it—you're just the least mite older."

"What do you think of that ?" he said, bitterly, pointing to the scar across his forehead.

"What do I think of it ?" cried she. "Why, I think it's a long, red beauty mark. I think it's just lovely ! If you belonged to me, Hector, as you did once, I would kiss that forehead fifty times a day. I'd make you shave off that ugly beard, so as to let that mustache out in all its pristine loveliness ; and there isn't another thing I'd change about you, to make you perfection."

He had to smile ; more at the extravagance of the flattery, than because he allowed it to flatter him ; and not a little at the ingenuity with which she made the answer. Besides, he found this sweet face and girlish prattle a relief after the long months in which he had kept himself from his kind. It was like coming out of a cave into an atmosphere full of sunshine

and singing birds and gaily colored flowers.   Gabrielle
began to affect him like new wine.

"Do you really mean," he asked, "that any price
which I could pay would induce you to receive me as
a lover, with these disfigurations?"

Gabrielle laughed her sweet, low, mellow laugh.

"What a way you have of putting things!   I
wouldn't be hired to love any man whom I didn't
wish to love.   You know we were great friends until
Walter's sister came between us.   I should have loved
you 'forever and ever, amen,' if you hadn't thrown
me aside.   As for those little scratches on your face,
they're not worth speaking of.   They wouldn't make
the slightest difference to me."

Greyburn's eyes brightened.   His face bore the first
real smile it had seen for months.

"You give me hope," he said, "that my life is not
wholly gone—that I can yet save something out of its
wreck.   But—I have committed a breach of courtesy,"
he added, as his eye rested upon Charlie.   "I should
have introduced my young friend here.   Miss Delaporte, Mr. Leslie."

"I am delighted to meet him, I'm sure," said the
girl, advancing, and offering her hand.

Charlie did not take it.   Indeed, he shrank from its
touch, more from instinct than willful impoliteness.

"Mr. Greyburn is disposed to be facetious," he said.
"I am his servant, nothing more.   I know my place,
and I also know that the customs of society do not
place me on a level with the friends of my employer."

The girl stood looking from one to the other in
complete bewilderment.

"Servant or friend," she said, "I offer you my
hand.   Won't you take it?"

Stouter hearts than Charlie's had melted beneath

the glance of those lovely eyes, but he showed no signs of capitulation.

. " I cannot," he said.

"And why ?" asked Gabrielle, smiling upon him like a very fairy. "What is there in that little hand which can harm a child like you ?"

" It is not for me to say," said the boy, lifting his eyes to hers, and never flinching before her gaze, " that there is wrong in your hand. I will leave it to you—is it a pure hand ?"

Gabrielle uttered a little cry of pain.

" Is it a hand which points to a better life ? Or does it beckon its followers downward toward the gates of death ?"

" You must not mind him," interposed Greyburn. " He is nothing if not preachy. I keep him as a foil to my sinfulness. He marches ahead where the sun can shine on him. I am the shadow creeping along in his wake. He is interesting and I love him. Besides, he saved my life at Chatham. As for heeding all he says, that were impossible."

" It were better if you heeded some of it," cried the boy. " I urged you not to enter this house."

" Why, what harm has happened to him here ?" cried Gabrielle. " One would think that I were a viper whose touch would poison him."

The lad turned once more to Greyburn. " Please go. It is nearly morning."

" There is no need of haste," replied the man. " We have nothing to do but sleep when we get home. I have found an old friend here and I wish to talk with her. You may go. Get a carriage, that will be best, and I will come later."

" No," said the lad, firmly, " I cannot leave you. I have followed you all night and you must come with me now. We will take the carriage together."

"I am not going," said Greyburn, raising his voice a little.

" *You shall.*"

The boy took him by the arm as if he would abduct him by main force.

" By what right do you say that?" queried the man, sharply.

" By every right.   Here is temptation, which to you means sin.   Come, I have counseled you for many weeks.   I conjure you, listen to me now."

"Go with him," said Gabrielle, seeing that he hesitated.   " You may get infected by breathing the same air with me."

"Come," repeated Charlie.   " Even she joins with me in asking it."

"I will not !" cried Greyburn, losing all control of himself.   " I have been a slave too long.   What have I to gain or lose ?   The woman who swore before God to love me shrinks from my scarred face.   This woman, as fair as she, offers me her affection, and I will accept it.   Go to my home, or where you will, I shall remain here."

The boy grew very pale during the last words.   He lurched dizzily toward a chair, tried to grasp it, and fell lifeless upon the floor.   The scene changed instantly.   Greyburn caught up the slender form and laid it on a sofa, while the impulsive girl ran to a cupboard for restoratives.   Before she could fetch them she was startled by a loud exclamation, and turned to see Greyburn with his arm extended toward her in a beckoning attitude.

Charlie lay in a dead faint.   Greyburn had unbuttoned the child's coat and loosened his collar, in order to give him all the air that could be got into his lungs.   The breath was so still that for a moment he feared it had departed.   Tearing open the shirt, he was about to apply his ear to the heart when he made the discovery which caused him to cry out.

"Good God !" cried Gabrielle.   "It is a girl."

Greyburn bowed his head in his hands and uttered not a word.

" Did you not know it ?" she asked, suspiciously.

He shook his head and she saw that he trembled a little.

" How long have you known her ?"

" Six months," he said in a whisper.   " I can't comprehend it.   Little Charlie."

" You must get a doctor."

" Yes, where ?"

" Just around the corner.   The first door.   There is a night bell."

The doctor was procured, and by his directions Gabrielle put the child to bed and applied the necessary remedies.   The medical man thought that he understood the situation when he found his girl-patient dressed in boy's clothes, and he said :

" Don't let her get excited when she wakes.   This masquerading business is always dangerous.   It acts on the nerves of a girl to be on the street in man's garments."

When the faint was changed into a quiet sleep under the influence of the medicine, and the doctor had taken his departure, Greyburn and Gabrielle conversed in low tones over the strange affair.   He told her all he had to tell.   When he finished, she said, with a woman's intuition :

" One thing is certain, Hector, the poor child had a reason for her jealousy of me.   She is terribly in love with you, herself."

" I am afraid so," he responded, gloomily.   " And yet, how can it be ?   She is the soul of virtue, and she knows that I am married."

" That makes no difference," replied the girl.

"Virtue can control a woman's conduct, but not her heart. It was so romantic. She saved your life, and all the forces of nature combine to make us love that to which we have given being. Did you never have the slightest suspicion that she was other than what she seemed?"

"Not the least. She has been with me on tramps of miles, lasting all night, and showed no more signs of weariness than would be expected of a frail boy. Think how she carried me through my illness at Macon and restored me to my friends. It seemed remarkable for a boy ; it seems doubly so for a young, inexperienced girl. What could have been the object of her assuming boy's clothing ! It is more like a romance than a real occurrence."

It was ten o'clock in the morning when Charlie awoke. As she glanced around the unfamiliar room the scenes of the preceding night came slowly back. She lay very still, thinking what to do and say, now that her secret was discovered. When Gabrielle looked in, Charlie smiled to her and put out her hand.

"I was impolite to you last night, I fear," said the sick girl, "but I meant well. You will forgive me, won't you ?"

"Don't speak of it," said Gabrielle. "What can I do for you !"

"Do you think I could rise ?"

"Not to-day."

"To-morrow, then, or whenever it is safe for me to get up, would you get me something to wear suitable for my sex ! You know," she added, blushing a littie, "I cannot be a boy any longer."

"I will get anything you desire," said Gabrielle.

"You will find money in my pocket-book. Has he —has Mr. Greyburn—gone away ?"

"No, he is near at hand and very anxious about your recovery."

"Will it be improper for him to come in here a minute?" said Charlie, hesitatingly.

"I cannot see why. You are ill. That excuses everything."

"Please speak to him, then," said Charlie. "And, would you mind? I wish to see him a little while alone."

Greyburn came in, closed the door softly behind him, and sat down in a chair by the bed.

"Dear little Charlie," he said, in tones of infinite tenderness, "can you ever forgive me for my harshness last night? I feel so guilty, after all your kindness to me."

"Hush!" said Charlie, taking the man's hand in hers. "We were both unreasonable. We did not understand each other."

"I cannot believe," he continued, "that the boy I have traveled with these long months is, after all, a woman. I could not understand how so much goodness could lurk in a masculine frame, but this hypothesis I never dreamed of."

"I knew you did not," Charlie smiled, "but it can no longer be denied. When I rise from this bed it will be to assume the garments of my own sex."

"Why did you don those of the other?'

"To get work more easily," she said. "As I told you, I left my grandfather's house at the age of ten years. What could a girl do? I tried in vain to get anywhere except into a kitchen. Then I put on a boy's suit and had no more trouble. As a boy I was a success, as a girl a miserable failure."

"What will you do now?"

"That," she answered, smilingly, "is for you to say. My contract with you should not be broken because my sex is changed."

"It is impossible," he said, decidedly, "for us to be together under these altered circumstances."

"Why ?"

"Because," he answered, turning his face away, "my reputation will blast yours wherever we are known. You must go where no one will ever hear that you lived these months under my roof, or you are ruined. I could not, after this, walk or ride with you in public and leave you a particle of character in the eyes of New York."

"Once more," she said, softly, "you will begin to lead a life of virtue. I will be your guide. You will win the regard of him that overcometh."

"No! no!" he cried, "it cannot be. You could not lift me up and I should drag you down. The love for me which is developing in your heart is a dangerous thing. Strike it down! crush it out, as you would an infant serpent, or it will throttle you! I am a wicked man. I must run my course, but I will never consent to destroy you with me!"

"You need not fear for me," replied Charlie, looking at him with an expression of ineffable tenderness. "I had a mother who taught me that the greatest of supplications was this, 'Lead us not into temptation.' She knew what punishment follows wrong-doing, even when the evil one appears in the brightest and most pleasing of shapes. No one could ever persuade me to sin, and if violence were used I would not hesitate to send my soul to that mother who gave it to me white, and taught me not to let it be sullied."

"I cannot listen to you," he said, in tones of expostulation. "No matter what your intentions or mine may be there would always be danger."

"You cannot refuse me," persisted Charlie. "You will not turn from your door one who loves you as I do."

"But you shall not love me!" he cried with vehemence. "I refuse to allow it. I will send you where you please, so that it be away from me ; and I shall, of course, bear all your expenses. My love is the only thing I shall refuse you, and that I *must* not give."

"Oh, yes ! you *will* love me," said the girl, raising herself upon her pillow, and looking at him with eyes from which the tears were flowing. "You *must* love me ! Do you not know why ? Can you not guess? *I am your daughter !*"

***

CHAPTER XXVI.

WHEN Clara Greyburn came to realize what she had done—that the being at whose appearance she had manifested terror, and whom she had driven from her door, was her husband—she fell into a fever which lasted for weeks. Mr. John Bird, who was instructed by Greyburn to arrange a settlement with her, came on from New York, waited several days, and then, by advice of Dr. Robinson, returned again to the city to await her recovery, which the good doctor warned him would be very slow. The lawyer made arrangements that all charges should be paid by himself and that he should be sent for at the earliest practicable date. The winter and spring passed before Clara's mental and physical strength were considered equal to the transaction of business, and the physician would have postponed the matter still longer except that her inquiries became so imperative that he feared lest her anxiety to know what had become of her husband might retard her improvement.

One day in June Mr. John Bird made his second

appearance at Chatham, and alighted from the stage coach in front of Mrs. Baldwin's house. Clara was still far from strong, and received him in an easy chair. The landlady left them alone, after showing Mr. Bird into the room, and the man of business proceeded with his errand.

" Mrs. Greyburn," he began, but she interrupted him.

" Tell me first if he is well ! Has Hector—has Mr. Greyburn—entirely recovered from his terrible accident ?"

" In one sense, yes ; in another, no," answered the lawyer. " With the exception of a few scars, which he will probably carry with him to the grave, his bodily hurts are mended. Mentally, his condition is not so good. He is moody, reticent and evidently unhappy. The loss to his facial appearance seems to weigh heavily upon his mind."

She caught eagerly at every word.

" How does he live—alone ?"

" Almost. He has only the boy for a companion ; the one who testified at the trial, you remember. They live with a servant or two, hardly ever appearing out, and seeming to shrink from publicity. As far as any of Mr. Greyburn's old companions are aware, he is literally dead to the world. I doubt if any of them know that he is in the city, and I am sure he doesn't desire that they should."

There was a slight pause and then she said :

" Do you include me in that list, Mr. Bird ? Am *I* one of those old acquaintances from whose presence he desires to hide ? Sir, you are a lawyer—*his*—lawyer—but you are a man, and I believe, a gentleman. I must talk to you in what may seem a plain manner, but I have no one else to speak to. Have you come to tell me that my husband will insist on our living apart, or is there any hope that in time I

may take my rightful place? Do not hesitate, sir.
You see I am very calm."

" The attorney coughed, and looked considerably
disturbed.

" I did not anticipate this turn in the conversation,"
he said, " but if I proceed with my business, as ordered
by my client, you can perhaps judge as well as I in
relation to the matter of which you speak. Mr. Greyburn instructs me to offer you whatever part of his
fortune you will consent to receive."

" I will never touch a penny of it !" she burst out,
indignantly. "I have told him so. You came here
when I was ill, and in his name ordered all my bills
charged to you. I shall not allow it. I have half of
a house in Springdale, which I can sell, and pay all I
owe here. As soon as I am strong I can teach school
again. Hector may hate me, but he shall never
despise me! I would rather starve than receive a
dollar of his money under such conditions !"

Mr. Bird coughed a good deal after this, and was
more disconcerted than he remembered to have been
in the whole course of his professional career.

"Of course no one can compel you against your
will," he said, finally. " But you must excuse a man a
good deal older than yourself if he tells you plainly
that you reason quite erroneously. As I have been
given to understand it, Mr. Greyburn drove here one
night with the intention of discussing these matters
with you. Instead of giving him the slightest en-
couragement—this is the way I hear it—you expressed
in a violent manner your wish that he should leave at
once. As you seem to desire me to speak plainly, I
should like to understand this point."

" It was a most unfortunate error on my part," she
replied, "and it has cost me hours of agony. I was
highly wrought up with the knowledge that Hector
was still living, and when the boy called and began

to talk with me I had no idea that my husband was within many miles. When he stepped into the room he was so changed that I never suspected who he was. He stood by that door, half in the shadow, and the only effect of his presence was to inspire me with terror. When he was beyond reach and they told me whom I had sent away, I fainted, and my long illness followed. Could Hector understand this, could he know how dearly I craved his presence at the very moment when my eyes failed to recognize him, would he not forgive me? Oh, Mr. Bird! don't you think he would?"

"He is greatly changed—I mean in appearance," mused the attorney. "The handsome face you used to know will never come back to him."

"Do you think I would mind that?" said the girl, eagerly. "Does he think—can that be his reason? Is he afraid that scars or disfigurements will affect my love? Rather would they make it deeper, by reminding me every hour that he owed them to my blind, foolish, wicked conduct."

Mr. Bird started.

"To yours?" he said.

"To mine. I drove him from my heart when he yearned for my affection. The evening before the accident he begged me to relent and I would not. In his distress of mind he found sleep impossible and arose in the middle of the night to walk in the open air. Oh! I am all to blame—all! all!"

"Mr. Greyburn does not so consider it," said the lawyer, comfortingly.

"And when he understands what I have told you, will he let me come to him?"

The lawyer slowly shook his head.

"I cannot encourage such a hope," he said, "without being false to my trust. 'Tell my wife,' said Mr. Greyburn, 'that we can never be happy together;

that I must live my life in my own way and endure my sorrows as I can ; tell her that I am a bruised and broken man, body and soul, and wish to be considered as one dead.' These were his words, and I am sure nothing will turn him from his decision."

A low moan escaped her lips.

" If this be so," she said, " let us bring this interview to a close, as it is very painful to me. Tell my husband that I shall never trouble him again. As soon as I am able to travel I shall go to some distant place where he will never hear of me. I have no one in the wide world now who cares where I go, or what I do. I wrote to my brother last week and he answered my letter in the harshest manner. He is my only near relation. Mr. Bird, I must bid you good-by. I really am not strong enough to bear more."

The lawyer persisted until he saw that further argument was useless. Unless he could say that he believed that Greyburn would consent to receive his wife as a wife she would not live on his bounty. There was no middle course. The weak little woman was very strong in her resolutions, and Mr. Bird left Chatham without accomplishing anything whatever.

He told the story to Greyburn with great minuteness, but found him as obdurate as his wife had been. " I can never make her happy, and I am better alone," he said. " Now, is there no way in which we can compel her to accept something? It seems preposterous for a woman to insist in the technicalities which she raises."

" There is one way in which something might be done," said the lawyer. He unfolded a plan which he had invented, and which, for want of anything better, was at once decided upon.

What this plan was, the reader may perhaps surmise when he learns that Mr. Bird called within a few days upon Mr. Walter Campbell to ask him whether he would sell his interest in the parsonage at Springdale.

"Yes, I'll sell it," said Walter, grimly, "and the sooner the better. I don't want to own a thing in common with either of them. Find out what the place is worth and make out your deed. I'll take the money and give it to the Magdalen's Home to establish a free bed in their name." He laughed discordantly at the idea.

When, a few weeks later, Clara offered her portion of the homestead for sale, the bidding was so spirited as to start from its propriety the staid old village.

"Gentlemen," said the auctioneer, "I offer you to-day a most desirable piece of property. This house is well known to you as the house of a former beloved pastor of the church in this place, and later of a"—here he caught the frowning eyes of several village matrons—"of a—of another perton who—who has moved away. The property consists of the house, garden, and about four acres of meadow. I offer one undivided half of the estate. Who will start it? Come, gentlemen, anything for a beginning."

"One thousand dollars," said a stranger, who stood in the crowd.

"One thou—look here !" said the auctioneer, "this is not the place for any foolishness. I offer one-half of this property and I ask for a bid. Let me say, before I go any further, that the terms are cash. Now gentlemen, we will begin again."

"One thousand dollars," repeated the strange bidder.

"You understand I am only selling half of the place ?" said the auctioneer, hardly able to credit his sense of hearing.

"Certainly," said the bidder.

"Well, then," said the auctioneer, recovering himself,

" I am offered one thousand dollars. Will any gentleman raise the bid ?"

" Two thousand," said a voice in the crowd. Everybody knew this bidder. It was Squire Sawyer, from
Brewster.

" It's all right," said the Squire. " I'm bidding for
another party, but I've got the money here. Go
ahead, Martin. I guess that'll take it."

The excitement in the little party was now at fever
heat. What was the matter ! Had gold been discovered in the orchard ? Had oil been prospected in
the rocky side hill ? Two thousand dollars for half
a place which would have sold high at eight hundred ! What could it mean !

" Squire Sawyer bids two thousand," said the confused auctioneer, " and ——"

" I bid three thousand," said the stranger.

" Who are you bidding for ?" demanded Mr. Martin.

" I should like to know that, too," added Squire
Sawyer.

" Cash," replied the stranger, taking a heavy roll
of bills from his pocket. " Go on with the sale, or I
shall miss the next train at Brewster."

" Three thousand I am offered," repeated Mr.
Martin, in a shaking voice, " for one-half of this
property. Three thousand—do I hear anything more ?
Three thousand ——"

" Thirty-one hundred," called out Squire Sawyer,
desperately.

" Four thousand," responded the imperturbable
stranger, and at this sum it was knocked down. The
purchaser gave the name of George A. Severance.
After receiving his papers and paying down the
money, he stepped into a carriage and departed, the
center of a hundred pairs of astonished eyes.

Mr. Severance had a few minutes to wait for his
train, and Squire Sawyer, who had followed him as

far as his own residence, strolled down to ask him a few questions.

"Who is the real purchaser of the Campbell parsonage?" he asked. "I am interested to know, as the only other bidder."

"Didn't you hear me give my name to the auctioneer?" said Mr. Severance, evasively.

"Yes, but there's some mystery about it. Now, I'd just as lief tell you whom I was bidding for, as long as the affair is all over. Of course, you know that five hundred dollars is more than the thing is worth, and I bid thirty-one hundred dollars. I was bidding for a fellow who used to live here—John Dinsmore, by name—who had a great attachment for the parson's daughter, though no one suspected it until that affair out South got into the papers. This Dinsmore is a cripple, probably for life, but he wanted to give the girl a lift, and sent word to me to run the place up as high as was necessary. I think he wanted to come back and live in it. Now, I've been confidential with you, and you ought to be the same. For whom did you really buy it?"

The iron horse came snorting and screaming up to the platform.

"Look in the Registry of Deeds next week, and you'll be convinced that I've told the truth," said Mr. Severance, as he stepped aboard.

"Would you take forty-five hundred dollars for the property if I can raise it within a week?" called the Squire, as the train started.

"No," said Mr. Severance. "It isn't for sale."

Clara received the money for her little home, with the greatest astonishment. The agent who arranged the sale wrote merely that two bidders "got to running each other," and that the sale was perfectly legitimate and honorable. The faintest idea of the real truth of the matter never occurred to her. She paid up all her bills at Chatham and departed, promising good Mrs. Baldwin to write whenever she got "settled" in her new place.

When Mr. Severance, who was one of the clerks in the employ of Bird & Bird, recited the particulars of the sale to Greyburn, he was much pleased. The explanation made by Squire Sawyer also interested him greatly.

"I'm glad that blacksmith didn't get a chance to live in the house where she was born and reared," he said to himself. "I'm *very* glad. And I don't see why, either ; for it never can make any difference to me."

CHAPTER XXVII.

WALTER CAMPBELL was in no enviable frame of mind that night when he left his beautiful inamorata embracing a drunken old woman in the dirt of the street, and rode away in his carriage toward his Madison avenue residence. It seemed to him that he had used Gabrielle extremely well, and that she made a very poor return when she thus disgraced him in the eyes of a common police officer and a motley crowd of street *canaille*. He thought, as he rolled away, how unpleasant his house would be with its fair mistress forever absent, as her return after what had happened was not among the possibilities. He did not like the picture which came to his mind. Selfish to a degree, he thought of nothing but his own convenience, and it seemed as if misfortune in one form or another was continually dogging his footsteps. While indulging in such gloomy fancies he happened to notice, strolling along the almost neglected pavement, no less a person than Mr. Chester Bolton ; and, signaling to the driver, he was driven to the curb, where he could accost him.

"Hullo !" said Bolton. "It's you, is it ? What's up ?"

"Get in here and drive up to the house with me," said Walter. "I'm in a pretty mess and I want to talk with you."

"All right," said Bolton. "By the way, where's Gabe ? Thought I saw you at the Fifth Ave !"

"You did," said Walter, "curse the luck ! You'll never see us there or anywhere else together again, though ——"

"Sho !" ejaculated Mr. Bolton. "What's the mat ? Course of true love, eh ? No ! Not jell, are you ? No hated rive ?"

"Nothing of the sort," said Walter. "I'll tell you, but don't you ever mention it. It might set the boys to laughing at me, if they knew it. There's only one man, a policeman, in the secret, and I can shut his mouth."

"All right," said Mr. Bolton. "Drive ahead. Produce your anec. I'll be dumb as a lob."

"Well, you see," said Walter, "after the theatre we drove down to Mendall's office for a minute, and were coming back, when we found a devilish mob in one of the streets, where an officer was trying to arrest an old woman who was drunk. I found that we had got to wait, so I jumped out to see the row. The old woman set up a fearful howl because some one had been saying that her daughter wasn't strictly V., and the next thing I knew—would you believe it ? Miss Mademoiselle Gabrielle was out of the carriage, hugging the old gal and calling her 'mamma !' "

"Joseph and his brethren!" ejaculated Mr. Bolton, with surprising inappropriateness. "Case of temp insan, was it? Down to Blackwell's now, I suppose."

"Not at all," replied Walter. I couldn't doubt what she said in the way she said it. The old woman knew her, too. All I could do was to leave them there."

"When she comes back to-morrow you must talk to her," said Bolton, with a vague idea that it was the proper thing to say.

"Come back!" repeated Walter. "Not to me! She may go with the sort of trash she belongs with. It makes me shiver to think I have had her so long. There should be a law to keep such creatures in their native element. Ugh! Who would have thought, with all her fancy airs, that she belonged in that sphere?"

They alighted at Walter's residence and ascended to his private parlor on the third floor, where, over a bottle of wine and a couple of havanas, they resumed their conversation. It dwelt a little longer on Gabrielle, until both gentlemen agreed that it was a waste of time to discuss that subject further, and turned it into another channel.

"I can't help thinking," said Mr. Bolton, "of the gay old times I've had in this house when Hector Greyburn owned it. It seems queer, don't it, to think how soon he went to the dogs."

"He was a fool," said Walter, in a tone which showed that he did not like the subject.

"At the last—yes," assented Bolton, "but not in the old days. His house was always the property of his guests. I never knew him to say a word, whatever happened, and sometimes things used to happen which would have made trouble anywhere else. Where the deuce did he spring from, all at once, and where did he get the quantities of money that he used to throw away?   That's the question that's bothered a good many of us."

"Stole it, probably," said Walter.   "He wouldn't have got it honestly, if there was any other way.   Be sure of that."

"Why, I didn't know you was so down on him," said Bolton, with some surprise in his voice.   "I remember, when you first came to town, you seemed to think he was old Jupe himself."

"I've had reasons to think he is old Nick himself, since," said Walter, pettishly.   "The way he used me at the end wasn't a thing to make me fall in love with him."

"Ah! I didn't think you knew," said Bolton, incautiously.   "None of the boys thought so, and, of course, none of us felt like coming to you with the news."

"Didn't think I knew!" repeated Walter, with a sneer.   "Didn't you think I could read?   The marriage notice was printed in every paper in New York."

"The marriage," echoed Bolton.   "The marriage! oh, yes!   But I meant the—other events, you know —preceding that.   There, of course—is—is where the —the—feeling comes in."

The hesitation with which Mr. Bolton launched upon his unpleasant theme was not lessened by the glare which appeared in his companion's eyes as he proceeded.   He wished heartily that he had never thought of Greyburn, or had smothered his ideas instead of giving them utterance.

Walter struck his fist upon the table with a loud noise.

"What in the name of the infernal devils do you mean by that? he shouted.   "The 'preceding events,' do you say?   What in hades were the preceding events?   D—n it, man, answer me!   What do you mean?"

"'Pon my soul!" cried Bolton, thrown completely

off his guard. "I thought by what you said that you knew it all."

"Knew it all ! Knew *what ?*"

"Why, that—that—they were at the Hampden together."

"At the Hampden ! Well, supposing they were at the Hampden ! What is there so terrible in a man and his wife going to a respectable hotel ?"

"They went before they were married, though," said Bolton, desperately.

"Well," said Walter, nervously. "What of it ? They went there to supper, perhaps ? To secure rooms ? Well, well ?"

"D—n the thing !" said Bolton, "I thought you knew. I'm getting into a pretty fix. If you don't know, go somewhere and find out. I won't say another word."

Walter gazed at him stupidly for a moment. A terrible conflict was going on in his mind. Suspicion followed suspicion, until he could bear it no longer.

"Chet," he said at last, in a lower tone, "tell me. What is it ? You claim to be my friend and I can't run around town asking such questions. You have something which I ought to know. Tell me !"

"I wish the imps had had me before I came here to-night," said Bolton, "but if you will have it so, I'll tell you. They were at the hotel together all of one night and didn't get married until the next day."

"It's a wicked lie !" cried Walter, indignantly. "Somebody has deceived you. I know it would be impossible. My sister married this man, which is bad enough, but she never disgraced herself with him in any other way. I could swear it ! Bolton, you don't know her, or you wouldn't even repeat so gross a slander."

"I've seen the register," said Bolton, "so there's no hope on that score. I wish there were. Campbell, I'm sorry for you, but you know Greyburn was a terrible fellow among the women. In marrying your sister he did what he could to right his wrong. From all I know of him, it is the best act he ever did."

"I don't believe it yet," said Walter, growing paler, however. "It is easy to fix a hotel register—much easier than to win a girl like that to shame. There is deception here, Bolton, somewhere. There must be. Own up now. The register could have been tampered with."

"I'd like to help you, if I could," said his friend, "but it's no use. You might as well have it out now as at another time. There's more proof than the register. Have you forgotten Middleby's wager? Perkyns paid Greyburn the money the morning before he was married."

Walter looked for a minute as if he had experienced a paralytic shock. He stared at Bolton like a drunken man. When he spoke, his tongue was thick and his voice unsteady.

"Do you say Middleby's money went to Greyburn? And on *her* account?"

Mr. Bolton bowed.

"Everybody knows it?"

Mr. Bolton assented.

"Where do you suppose Greyburn is?"

"No one can tell," said Bolton. "He disappeared after the acquittal of the man charged with his murder."

"Dinsmore?" said Walter.

"Yes, I think that was the name."

"*He* knew."

"You think so?"

"No doubt of it," said Walter. "It wasn't like him to try and kill a man without cause. I wish I could find Greyburn."

"What do you want of him?"

"I want to see him," said Walter, still in that thick, low voice. "He is my brother. I want to shake hands with him. He has done me great honor in marrying my sister. It was very kind of him to save her from disgrace after her folly. I want to meet him and tell him how much I appreciate it."

"You want to keep away from him, that's what *you* want," said Bolton. "The affair has all died out now and you don't want to make it public again. I hear that his lawyers offered his wife any sum she pleased, to be settled on her, but she refused to take anything and has also disappeared. He seems to have been perfectly honorable in everything connected with the separation."

"Oh, he's honorable!" said Walter. "He knows what's right. A few dollars will heal a family disgrace. He won fifty thousand dollars by my sister, and, like a gentleman, he offers her part of it. He is magnanimous, noble! I must find him and thank him personally."

"I wish you'd drop the mat, I do, really," said Bolton. "I feel as if it was my fault that you ever heard of it. Of course it isn't pleasant when these things come into one's own family, but you know they do happen, and happen every day. You've had your share in them ; so have I ; so has Greyburn. 'Pon my soul, Walter, we are not the ones who should cry baby."

"You're right," assented Walter, still with that terrible calmness. "We have often, I remember distinctly, gone into the houses of our dearest friends—or those whom we pretended were dearest—and treated their sisters as if they were those of perfect strangers. We have shaken dice for the honor of our mothers. When we have been invited to dinner we have invariably stolen the silver. When they have asked us to remain over night we have always risen in the darkness and strangled the children, taking occasion at the same time to stab our hosts to the heart as they lay asleep. It's a little thing that Greyburn has done to me—not worth talking about. Of course, as you say, I'll drop the matter."

There was something almost blood-curdling in the manner in which Walter uttered these ironical words. Mr. Bolton rose, shivered a little, said he was sorry, and hoped his friend would feel better by the next morning. Then he looked at his watch, declared that it was getting altogether too late, and took his departure, feeling very uneasy over the result of his unhappy error.

The next day Walter was not at his desk at City Hall, and a messenger, who was sent to inquire about him, returned with the answer that he was not well. Mr. Mendall, upon learning this news, also called at the house, but was informed by Williams that Mr. Campbell would positively refuse to see anybody. The succeeding day he still remained in his room, still claiming illness, though no medical man passed over his threshold. In the afternoon he gave Williams a note to deliver ; and early in the evening a dark complexioned man of medium build rang the bell and was at once escorted up to Walter's room.

This man was Mr. Maurice Stager, a private detective. As soon as the customary salutations had passed, they proceeded to business.

"I want you to find Greyburn," said Walter.

"Umph ! Have you any idea where he is ?"

"Not the slightest."

"Not a very encouraging outlook," remarked Stager.

"Then you don't think you can find him ?"

"Oh, I can find him, but it will take time, unless I get a good clue to start with. I can go right out to Georgia and then trail him along. We might put a personal in the *Herald.* Or, perhaps you want this thing perfectly quiet."

"That's just what I want. You must not say a word to any one that we have spoken on the subject."

"Do you mind telling me what you want him for?" said Stager.

"He is my brother by marriage."

"Yes, I know that."

"You know the rest, too, probably," said Walter, finally. "How he went to the Hampden ——"

"And stayed there with his girl the night before he married her? Yes."

"Well, I haven't seen him since ; and I wish to speak with him."

"All right," smiled Stager, knowingly. "I'll go to work at once."

<hr>

CHAPTER XXVIII.

The next morning Walter was back at his desk, but the effect of his illness was marked by his fellow clerks in his reserved demeanor, as well as the unusual paleness of his face. To Mendall, who met him as he was leaving in the afternoon, his answers were short and hardly polite.

"I hear you've been ill," said the banker.

"Yes."

"I called to see you, but Williams said you could not be disturbed."

No answer.

"You are better to-day, I hope?"

"Yes."

"And Gabrielle? How is she?"

"I don't know nor care," snapped Walter. "She's gone, and I'm glad of it."

"Gone !" echoed the banker.

"That's what I said."

".Since when ?"

"Several days ; nearly a week."

"So that's what's the matter," said the banker with a look which was meant to be roguish. "Well, don't mind her. There are plenty just as good. She was expensive, too."

"Bah !" snarled Walter. "I didn't want her. I sent her away. Don't take me for a fool !"

"Certainly not," said Mendall. "But where is she ? Where did she go ?"

"To the slums which she came from, I suppose ! Do you want her ? Go down around the wharves where such vermin breed Look along the streets below the Five Points. You'll find her there, probably, with the sailors and stevedores."

He departed with the utmost abruptness, leaving Mendall very much astonished, and not a little indignant at his curt manner.

"The little jackanapes !" he muttered. "I wish I could get along without him. I wonder what he'll do next? The idea of his treating *me* in this way ! Wouldn't let me into my own building yesterday !"

A passing policeman touched his hat to the banker.

"Hallo, Daniels," said Mendall.

"How do you do," responded the officer.

"Did you notice young Campbell ?" said Mendall. "He's all broke up to-day. Lost his girl, he says."

"Oh, I know all about that," said the officer, glad to air his knowledge, and proceeded to give the banker an account of the affair with Mother Delaporte."

"You don't tell me !" said Mendall, as he concluded,

"Where is this Barnes court where you say the old lady lives?"

The officer described its location, and the banker started at once in that direction, first cautioning Daniels not to mention the affair to any one. As the officer had secured his position through Mendall's influence, he promised compliance, and the banker had full confidence that he would keep his word.

Mendall found Gabrielle still at her mother's. With characteristic good-nature, she allowed the banker to clasp her in his arms as he entered the hall, telegraphing him a warning at the same time that he must be sure and not repeat the operation in her mother's presence. When they entered the room where Mrs. Delaporte was sitting, Gabrielle introduced her visitor, and the old lady rose to welcome him with every mark of courtesy.

"Mr. Mendall is an old acquaintance of mine, mamma dear," said Gabrielle. "He tells me that he and his wife wish a housekeeper, and he wants me to agree to fill the place. He is not like Mr. Campbell, to despise us because we are not rich."

The banker listened with astonishment and delight to this speech. The soft, sweet way in which she addressed her mother, charmed him. There was nothing of the aristocrat in Mendall's composition. The flower he sought lost none of its fragrance when he learned that it grew upon a dunghill.

"Is it not time, mamma," Gabrielle continued, "that you took your medicine? It is nearly six o'clock. My mother is not well," she explained, "and I have to be very careful of her." So, speaking alternately to her mother and to Mendall, she escorted the old lady into another room, from which, in about fifteen minutes, she returned alone.

"All quiet along the Potomac?" he asked, slyly.

"Yes," she smiled. "My mother is sound asleep,"

"It must be wonderful medicine that you give her."

"It is gin," she said. "Nothing else soothes her. She is out of all trouble now until to-morrow morning. No care, no sorrow, no pain will disturb her for fifteen hours."

"What do you think I came here for?" he asked, changing the subject.

"To get me to live with you," she replied, vivaciously. "And to offer me that pretty house on Madison avenue, to be all my own, with a deed recorded in my name, if I consent."

His countenance fell a little.

"Not that house," he said. "That one is too big, and, besides, Walter has a claim upon it, and I couldn't get him out. I'll buy you a nice little place, though, somewhere else. Something in the bijou style."

"Worth how much?" said Gabrielle, calculatingly.

"Oh, a nice one. You wouldn't understand the figures if I told you. What do a nest of martens know about the cost of their box? I'll guarantee it will suit you."

"And you will furnish it all new? And I may go and pick out just what I want in the way of furniture?"

"Yes, yes!" he said, impatiently.

"And the title deeds shall be mine?"

"What do you want of title deeds? You would lose them if you had them."

"Oh, no, I wouldn't! Say, am I to have the title deeds?"

He gave in under her bewitching smile, and said yes, she should have them.

"And now, for how long am I to sell myself in exchange for this piece of real estate?"

"How long?" he echoed.

"Yes. It's a bargain and sale, you know. You are going to give me so many dollars' worth of property for my company. So I ask—for how long?"

"Why, forever!" said he. "I never want to lose you."

"Then," she said, with a pretty toss of her head, "I decline your offer. It isn't high enough."

"How strange you are!' said Mendall.

"Not at all. This is business. Your house and furniture will be worth—how much? Perhaps eighteen thousand dollars or twenty thousand dollars. In exchange, you want me for life, and you want too much! You are driving too hard a bargain. I can do better."

"But your expenses—your dresses—jewelry, servants, household charges, etc.—they will cost a pretty penny," he said.

"Still not enough for a life lease," she responded with a laugh. "And you quite forget that I must have spending money."

"Oh, that is one of the etceteras, of course," he admitted.

"Well," she said, "we won't quarrel. Pick out your house and let me see it. If it doesn't suit, negotiations are off. If it does, and the other preliminaries are all right, I will take the deeds, and you shall have me till—till I get tired of you."

"Which may be the next morning."

"Precisely. Now give me a kiss and go. Get the house this week sure and let me know at once."

She rose on tiptoe to kiss the bronzed face which he bent down to her, and he half lifted her petite form from the floor with his strong arm.

"You will love me a little?" he said, as the contact with her red lips brought back the youthful touch to his veins.

"Love you! I shall adore you. Especially if the house suits. It must be in a good location and where

there is plenty of sun.   Don't be long deciding ; and
don't come here again until you come in a carriage to
take me to see the place.   Good-bye."

The banker drew a bill from his pocket-book and
pressed it into her hand.   There was a figure five and
two cyphers in the corner.

" I will have a house ready for you to-morrow," he
said, warmly.   " Now, once more."

" You've had enough," she responded, evading the
attempted embrace, and wafting him a kiss across her
fingers instead.   She placed the money in the bosom
of her dress and sweetly but firmly bowed him out.

Within a week she had the coveted deeds in her
possession and soon after was comfortably installed
in her cosy home.

Meanwhile, Maurice Stager hunted for Greyburn.
He went to Johnsbury, to Chatham, back to Johnsbury again, then to Macon, getting more and more puzzled.   It became evident that the party for whom he
searched had gone back to New York, but had he remained there ?   Could he be in a place where so
many people knew him and yet escape notice ?   Stager
came back to the city, where he met Mendall one day
by accident.   In the course of a brief conversation
Mendall disclosed to Stager the facts relating to the
discovery of Charlie's identity, which he had learned
through Gabrielle.   Further investigation showed
the detective that both Greyburn and the girl had
suddenly been missed from their residence and gone
no one knew whither.

When Stager came back to his employer and told
him what he had learned, Walter drew a deep breath
of joy.

" You need not hunt any longer for Mr. Greyburn,"
he said, gaily. " I have a new piece of work for you,

for which I will pay double the reward that I promised for the other."

"What is it?" asked the detective.

"*Find me his daughter !*"

———————◆———————

CHAPTER XXIX.

The revelations which Charlie made in the little bedroom in Barnes court completed the change in Hector
Greyburn which his love for Clara Campbell had im-
perfectly begun. All of his life seemed to centre
upon his daughter. Her every movement, as she went
about the house, was followed by his watchful eye.
When she retired at night he would go to her door
and catch the sound of her quiet breathing before he
consented to seek his own rest. Could he have lain
like a dog on the mat before her chamber he would
have been quite content.

The first day that she felt well enough to talk so
long, she told him her story :

"I was brought up at my grandfather's in the
northern part of the State. I played around his farm
as any child might until I was nine years old, when
my mother died. I was always under a cloud. My
childish days were darkened with a something which
I could feel, but not comprehend. Neighbors whispered when they passed me. Strangers looked over
their shoulders and made remarks when I was pointed
out to them. Children at school threw taunts at me,
none the less aggravating because I did not then
know what they meant. My mother never went into
society. When we had company she did not come to

the table. Her life seemed to be made up of incessant tears. I knew that she was included in the ban which hung over my head, and I knew that in some way I was the cause of her trouble, as she was of mine.

" Driven from other companions we learned to be much together. We climbed over the hills and lost ourselves in the big woods, day after day, all the summer. After two terms at school she said I need not go again. She taught me after that herself, and I learned much faster than before. She was always frail, as I remember her, and she faded gradually until the end.

" I was older than most children of my age, and we seemed more like companions than is usual with a mother and child. One day, only a few months before she died, I asked her :

" Why do they say that I never had a father ? The children always tell me that. Was it so ?"

" I never saw her weep as she did that day. 'My poor child,' she said, 'you are punished for your mother's sins."

" Then she told me, as well as she was able to reach my childish comprehension, that there had been a bad and cruel man who would have been my father but that he was so wicked. She said that she knew her life would not last much longer, and she wanted me to fall on my knees and promise her before God that I would sooner die than ever do wrong. I promised, with uplifted hand, in the attitude she prescribed. Then she told me the name of the man who had wrought our shame. She made me promise never to forget it, and to pray every night as long as I lived, ' God keep me from being such as he made my dear mother.'

" When they buried her in the village churchyard my life was wholly desolate. My grandfather was a stern man whose disposition had not been sweetened by his adversities. Existence with him became unbearable and I ran away. To get better opportunities I assumed a boy's dress. I had lived apart from the world, and it was as natural for me to associate with one sex as the other. I think no one ever suspected my secret until my swoon revealed it to you.

" My work in saving your life at Chatham was done without hardly any premeditation. You were a stranger to me, but I saw that you were in danger, and did what I could under the circumstances. I intended, as soon as you should recover, to take an honorable leave of you and pursue the next path into which fortune led me. When I learned from Sarony who you were—when he pronounced the name I had heard from my mother's lips—I shrank from going back to you, and wrote the letter which you received from Mr. Bird. I had hardly any money of my own, and after what I had discovered I would not touch another penny of yours. The next day I saw an account of Dinsmore's trial in a newspaper and hastened to Georgia to save him. I told my story to the conductors and they passed me without a ticket all the way. As soon as I saw that I was no longer needed, I started for the woods, where you found me, with the distinct purpose of lying down to die. I had no money and I would not beg. I had never known but one friend and she was in heaven.

"While I was protesting to you that I would not be disturbed, I seemed to hear my mother's voice, saying, 'Go with him, you can do him good.' I yielded, but even then I could not endure that you should touch me. You remember how I insisted that you should call the coachman. The rest, you know."

Greyburn heard her story with mingled emotions. Her allusions to her childhood and her mother's sorrows touched him deeply.

"My child," he said, wiping the tears from his eyes, "I deserve all the odium with which your mother's teachings have taught you to regard me. I met her at a time in my life when the ruin of a confiding girl was the pastime of any summer's afternoon. It is the old story—too much trust on her part, too much villainy on mine. Day after day she prayed me to marry her for the sake of the child, until I grew weary and brought a new love to share our home. Your mother could bear no more. She went back to her father's house. In my new attachment I soon forgot her. You see, I confess everything."

Soon after this, Greyburn disposed of his furniture, gave up the rooms he occupied, and, with his daughter, bade farewell to New York. They went first to the village of Fairfield and visited the little cemetery. In a quiet corner they found a tall shaft of granite, marked "Walbridge," and smaller stones reading:

"William H. Walbridge, died January 12, 18—, aged 73."

"Susan, beloved wife of William H. Walbridge, died March 3, 18—, aged 61."

"Charlotte Helena, only daughter of William H. and Susan Walbridge, died August 7, 18—, aged 26. 'There the wicked cease from troubling.'"

Greyburn broke down a little as he read the latter inscription, but a touch on his arm recalled him to himself.

"She gave me her own name—Charlotte Helena. When I became a boy I called myself Charlie, but mother always called me Lena."

"Here lies the woman whom I so greatly injured," he said. "In her presence, Lena, can you—do you—forgive me?"

"With all my soul!" she answered. "But my mother is not here." She pointed to the cloudless sky.

"There ! she will wait for you and me until we shall be ready to join her."

"For you, yes," he said, "but not for me. I have sinned too deeply."

"Though they be as scarlet," she whispered. "But see, they are bringing the stone."

A wagon came up the graveled road. Several brawny men lifted out a piece of marble, cut in the prevailing form of memorial tablets. The workmen removed the stone which marked the grave of Lena's mother, and placed the new one in its stead. The work occupied but a few minutes, and when the men were gone Lena bent down to examine the stone. There was a pure white lily, broken at the stem, and below it these words :

"To Charlotte Helena, dearly regretted wife of Hector Greyburn, who died August 7, 18—, aged 26 years. This stone is raised by the husband who wronged her."

"You should not have used the last words. They are too harsh," said Lena.

"It is in expiation," he replied. "I have called her my wife, and by all the laws of Heaven she was so. Those who come here and see that the stone is changed will also witness my repentance. Let us go."

It was at Boston that they finally settled. Lena was to have the best of educational advantages. They installed themselves in a quiet house at the Highlands. Lena applied herself to her tasks with avidity. Greyburn hardly ever left her for an hour excepting at night. He held his book and pretended to read while her tutors gave their lessons. He walked or rode with her daily. She filled his whole life, and when she was not in view all else became a blank.

So passed the autumn and succeeding winter. When the roses came again Lena had blossomed into a beautiful young woman. Her hair, which had been cut in boy's style formerly, now reached to her waist unbraided, or shone like an aureole when it encircled her queenly head. Her figure had developed into one of surpassing loveliness. She had made such progress in her studies that her teachers were astonished. The devotion which she and Greyburn showed to each other was marked by all who knew them. There was but one thought in his mind, one aspiration in his soul, one prayer on his lips—Lena !

It is at the zenith of our happiness that we seem the most certain to experience the reverse. One evening Lena stepped out of the front gate and strolled slowly down the street, waiting for her father, who was getting ready for their usual walk. She had gone but a little way, when a carriage passing by, stopped, and a man stepped out.

"Could you give me assistance for a moment?" he said. "A lady has fainted."

Wholly unsuspecting evil, Lena went instantly to the carriage door. As she reached it, a sponge saturated with chloroform was pressed over her mouth and nose and she became unconscious. The man who had accosted her, and another inside the carriage drew her hastily within the door, and the vehicle rolled rapidly away.

Greyburn came out of the house a few minutes later and looked up and down the street for his daughter. They had not agreed upon any particular direction for their stroll, and he was a little surprised that she was not to be seen. He went back into the house, and ascertaining that she had certainly passed out, he returned to the gate by no means reassured. A police officer making his evening rounds came along, and Greyburn learned that he had passed no lady answering Lena's description. The officer soon learned the cause of his uneasiness.

"Something has happened to her," said Greyburn,

with a very pale face. "She would never have walked so far away alone."

"What do you imagine?" asked the officer.

"I don't know," he replied, despairingly. "Are you sure that you did not pass her coming up the street?"

"Positive," said the officer. "I met only a boy, and that was some distance below here. Nothing but a boy—and a carriage."

"Then," said Greyburn, paling still more at the thought, "my daughter is in the carriage. Could you see its occupants?"

"I could not. But why do you suspect this? Did you fear an—elopement?"

"No," replied Greyburn, quickly. "She has been stolen. What can we do? Speak, man! The treasure of my life is lost!"

"First, let us be sure that she went in the carriage," said the policeman. "Who would have taken such means to secure her possession!"

"I don't know, I couldn't guess," exclaimed the tortured man. "But I know that she is there. This is the first time that she has ever left me for a moment since we came to Boston. We must find that carriage. Tell me what to do. Help me to find my child and you may name your own reward."

"Come with me to Station IX.," said the officer. "From there we can send word to headquarters, and thus all over the city."

They repaired with all possible speed to the station, and soon every police officer in Boston knew that a young lady, sixteen years of age, slender, rather tall, with chestnut hair inclined to be wavy, and dressed in brown silk, was supposed to have been carried away in a public carriage from the vicinity of Warren street, about seven o'clock that evening.

The officer could give no description of the carriage, horses or driver. It was rather dark when they passed him, and there was nothing about them to especially attract his attention. The Lieutenant in charge of the station, having done all that he could in recording the description and sending messages, ordered the officer to return to his beat, and suggested to Greyburn that he had best get a carriage and go to the central office at City Hall.

The unhappy father complied with these suggestions, and half an hour later was in consultation with Deputy Chief Quinn, who had already despatched several of his detectives in search of the lost girl. The absolute despair which was painted on Greyburn's face drew genuine expressions of pity from the Deputy, used as he was to sorrow and crime. ·

"And you can imagine no one who might have done this thing ?" said he. "Try to think."

"I have tried," said Greyburn. "There are men who might wish to revenge themselves upon me, but who could harbor ill to that innocent girl ? She knows no one. We have lived secluded. I tremble to think what must be the motive for her capture."

He wiped the perspiration from his forehead and shook like a palsied man..

"Some one may have taken her to hold for a reward," said the Deputy.

"God grant it !" said Greyburn, solemnly. "I would give every dollar I have—yes, bind myself to work and earn as much more, to have her safe in my arms again."

"We will hope that that is the secret of this mystery," said the Deputy, "but think once more. One of your enemies might try and revenge himself on you through her."

"Yes," he admitted, " but those who might do that do not know that we are in Boston. We have lived here quietly, even passing under assumed names, in order to avoid everybody we have ever known."

"Will you tell me your real name?" said Mr Quinn. "It may help us."

"It could not," replied Greyburn, desperately. "Find me my daughter. She went out into one of your streets and disappeared. Good Heavens! to think that I must stand here, while she is in, God knows what peril! I have told you all I can. I will pay any reward in reason for the first news of her." Then he staggered a little and added : "I will return in a few minutes, but I must get the outdoor air or I shall faint." So saying the unhappy man left the office and passed out into School street.

Mechanically he walked along. The cool air of the night swept over his heated face, and brought a slight sense of relief. His loss was too great for him to realize yet. He walked on. The old days at Macon and Chatham Corners came into his mind. He seemed again to stand in the court-room and see that boyish figure in the witness box. He seemed to kneel once more in the grass at the foot of the tree and beg the child to let him save his life. Then he was back in New York City with Charlie. Then they were at Gabrielle's, and the boy changed into a young woman, who was throwing her arms around his neck, and crying, "I am your daughter!" Then they were in Boston. And at last, he came out of the house to find her gone, and to learn that she had been stolen.

Hush!

He stopped in his walk and looked around. He did not recognize the locality. Had he been asleep and dreaming? He pressed his hand to his head. It was very hot! Was he dreaming still? Was it all a dream, and Lena now safe at home? His brain felt a little as it did after the fall over the Chatham rocks, during those weeks when he did not know who or what he was.

He looked at the houses. The street was a very quiet one, and hardly any passers were to be seen. How could he have walked here without knowing it ? Horrible thoughts began to suggest themselves. Was he insane ? Lena was lost, and he who ought to be engaged in searching for her was wandering almost in a trance, and whither even himself knew not.

Lena !

The door of the house in front of which he stood opened and a man stepped out. Was this another dream ? The face was one he had known—but here ! And at this time ! He resolved to test whether it were real or no, and, springing up the steps, he caught the man by the shoulder and turned him as quick as lightning toward the broad glare of the street lamp.

" WALTER !"

CHAPTER XXX.

ONE was as white as the other. In the face of the younger man the elder read guilt. In the face of the elder the younger read something that was not vengeance, not despair, not horror—but a worse thing than all three.

" Walter Campbell !"

" What do you want ?"

" My daughter."

" What do I know about her ?"

" Give her to me !"

The grip on the shoulder tightened. There was no

way to escape the maniac, and Walter's thoughts took another turn.

"Come in. We don't want a row in the street."

They stepped into the parlor, Walter closing the door behind them. The grip had never once left his shoulder.

"Now," he repeated, mustering more courage, " what do you want?"

" My child!" said Greyburn, glowering into his eyes like a tiger at bay.

" Take your hands off, or I will say nothing. If I am to reply to your questions, you must treat me like a gentleman."

"Give her back to me," he said, releasing his hold, and changing his voice to a pleading tone.

" Who?" demanded Walter, striving to collect his thoughts and decide what was best to do.

" Lena, my child. Why do you delay?"

" I have not seen her."

" Now you are lying !" said Greyburn, fixing his eyes upon him with increased fierceness. " You seized her this evening and took her away in a carriage. Where is she ?"

"Who told you that story ?" said Walter.

" It is true," said Greyburn, earnestly. " Don't deny it ! I will never let it do you harm, only give her back to me ! I pledge you my sacred word. Don't you see how I suffer !"

Walter Campbell stepped back several paces and the color came into his white face.

" *You* suffer !" he cried. " *You!* And you ask sympathy and aid of *me ?* Whose sister did *you* lure to her betrayal ? The honor of whose family did *you* tarnish forever ? What brother's name did *you* make the laughing stock of New York ? Come a step nearer and I will kill you !"

When Greyburn recovered enough from this outburst, which filled him with renewed alarm, to see what was going on, he beheld Campbell standing in front of him with a revolver in his hand.

"I do not fear your weapon," said Greyburn, sadly. 'As to what you say, you have been misinformed."

"What! Have you the effrontery to deny what all New York knows? Are you a coward as well as a villain?"

Greyburn shook his head deprecatingly.

"If I stood with a loaded pistol in front of an un-armed and nearly crazed man whom I had wronged, I wouldn't ask him that question."

Walter threw the pistol upon a sofa at the farther end of the room and said :

"Now we are on equal terms and I ask it again."

"And I reply as I did before, that you have been misinformed. I never betrayed your sister. I never said a word to her that was not dictated by blind, re-sistless love. She became my wife as pure as an angel. She was too pure, too good for me, and we separated. They who have told you differently are to blame. If this is your revenge for Clara, it is ill done. Give me my child and let me go !"

The young man looked upon him with contempt written in every feature.

"Did you not wager to defile her ?" he said, bitterly. "Did you not covenant with Otis Middleby for so much money to make her name a by-word ? Did you not go to Clarence Perkyns and claim the forfeit ? Answer ?"

Greyburn drew a disheartened breath.

"Walter, that I did wrong I do not deny, but you accuse me of too much. You were there when the wager was made. You are aware that I did not know what name was to be inserted in the compact. You remember—you saw me—how affected I was when I found it to be that of the woman I loved the best in all

"Give me my child." *Page 322.*

the world. You know how they had surrounded me. They had half of all I was worth in their hands. I did claim the money. I did make them think I had a right to it, but my dishonor went no further. I deceived them as they tried to deceive me. I could convince you, had I time and the witnesses, but while we are talking, where is my child? Tell me that she is safe ; assure me that no one will harm her, and I will wait as long as you please."

"You don't believe me, then," said Walter, "when I tell you that I haven't seen her? Well, let us suppose that you are right. Let us suppose that I have her safe somewhere under lock and key. I may have good cause, for all you know. *I may have bet money on her !*"

The sarcasm with which he uttered these words and the cruel effect which they had on his victim may be imagined.

"Walter—Walter," he stammered, "you are carrying this thing too far. You ought not— you ——"

"Or, supposing—merely supposing," continued Campbell, "that I am as noble a man as you, I may keep the girl over night where the associations will blast her reputation, and then, as a balm to her sorrows, offer myself to her in the morning in marriage. *That* you wouldn't call unfair. That would be honest, honorable, worthy of commendation, wouldn't it ?"

"Walter !"

"And," he proceeded, in the same caustic vein, "after doing this high-minded thing, I might live with her for a few weeks and then, concluding that she was 'too good' for me, desert her. Do you see ?"

Greyburn threw himself at his companion's feet.

"Revenge yourself on me," he cried, "and not on an innocent child. See ! I am at your feet ! I beg,

I entreat you, give me my daughter. You may take all else I have. I freely promise it to you. Give me Lena and let me go !"

Tears and sobs, the tears and sobs of a strong man unused to weeping, mingled with these entreaties. Walter smiled grimly down upon the suppliant figure.

"You are touched at last !" he said, between his set teeth. "You have a vulnerable spot and I have found it. Why, what a fool you are ! One girl's honor, more or less, what is it worth? How often you have instructed me in that school! Can't you take one single glass of your own medicine? How many women have *you* lured to their ruin? A dozen? a score? a hundred? See how sweet it is to have the viper rear his head on your own hearthstone !"

"No, no !" cried Greyburn. "Say not so ! I never was a kidnapper. I never used force. Walter ! I beg, I implore you, give me Lena and let me go !"

"You never used force !" repeated Walter, bitterly. "No, you had more subtle weapons ! The rattlesnake fascinates the bird for whose quick flight he is inadequate. The spider spins his gossamer for the fly who could never be caught by the fleetness of his feet. Of that ilk are you. Why then should you complain that the hawk or the panther seizes its prey boldly and openly. Is their way less honorable than yours ?"

"Oh, Walter !" cried the unhappy man, writhing under the torture of his words, " for what evil I have done Heaven is meting me my punishment. I would blot it all out were that possible. Since I recovered my child I have lived a life of honor, learning from her pure mind how much better it is than sin, which pleases for the time only, to scorch and curse at last. I am sufficiently abased. You know what it has taken to make me kneel. You know that, for my own life, though it were menaced by the slow agonies of torture, I would not beg, if one word would save it.

Once more, for the sake of all you hold dear, in the name of your mother in heaven, I ask you—give me my child and let me go !"

For answer, Walter threw a look of hate and contempt upon him, and pulled a bell rope which hung near where he stood. Two stalwart fellows answered the summons.

"Secure that man !" said Walter. Greyburn sprang to his feet and glanced hurriedly at the men, who advanced toward him.

" Stand off !" he cried, all his manliness returning. " Touch me at your peril !"

The men did not seem to relish their task, and at this sign of resistance they halted, looking to Walter for instructions.

" D—n you, why don't you obey ?" he said, angrily. " You are to be well paid. Secure him, as I tell you. He is not armed."

Thus assured, the men with one impulse dashed upon Greyburn. He struck the foremost a blow with his right fist which sent him reeling to the floor, and gave the other a "left-hander" under the chin, which caused him to retreat with a loud yell of pain. Seeing the fate of his employes, Walter bounded to their assistance, but Greyburn reached the sofa where the revolver lay, and its ugly muzzle confronted the young man. With the pistol in his right hand and his left on Walter's throat, the now thoroughly aroused Greyburn stood, demanding his child in louder tones than ever, wholly unmindful of the fact that the person he was addressing had lost all power, from the compression on his vocal organs, to make any answer whatever.

The grip on Walter's throat was like a clasp of iron, and rendered him entirely powerless. Had it continued much longer, he would never have been able to speak again in this world. An interruption caused the pressure to be withdrawn.   It was a loud peal at the door-bell.

The man who had been knocked to the floor was still insensible.   The other started at the sound of the bell to escape through a rear door, but Greyburn leveled his revolver at him, and cried :

" Answer that bell, or you are a dead man !"

" Don't shoot !" cried the fellow, dropping upon his knees in abject terror.

" Answer that bell !" Greyburn cried again, in a voice of thunder.

The bell pealed louder than before, and the frightened wretch did as he was bid.   Directly the door was opened, half a dozen policemen in citizens' clothes sprang into the house, and in less time than it requires to tell it, had each of the occupants securely handcuffed.

" Not a sound !" whispered each officer.   One, a sergeant, who seemed to be in command, noticed the unconscious man on the carpet and said : " So you have been fighting among yourselves, eh ?   Pity you hadn't all got killed.   Say, where's the gal ?"

" For God's sake," said Greyburn, who at last found words to speak, " who are you ?"

" We're police officers, as I guess you'll find out to your sorrow," responded the official, opening his coat to show a badge.   " Come, where's the gal ?   Be quick about it.   It'll be just as well, you know. We've traced her here and we know she's in the house.   Do you want us to bust in all the doors, or will you give her up like sensible men ?"

" Thank Heaven !" cried Greyburn, devoutly.   " I am her father, and will reward you well.   Take these things off my wrists.   Walter, tell them where she is.   What can you gain now by delay ?"

The sergeant looked incredulous at first and then seemed partially convinced.

"Take 'em off," he whispered, "but look out for him." Visions of losing the reward by making a possible mistake came into his mind.

"Walter, where is she?" Greyburn asked again.

"What good will it do me to tell?" he replied, doggedly. "Will you make these cops let me out of here?"

"I can't do that, but I will do all I can to get you free afterwards. Where is she? Every second is an hour to me."

"She's in the top story, in the large back room," was the sullen reply. "She isn't hurt any. You'll find her all right except a little dizzy from the chloroform. Take these irons off and I'll give you the keys."

Greyburn grasped the keys and started up the stairs, closely followed by the sergeant and two of his men. The others remained with the prisoners.

"How came he here?" said the officer, who guarded Walter, pointing to the staircase.

"I don't know," was the reply. "The devil sent him, I reckon. He's choked me nearly to death. If you're a man take me to the door, where I can get a breath of air. I'm swooning away."

He looked terribly pale and the officer willingly complied with his request. As they reached the doorway, Walter put his hand into his vest pocket and produced a roll of bills. No words passed between him and the officer, but they understood each other. The money was placed in the policeman's hand almost before he was aware of it, and his prisoner fled down the street. Several pistol-shots sent in the direction of the cloudy sky above, and a brisk chase up a side street where Walter had *not* gone followed, and the officer returned after fifteen or twenty minutes very much out of breath.

"Dern the cuss!" he said to his associates. "He pretended to be so near dead that I thought he was going to faint, when all at once he tipped me over and run like a deer. I fired at him four times and I think I winged him, but he got away. He went like the wind. I guess I'll go to the station and leave word. They'll be sure to catch him to-morrow."

When Greyburn reached the door in the attic, his hand trembled so violently that he could not use the keys. The sergeant took them and turned them in their respective locks. The room was perfectly dark, and a shudder passed over even the stout-hearted sergeant of police as he entered it. A girl's voice, and a very weak one, broke the silence of the terrible place.

"Not yet!" it cried. "Give me—a little—longer. I cannot—escape. The windows—are all—barred, and the—door is—strong. Come—in an hour and I —will not—ask you to wait—longer."

Greyburn's eyes were brimming over with scald-ing tears. He made his way in the direction of the sound, while the sergeant was searching in his pock-ets for a match. The girl heard him approaching and cried out again in terror, and yet hardly above a whisper :

"Oh, not yet !   Please, please, not yet ?"

"Lena !" he called.

"Whose voice is that ?" she cried. "Speak !"

"It is I, darling, your father."

The flash of the match showed the girl lying upon a bed on the farther side of the room. Her hair was disheveled, her dress torn, and her white face hardly looked as if she was still alive.

"Father !" she gasped, trying to lift herself from the pillow. "Oh, have you come at last !"

The policeman found the gas-jet and lit it, and then, at a motion from the sergeant, all thoughtfully retired outside and closed the door.

"Lena, has he hurt you ?" were Greyburn's first words. "You are very pale. Has he done you wrong? If he has," he sprang to his feet with a wild look, "I will kill him now."

The girl put out her hands and recalled him to her side.

"'Vengeance is mine; I will repay, saith the Lord,'" she repeated, faintly. "Papa?"

"Yes, my darling," he answered, broken down at the childish word she had never used before.

"Papa, listen to me and hear all I have to say. You know what I promised my mother before she went away—that I would choose death rather than do wrong. Papa, I have kept my word."

"It is well for *him*," he muttered.

"They seized me, with some drug to make me insensible, and brought me here. The man who led them offered me insult—no! don't speak—hear me out. I persuaded him to give me an hour in which to compose myself. The drug I had taken made my head unsteady. He gave me the time. God answered that prayer. Papa, I shall go to my mother pure."

She pressed his hand against her cheek, while he sobbed out that she was all purity, all goodness.

"Papa, my voice is weak. I can only whisper."

"I know it, my angel! I will send for a carriage and take you home, where a doctor shall prescribe for you. They have frightened you to death—poor little white dove!"

"Papa," she whispered, as he stooped low to hear the words, coming yet fainter than before. "Be brave, be strong. See, I do not cry. I am going to my mother."

The terror in her words seemed to turn him into stone.

"It is not the fright," she continued, speaking very slowly. "I could not do wrong. I knew God would forgive me, and I had no hope in that man's mercy. Papa, I am bleeding to death."

He roused himself to call loudly for help and to tell the men outside to go—for the love of God !—and get a physician.

" There's no need,"she whispered. " Before he can get here I shall be gone. Listen, papa. I am going to my mother. What can I tell her—for *you ?*"

"Oh Lena ! Lena !" he cried, "your words are killing me !"

"Shall I tell her that you will always do right? that you will meet us there? that ——"

The sergeant, who had sent his men in opposite directions for medical aid, stole into the room, and stood with uncovered head, watching the heartrending spectacle.

" They have murdered her !" cried Greyburn.

The girl roused herself a little.

"Understand," she said, in a whisper hardly to be heard even in that still room, and showing a small stilletto, " I—did it—myself. I always kept it by me. I promised my dying mother that I would sooner die than ——"

She fell back.

A moment later a physician entered the room and looked at the quiet face.

" I fear I am too late, sir," he said.

CHAPTER XXXI.

MONTHS have gone by, and the violets are blooming on Lena Greyburn's grave. Hector has borne his loss, as such losses must be borne, so long as Death stalks into our homes and makes our hearts desolate. He would have welcomed the destroyer gladly, had it come for *him*, but his fate was to wait and to suffer.

Lena was buried at Fairfield, and in this secluded village Greyburn made his home. He boarded with an aged couple, who respected his evident wish for privacy. Month after month he lived there, staying a great deal in his rooms, and never receiving a visitor of any sort. The only thing for which he ever left the house was to take an early horseback ride, a thing absolutely necessary for his health, and a walk in the evening to the cemetery, where he would sit often very late, lost in reverie, by the side of her with whom all his love, all his life, all his ambition lay buried. Twice during the first few weeks the sexton, who could see from his residence all who went in and out of the cemetery, found Greyburn at nearly midnight unconscious on his daughter's grave. On being roused by the application of simple restoratives, he was able to walk home with assistance, but seemed like a man dazed, and never alluded to the circumstance when he met the sexton afterwards.

Mr. John Bird came up to see him—once—and made arrangements about sending at regular intervals the small sums of money required for his inexpensive way of living. He also sent a number of books, which proved the only solace left to his disconsolate client. Greyburn had never been a great reader, but now he devoured volume after volume. History, philosophy, science, religion or romance—it was all one to him. At first he read thoughtlessly, but soon the medicine of aroused thought began to work, and he turned to his books with something akin to satisfaction, if not pleasure.

It will seem a strange thing, but not one idea of vengeance on Walter Campbell ever entered his head. He did not forget, in those horrible hours when the minutest particulars of his tragedy used to run through and through his mind, that Walter was the real murderer of Lena. He recalled the abduction, the imprisonment, the threats which had driven the unhappy girl to suicide. But through the confused channels of his memory there was no trace of vindictiveness, no special blame for any one—unless, indeed, himself. For Hector Greyburn had come to realize that had his own life been different, had his own acts been other than what they were, the present deplorable condition of things could not have existed.

He thought of Clara, as he thought of everything and everybody. He wondered where she was, and whether she ever thought of him. He wondered if she had read in the newspapers of Lena's death, or had heard in any way the part her brother had in the matter. He hoped that she would not write or come. Not that he felt any sentiment of animosity toward her—not by any means—but he did not wish to be disturbed. He was so changed that his only desire was to be left alone. You might have searched his heart and found in it no particle of hatred toward a living soul, but he would make no new friendships nor renew old ones.

Among the books which he read with the greatest interest was the Bible. He had a superficial knowledge of its contents, but now he read it with the greatest interest. He surprised Mr. John Bird by a request for half a dozen of the best commentaries, and when he received them, he studied the Holy Book by their aid with the zeal of a theological student. One Sunday he appeared at the village meeting-house, to the astonishment of pastor and people, but as he engaged a seat and never missed a service after that, the wonder soon died away. When the minister called to express his gratification at Greyburn's sudden interest in religion, he found him buried in his Bible and commentaries. The conversation was very brief, however.

"I thank you for your call," Greyburn said, "but I am living alone and make it a rule to receive no one. You will not take it unkindly when I say that hereafter I can make no exception."

Where was Clara? In a country town out in Wisconsin she was again living the quiet life of a school teacher. When she left Chatham she would not take with her of Greyburn's property, even his name. She was known to her scholars as Miss Campbell. With her modest salary, and the proceeds from the sale of the parsonage placed in the savings bank, she reckoned herself out of the reach of poverty, as her wants were very few. Fully convinced that her husband would never relent, she resigned herself to circumstances. While hardly what one could call happy, she experienced that quiet comfort which must always proceed from a pure mind and clear conscience. If there were nights when she wept herself to sleep, they were followed by mornings when she rose with renewed strength and confidence in the ultimate goodness and wisdom of all the dispensations of Heaven. She would not even read a newspaper, for fear that something in it might disturb that serenity of mind which she sought to cultivate. Thus it happened that even the circumstances attending Lena's death, which were reported by the Associated Press and spread broadcast over the country, failed to reach her eyes.

John Dinsmore : When his trial was over, and he was pronounced a free man, he elected to return to New York city, where he sought to keep himself informed of what the principal personages in this story were doing. His success was only partial. He learned that Clara had separated from her husband, and that Hector was living with Charlie, but when Greyburn and his newly-discovered daughter left the city, the blacksmith completely lost the trail. Dinsmore was a very religious man, albeit his faith was more in a God of vengeance than a Saviour who delights in forgiveness. When he read in the newspaper the story of Lena's death, he offered a devout prayer of thanksgiving. He moved his soundless lips in praise to the Almighty, that the wicked had at last been overtaken in his sin, and just punishment meted out to the destroyer. Unable to walk without crutches, and then only very slowly ; not capable of enunciating a single syllable ; changed in a moment from a brawny man with a giant's strength into a creature more helpless than a child—Dinsmore forgot it all when he read of Greyburn's loss. It proved to his mind that the Omnipotent does not sleep, and that there is something more than empty sound in the words, "I will repay, saith the Lord !"

Walter Campbell kept in hiding for several weeks after he escaped from the police, but learning through Stager how quietly Greyburn was living at Fairfield, and feeling sure that the prosecution against himself would never be pushed, he turned up one day at his desk in City Hall, which Mendall's influence had retained for him. But he was not a happy man. The money which he once believed would give him all he wanted in this world, failed to satisfy. He plunged into the wildest dissipation, and was almost useless in his position, as well as a sore trial to Mendall, who could neither induce him to reform nor rid himself of what soon became an intolerable nuisance.

A crash in the affairs of the men who had been enriching themselves at the expense of the public treasury came soon later, and all the world was astounded at the developments which the *New York Times* made in relation to what was popularly called the "Tweed Ring." Most of the parties inculcated directly, big and little, fled the country ; a few were arrested and sentenced to terms in jail ; others surrendered a part of their gains ; some died in foreign lands. A very large number who profited by the rascalities were never prosecuted, but were left to enjoy their wealth unmolested.

Among those who fled at the first alarm was Jacob Mendall. It may be as well to state here that he never returned, but died within a few years in a European city. Walter was accepted as a government witness, and after a week in jail was released on bail. The house on Madison avenue was attached by the sheriff as Mendall's property, and he had to vacate it. With his occupation gone and not even a roof over his head, Walter's decline was rapid. But for occasional aid received from the District Attorney, who relied somewhat upon his evidence in the forthcoming trials, this youth, so recently revelling in luxury, might have had to go to the police station for a bed and breakfast. He would have applied even to his sister in his extremity, for his pride vanished in the face of cold and hunger, but he had no means of obtaining her address. All his other friends, as is usual in such cases, gave him the go-by as soon as his cash was exhausted. Some of them would not have minded his disgrace, but none could forgive his impecuniosity. One day he sank so low as to write a note to Gabrielle Delaporte, asking her for a " loan " of fifty dollars. She sent him the money, with a few lines to the effect that he must never apply again, and that he must not dream, on any account, of coming to her house. These chilling words from the beauty on whom he had lavished thousands quite crushed him, and he did not venture to disregard her injunctions.

CHAPTER XXXII.

GABRIELLE heard the crash which crushed her late friends to the earth with the utmost indifference. She was possessed of a cosy residence, quite a stock of valuable jewelry and furniture, and a snug sum of money invested in eligible securities. What was it to her that Jacob Mendall was hiding in Paris, Walter Campbell begging the authorities for the price of a drink, and Hector Greyburn living desolate and broken-hearted within sight of his darling daughter's grave ? Gabrielle was absolutely incapable of feeling any suffering which was not her own. Her early life and later experiences had made her what she was. During those days when other women tore their hair and wept their eyes red because husbands and lovers were in trouble with the law, she sang like a linnet in her elegant parlors, ate her dainty repasts, tried on new costumes and jewels before the long mirrors, and rode every evening in Central Park in her private carriage, with the indispensable Williams on the box and a brass-buttoned footman beside him.

One evening, when she returned from her drive, she called in her French maid—a recent addition to her household—and passed an hour in making herself as beautiful as possible. She tried on four different costumes before she could get suited, and discussed with great animation the arrangement of her jewels. When all was finished, she looked superbly, if such a word can be applied to one hundred and twenty pounds of avoirdupois, for Gabrielle, though exquisitely shaped, was not a large woman. She looked with perfect satisfaction at her reflection in the mirror, as her eyes swept over everything from the ornaments in her hair to the satin slippers on her feet.

"If he is a man, he must be moved to-night," she murmured.

Then she went to the front bay-window, drew the curtains about her and peered down the street. Many people were passing, but the one she looked for was not in sight. She arose impatiently after a little while and sought her writing-desk, from whence she took a note and read it over carefully, and whispered to herself, "It is almost nine o'clock. Why should he be so late?"

As she thus mused, the door bell rang and she gave a joyous start.

"It is his ring," she cried, softly. "I would know it among a million." She glanced at the mirror once more. "Gracious, what a color! All the blood I have is in my cheeks!"

A servant entered and handed her a card. She told the girl to say that she would come presently, and, as she left the room, Gabrielle kissed the name on the card passionately. Then she tried to control herself, and, after a minute's practise before the pier-glass, succeeded in resuming her ordinary demeanor.

"Mr. Arthur," she said, in her sweetest manner, as

she entered the room where that gentleman awaited her, " I am very glad indeed to see you. But are you not quite late ?"

" I *am* a little behind time," he admitted, looking into her eyes, and holding her hand a second longer than was necessary, " but the sun sets very late at this season of the year, and ——"

" And you did not wish to be seen calling here now that you are a full-fledged clergyman. Don't dispute it. That was your real reason. And you were quite right."

" I don't know why I should object to being seen calling here," said Mr. Reycroft, confusedly. " Surely a clergyman ought to be trusted to go wherever he feels that his presence will benefit."

" Quite so," said his fair companion. " And yet, the most important lady in New York would make a terrible fuss if she knew that you would even look up to my window. You know whom I mean—Mrs. Grundy."

" It is in your power," said the clergyman, pointedly, " to silence even Mrs. Grundy's voice ; I mean, by giving her no further cause for comment."

" Excuse me," replied Gabrielle, with her usual vivacity, " but you know very well that she would never forgive me though I should blossom into a saint and live like an anchorite from this day on. As for that matter, she might bend her condescension a little even now. Since Jacob left, six months ago, I've been here all alone except the servants, and Diana herself could not have given less cause for complaint. Not for reasons of a lack of suitors, either, as you might think. Every mail has brought me the most persuasive missives, and I have been obliged to say " not at home" to a hundred callers. I am growing poor, too—I mean in money," she explained, clasping her plump left arm with her right hand and laughing—"just spending all my income and eating into the principal in the most unbusiness-like way. Here is a tax bill which came this morning, three hundred dollars, to pay on this house and lot. Isn't it outrageous! I think the municipality is bound to ruin me."

Mr. Reycroft looked at the bill.

"It is paid, I see. So that need not worry you, and there won't be another for a whole year."

"Yes, it's paid," she laughed. "A despairing admirer of mine, a down-town merchant, happened to be here when the collector called. Nothing would do but he must settle it. Oh, you needn't look at me in that way! I can't bear him. He demanded a kiss for his three hundred dollars, and I gave him a boxed ear instead. Probably he'll be around to-morrow again. Ugh!"

Mr. Reycroft looked at the girl earnestly. He was trying to see how much seriousness there was under her bantering tones.

"Miss Delaporte ——"

"Stop," she said. "You shall not say one word to me unless you can call me Gabrielle."

."Gabrielle, I wish to talk to you seriously."

"It's the only way you ever do talk to me," she interrupted.

"Perhaps," he continued. "But this time I want you to answer me seriously in return. Will you?"

"Yes."

The color, which distressed her a few minutes before, faded all at once away.

"I want you very much," he said, earnestly, "to promise me that you will spend the rest of your life in purity. You can do untold good in this city if you will give yourself to the forces of right."

"Haven't I told you," she answered, evasively, "that Mendall was my last lover? Of what do you complain? Why, am I not living as you desire?"

The clergyman hesitated.

"Is your life what it might be in its influence?" he said. "Ought you, for instance, to meet a gentleman in that dress which you are wearing now?"

Gabrielle started to her feet and faced the nearest pier-glass. Her arms were bare and the neck of the offending garment was cut very low; not lower, however, than is seen at many fashionable balls.

"I thought you would like it," she said, with a little quiver of the lip, like a disappointed child. She caught up a big knit shawl of white zephyr, and wrapped it around herself. "There! I hope you are satisfied now! I'll wear a Queen Elizabeth ruff here-after."

He smiled in spite of himself at the absurdity of her tone and manner.

"That is better," he said. "Now listen to me, Gabrielle, I have much faith in you and believe that you will keep any promise you make. Say to me that you will never have another lover. That will be an excellent beginning. Afterward, we can proceed to something more than mere negatives."

"I had decided to do what you asked before you put the question," she responded, a little wearily. "I am very tired of men. There is but one in the world that I could care for, and I am certain he would never like me."

He looked a good deal more disturbed than could have been expected from the nature of her answer.

"That man is Hector Greyburn?" he said, interrog-atively.

She looked up, stamped her dainty foot impatiently, and said:

"Of course not!"

"Then it is Mr. Campbell."

"You haven't seen him lately, I think," she answered, "or you wouldn't make such a ridiculous guess. He is a little drunkard, living on what he can borrow and beg. If you had happened to meet him this summer I should feel quite insulted."

"Then it is evident that I do not know the man to whom you refer," said Mr. Reycroft.

"You know him well," said Gabrielle, turning her head in an opposite direction, "but his name is of no consequence in this discussion, for, as I said, he wouldn't look at me. He would count me the dust beneath his feet. And yet, I love him. Yes; after years when I have only endured or tolerated my lovers, at the most, I love—and love hopelessly."

She stopped and burst into tears.

The Reverend Arthur Reycroft was as pale as his companion.

"His name—I insist upon his name!" he cried, huskily.

"You do?" said the girl, looking up, her face all damp with the unaccustomed torrent from her eyes. "You insist? But I shall not tell you."

Gabrielle had spent an hour with her maid's assistance in preparing herself to look lovely in Arthur Reycroft's eyes. Dress, jewelry, and her brightest and most winning smile, had been lavished in vain. All that she had gained by her pains was to be told that she ought to be ashamed to meet a gentleman in such a costume. But now, with her hair half dishevelled, with her cheeks covered with tears and her eyes flashing something which was almost defiance, she captivated and enthralled him; and before he realized what he was doing, he was at her side, lifting her in his strong arms and soothing her against his breast, her fair head lying upon his shoulder and his kisses raining upon her mouth.

"Gabrielle, tell me! am I right? Is it *I* who am so happy as to possess your heart! Is it—can it be —*I?*"

She tried to release herself from his grasp, but he insisted that she must answer.

"I have said that I will not tell you," she protested, looking saucily into his eyes for one moment. Then, growing suddenly sober, she added, "You forget what you are doing, Mr. Arthur. You forget who you are—and what I am. When you recall this scene you will regret it and blame me because I permitted it."

"I will never blame you," he said, passionately. "I love you so intensely that the world's opinion is nothing in comparison. This is not the fancy of the hour; it has been growing upon me for two years. If, as you have said, you will consent to love one man only, and I am that happy one, I will devote myself to you, and a thousand Mrs. Grundys shall not stand in the way."

The girl was not prepared for this tremendous outburst.

"Let me get a chair," she said, striving gently to disengage herself from his clinging arm.

"Not until you say that you will be my wife," he answered, firmly.

"Your wife !" She sprang suddenly away. "Your *wife !* That I will never be ! Are you quite mad ? You are a clergyman and a gentleman, occupying an exalted place in the world. I am a street girl, with all the name implies. I love you—I cannot help owning what you already know—I will love you as long as I live, and love you only, but marry you— never !"

He looked quite bewildered.

"What do you mean—do you think ——" he stammered.'

"I think nothing," she said, "except that our love is hopeless. I will give you myself, my life, if you will take it, but it must be in such a way that when you weary of the bargain you can give it up. I will not let you tie yourself so that you cannot loose the cords if they become irksome. There is nothing about me fit for a clergyman's wife, and if you were in your sober senses you would know it. I know what you are going to say—that you would give up the ministry for my sake. Such an idea is the result of temporary dementia. I am more sensible than you, and I must make you listen to reason."

The clergyman gazed at the girl with unutterable affection.

"Gabrielle," he said, "I am nearly thirty years of age, and I never cared for a woman before I met you. My father left me a fortune which makes labor no necessity. I adopted the ministry because I thought that I could do more good to my fellow men in that sphere of life than any other. Consent to marry me, become my inspiration and my valued assistant in the work of reforming the world, and I shall go to my task with twice the strength and courage I have hitherto had. If you object to the ministry I will willingly resign it, as it is not the only field of usefulness open to me ; but, my dear, dear girl, do not refuse the heart and hand I offer you—a heart never touched by another, and a hand of which no true woman need be ashamed."

He reached out toward her, but she only shrank farther away.

"Again I tell you that you are mad !" she answered. "I doubt not that your heart is pure, that your life has been all you claim for it—but mine, what has that been ? I have concealed nothing from you. Let me tell you that men do not marry women like me. They must not, they should not ! You have thought me heartless ; and so I am to all but you. Arthur Reycroft, I love you. I will repeat it a thousand times, if you wish, and no number of repetitions can convey to you the depth of my passion. Do you think that such a love is a mere selfish thing ? Every breath I draw is permeated with my affection for you, and I would rather fall dead at your feet than become your wife and see you gradually growing to dislike, and at last to hate me."

"I should never dislike you," he replied, earnestly. "My love is deep enough to last an eternity. But what would you have—an unholy alliance which would torment me hourly with the stings of conscience ?"

She shuddered a little and said :

"How horribly you name things ! I told you that our love was hopeless."

"If I were not a clergyman, you would marry me ?" he said.

"No, I would not. Neither would I have you for the world leave that profession."

"But you would have me," he said, "if I understand you, continue to preach one thing in my pulpit and act another. You would have my life a perpetual lie. You would have me violate the most sacred injunctions of my creed."

"It is no more than others do," she pouted. "There's Bishop ——"

"Don't, I beseech you," he interrupted. "I don't wish to hear the name."

There was a few moments of silence and then a new resolve came to Gabrielle. She went to him, placed one hand on his shoulder and stroked the hair back from his forehead with the other. She was astonished to find how hot and throbbing were his temples.

"Mr. Reycroft," she said, softly, "I am to blame for introducing this discussion and it is for me to end it. Do you know what the hour is ?"

"It matters little," he said gloomily. "One hour is the same to me as another now."

"It is half past one, and—my—bedtime." *Page 345.*

She drew a tiny gold watch from her bosom and showed it to him.

" Half past one o'clock at night. Not the hour that the Rev. Arthur Reycroft should find himself in the house of a cocotte."

It did not seem to startle him, as he made no move to leave.

"Do you understand ?" she repeated. " It is half past one, and—my—bedtime."

He looked at her with an expression which was very new to his eyes.

" Do you turn me out ?"

" No," she replied. " But if you stay I must prepare for sleep. Probably you won't mind."

She threw off the worsted shawl, and exposed her white arms and neck. Then she began on the buttons of her dress.

" You would not dare !" he muttered with a gasp.

" Not dare ? Do you think I am going to sit up all night ? I always disrobe in this room."

She proceeded leisurely, and he set his teeth.

" The servants are all a-bed," she said, with forced composure. " I usually have Ernestine to help me, but I can get along very well without her. If you were real polite, you would turn your face away for a little while. This is one of the cases where it is excusable."

He never moved.

She finished disrobing, and then put on a loose gown of crimson silk, bordered with ancient lace, and began to take down her hair.

" Confession is good for the soul," she said, with a poor assumption of gaiety, shaking out the braids, which fell almost to her feet. " I told you a little while ago that I loved you. Well—I don't."

Even that did not move him. If he heard, he gave

no sign, but sat with his eyes fixed upon her as if charmed.

" No," she proceeded, after a slight pause, with her voice trembling violently. " I do not love you. I only said so to see what you would do. I made it all up—tears and everything."

She laughed a little, not very naturally, and the tears gathered in her eyes again before she had finished.

" You see," she continued, turning toward him, " how easily I can cry. Didn't I fool you well ?"

It was sadly ludicrous to see the smiles and tears struggling for mastery on her cheek.

" Mr. Reycroft," she added, presently, " I hate to ask a gentlemen to go, but ——"

She hesitated, a little startled at his appearance. She found courage to touch his shoulder, and the slight motion of his body showed her that he was unconscious.

Gabrielle was not easily frightened, but she was a good deal disturbed at this turn of affairs. She rang for Williams and Ernestine and, snatching a bottle of camphor from the mantel, applied it to the nostrils of the sick man. Williams came in a few minutes and, after helping to get Mr. Reycroft's inanimate form upon the nearest bed, went in haste for a physician. The French maid took a pair of scissors and cut away the collar and the upper part of the shirt in order to allow the fullest opportunity for breathing, but all they could do had apparently been of no effect when the doctor arrived.

Luckily Williams had met Dr. Eldredge, one of the best physicians in the city, returning from a visit to another patient. The doctor made a hasty examination, wrote a prescription and dispatched Williams with it. Then he motioned to Gabrielle to have Ernestine leave the room.

"Tell me as quickly as possible all that you know about this," he said, when the door closed behind the French woman. " I recognize Mr. Reycroft, and I know him to be a man of apparent soundness of health. It must have taken a great mental shock to prostrate him like this. Speak freely, and remember that as a physician I shall disclose no secret which I may learn professionally."

Gabrielle colored to the roots of her flaxen hair.

" He asked me to marry him, and I refused."

" *He*—asked *you*—to *marry* him !"

" Yes. Wasn't it ridiculous ?"

The tears were flowing freely again.

" Preposterous !" agreed Doctor Eldredge. " He is the wealthy son of a proud family, a rising light in the Christian ministry ; and you ——"

" It is easy to see what I am," said Gabrielle, very quietly. " And yet, he is here, in my house, at two o'clock in the morning."

" Not for marriage, I should say," said the blunt physician.

" You asked me and I told you," said the girl. " It is the truth. For his sake, when he recovers, I beg you to keep my admission sacred."

" Perhaps he will not recover," ventured the doctor.

" Surely you jest !" cried the girl, now thoroughly alarmed. " A man in health could not die because of a mere disappointment."

" A man in health would not ordinarily get into this condition, but when the shock is great enough to put him there, the most serious consequences are to be apprehended," said the doctor, gravely. Williams came at this juncture with the medicines, and the physician busied himself with his patient for the next half hour without continuing the conversation.

Perceiving at last signs of returning consciousness, he whispered to Gabrielle that it would be wise for her to leave the room for a few moments. She had been weeping quietly by herself, and complied without hesitation.

When Mr. Reycroft opened his eyes he looked at the doctor ; then his glance passed about the room, as if he missed something.

" Where is Gabrielle ?"

" She is in the house. Do you wish to see her ?"

" She will not marry me," he said, looking a little vacantly at the physician.

" We will see about that," responded Dr. Eldredge, cheerily. " I will go and call her."

He met Gabrielle in the hall.

" Do you wish to save that man's life?" he demanded.

" I would give my own to do it," she replied, wiping her eyes. Her lips were trembling.

" Come in where he is. If he asks you to marry him, promise that you will do so. Never mind whether you intend to keep your word or not. Sick people must be humored. If you fail, he may be dead to-morrow, or he may be in a lunatic asylum."

She followed him to Mr. Reycroft's bedside. His eyes lit up as he saw her. She stooped down and kissed his lips.

" You will not marry me !" he repeated, faintly. " Did you not say so ?"

She looked up at the doctor. He regarded her with a stern expression and nodded his head abruptly.

" I did not mean it," she said with great effort.

The clergyman's eyes kindled with seraphic joy.

" My own—my darling !" he murmured, taking her hand and putting it to his lips.

Five minutes later, he was in a sound slumber.

" He is saved !" said Dr. Eldredge, triumphantly.

CHAPTER XXXIII.

One lovely Sunday morning, not long after the visit
of Rev. Arthur Reycroft to Miss Gabrielle Delaporte,
described in the preceding chapter, the congregation
over which he presided gathered as usual at their
house of worship in a small town near the metropolis.
It was rather a fashionable congregation and took
great pride in its pastor, who was considered one of
the ablest speakers of his age in his denomination, and
had refused several "calls" to other and larger
churches because of the deep interest which had
grown up between himself and his people. He had
been absent for several Sundays, his place being filled
by special arrangement. To-day he was expected to
return, and the house was crowded in every part by
an expectant audience.

It was a few minutes beyond the usual time when
the minister arrived. As he went into the pulpit
everybody noticed that he looked quite pale and care-
worn. He gave out the opening hymn in a low voice,
and after it was sung rose and stood at his desk. It
was the time for the invocation. The more devout
among the congregation had already bowed their
heads, when the pastor's voice broke the stillness.

" My friends, I came here to-day fully intending to
officiate as usual, but I find myself unable to do so. I
cannot address the Throne of Grace in a public manner and give you words of counsel and instruction
when conscience smites me for sins of my own. For
the kindness you have shown in a hundred ways you
have my sincerest thanks, but I feel no longer worthy

to occupy this pulpit. Unless there is some other clergyman in the audience, or some layman who feels competent to continue the service, I must dismiss you."

To say that these words created a sensation faintly expresses that effect. Men looked at each other as though they could hardly credit their hearing. It was a crushing blow, all the harder because totally unanticipated. As the young clergyman descended the pulpit stairs, with faltering steps and pallid countenance, an aged deacon rose and said, "Let us unite in prayer." The fervent petition of the old man, begging forgiveness for his pastor, whatever his unknown sin might be, and asking that grace be given him to withstand future temptation. was a great relief to all present. Mr. Reycroft took a seat in one of the side aisles, and waited for the audience to pass out before him.

At this juncture a gentleman, who was a stranger to most of those present, and who had come to town that morning on horseback, walked with a quick step up the broad aisle and entered the pulpit. Mr. Reycroft half started to his feet as he recognized the stranger, but something in the latter's manner induced the minister to sit down again. The gentleman opened the large Bible, and saying, "We will read a portion of the eighth chapter of the Gospel of St. John," proceeded, amidst oppressive silence, to recite the simple story of the sinful woman whom the Scribes and Pharisees brought to Jesus, demanding of him whether she ought to be stoned to death according to the Law of Moses. He read with clearness, and his manner was impressive. When he came to the words, "He that is without sin among you, let him first cast a stone at her," his eye roamed over the large congregation, and several present felt as though his glance rested especially upon them,

Some of the nearest noticed that he had a scar across
the length of his forehead, and that other marks were
visible upon his face, caused apparently by not recent
bruises. He closed the reading at the end of the
words, " And Jesus said unto her, Neither do I condemn thee ; go and sin no more," and turning backward the leaves of the Holy Volume, he proceeded :
" I will now speak to you briefly on the words found
in Exodus, twentieth chapter, fourteenth verse :

" ' Thou shalt not commit adultery.' "

There was a sudden stir in the church. Several
elderly ladies rose and walked out. A woman with
three young daughters tried to persuade her husband
that he ought to take his family and do likewise, but
he did not seem convinced. The deacons exchanged
looks of bewilderment. The occupant of the pulpit
waited a few seconds, partly to secure order and
partly to allow his text to impress itself upon his
hearers. Then he continued :
" Thousands of years ago the Almighty Father of
heaven and earth wrote with His omnipotent finger
ten special commands for the government of His children. He forbade them to have other gods, to make
images to adore, to take His Holy Name in vain, to
commit murder, adultery or theft, to bear false witness or to covet what belongs to others ; and he en-
joined them to rest on the seventh day and to honor
their parents.
" These commands were given amid thunderings
and lightnings so terrible that the people feared lest
their end was come. They are plain, explicit, direct.
There is no room for argument, no opportunity for
equivocation.
" I believe that the most vital of these injunctions
is the one usually called the Seventh Command,

which I have read to you. So far as human sight can reach, the violation of no other carries with it such a weight of sin and suffering."

The husband of the woman with the three daughters yielded to his wife's persuasions and they quietly left the church. A number of others took occasion to follow their example. The speaker paused until quiet was restored, when he proceeded :

" If a man or woman should worship all of the gods in the heathen mythology ; if they should ask Ceres to bless their fields, Neptune to give favorable winds to their ships, or Bacchus to furnish increase to their vineyards, no human eye would be filled with tears, no brother or sister would be condemned to misery. If they should bow down to images of wood or stone, the worship of those senseless things would injure the idolaters alone. Taking the name of God in vain is a wicked and foolish act, but its consequences are between him who does it and his Maker. A wise and beneficent law enjoins us to rest on the seventh day, but a man may work each Sabbath and yet do his neighbor no injury. Honoring our parents is a high privilege and duty, but only the old people who gave us birth will suffer if we forget to do it. Murder is a most terrible crime, but Christ has bidden us not to fear them that kill the body so much as them that can also destroy the soul. If my neighbor steals what is mine, or covets my goods, or bears false witness against me, the injury is not irreparable. But the results of that awful crime—adultery—who can follow to their end ?"

Fifty or sixty persons more, whose curiosity was evidently satisfied, took the opportunity of the slight pause at the end of this sentence to go out. The speaker did not seem in the least disturbed, but proceeded with increasing vehemence :

" In the neighboring city of New York there are

twenty-five thousand unhappy women this day living on the wages of sin, a standing disgrace to the men of that city, without whose concurrence they could not continue in their wicked lives for an hour. Children are born of these unions, to die of neglect or grow up worse than orphans. Truly the sins of the fathers are upon these little ones to the third and fourth generation. And not in the lower ranks alone is this most detestable vice found. Among the men highest in repute, and among the women who lead society, it stalks like a spectre, breaking hearts, disrupting families, tearing down every barrier which religion and morality strive to erect around the hearthstone."

Nearly every lady left the church during these remarks, but the speaker did not pause again.

"Let me tell you of a man I knew who came to New York in his youth and lived the life of a profligate for years. His curse fell upon more than one young head, and the extent of the evil wrought by his violations of the Seventh Command only God may know. He became the father of a daughter, whom he abandoned with her mother when a new fancy met his eye. In the mysterious ways of Providence this daughter, grown to young womanhood, became the means of saving her father's life and converting him from the errors he had followed so long. She grew to be as the apple of his eye. But in revenge for injuries inflicted upon his sister, another man abducted this girl, and when in danger of what was to her a worse fate than death, she made her own end with a stiletto. From only one of the many sins of that miserable father, a beautiful woman and her daughter lie in early graves, a man who had the strength of a Hercules goes on crutches and with voiceless tongue, and another wanders an outcast on the face of the earth. Where will these dreadful results find an end? As well might the man who flings a stone into the ocean endeavor to measure the circles which spread out over the deep."

The men did not go. They listened to him with eager faces.

"You are all careful of your daughters, but what good will that do you if you neglect to warn your sons? Not one of your homes is safe. Girls, as well taught as yours, are walking the street of yonder city to-night. Until the standard of masculine morality is raised you may hope in vain for the purity of your families. If your daughter is accused by popular report of unchastity, you are horrified, and well you may be. If your son is so accused, you smile and say, 'The young man must sow his wild oats.' His wild oats—yes—and somebody else's daughter will reap the damning harvest—somebody's girl, who but yesterday said her prayers at her mother's knee and lay down to dreams as pure as those of the angels."

The speaker's voice rose louder and louder as he proceeded :

"I charge ye, men, protect your sons. If I had a boy who was profane, I would talk to him ; if he got intoxicated, I would try to cure him ; if he committed *murder*, I would strive to save him from the gallows, for he would be still my son. But if he became a seducer of women, I would—no, I would not kill him, though I think a wolf deserves death no more than he—but I would pray God to end his life.

"This is not a popular subject. I have said no word unfit for the pulpit of a Christian church, no word that any Christian minister ought not to say, but half of the people who sat in these seats when I began have left them. I am sorry for the delicacy of ears which find themselves offended by an application of one of the most solemn adjurations of the Most High ; but I hope that the good seed which I have tried to scatter has not all fallen on stony ground ; that some grain may spring up and bear fruit to the salvation of souls, which might otherwise have perished because unwarned of their danger."

The congregation went slowly out. Greyburn—for it was he—went down the pulpit steps to where Arthur Reycroft sat, and put one arm around his neck as a woman might have done.

"Did I do right in speaking to them?" he asked.

Mr. Reycroft looked up with a countenance like one despairing.

"What a change!" he articulated. "You preaching purity, and I——"

"How bad is it?" said Greyburn, soothingly, and speaking in a low tone. "Walk along with me and tell me all. It will do you good."

They strolled out together and went down a shaded road in the rear of the church.

"You remember the young woman whom you brought to show me one night when I first knew you?"

"Gabrielle?"

"Yes."

"Well?'

'She possesses me, body and soul."

·What do you mean?"

"I mean that I love that girl and that this love is incompatible with the place I have occupied."

"Is the attachment really so strong?" said Greyburn, incredulously.

"Judge for yourself. When she declined to marry me—as she did at first—I had an attack of catelepsy, and lay for a week in bed at her house, under the care of a physician. It is contrary to his advice that I am out to-day."

Greyburn was silent for several minutes.

"You must drop her," he said, firmly, when he spoke again.

The clergyman clasped his hands together.

"So easy to say—so hard to do," he answered.

"What became of Mendall?" inquired Greyburn, with a desire to change the subject until he could collect his thoughts.

"Escaped to Europe when the *Times* disclosures were made. Are you in any personal danger? I have guessed lately at the meaning of the hints you gave me once."

"Not the slightest. I bought and sold land where improvements were to be made, but I mixed in no contracts and shared in no steals. However, I do not feel guiltless and shall do something soon to ease my mind. Did you hear anything about young Campbell?"

"Yes," said the clergyman. "I heard that he was dissipated and penniless. What a terrible retaliation he made upon your daughter."

"I must find and try to save him," said Greyburn, quietly. "I am much to blame for his present condition, and he is also, you remember, my wife's brother."

"Where is she, your wife?" asked Mr. Reycroft.

"I have no idea. That is the woman you should have married, Arthur."

The clergyman shuddered.

"Come," added Greyburn, "you have no right to be in this frame of mind. Look at me. My heart is buried under the sods of the Fairfield cemetery. For long months I have hoped and prayed for death. A few days ago I roused myself and determined to ascertain whether there was not something I could do in the part of life which is left to me to atone for the years I have wasted. I wanted advice from you and came to your church to-day to seek it, little anticipating this denouement. If *I* can endure the weight of *my* past, thickly sown as it is with briers and thorns, surely *you* can rise after one slip."

Mr. Reycroft blushed and stammered. "There has been nothing criminal ; but had she persisted in her refusal to marry me, I know not what might have happened, as I was madly infatuated that night. Dr. Eldredge admits that he was seriously alarmed about me."

"But you are calmer now," said Greyburn, "and more sensible. You have been following a will-o'-the-wisp, Gabrielle has had a dozen lovers and will have a dozen more. Marriage with you would please her for a few weeks. After that she would go back to her old ways, leaving you to the reflection that you ought to have expected as much. I know her. She is pretty, brilliant, fascinating. A dangerous plaything for a man of the world, and a fatal one to a good-hearted, innocent fellow like you."

"I have hopes to reform her," ventured Mr. Reycroft. "She has a noble nature underneath the frivolities which her experiences have brought to the surface."

"You are incredulous, but she is becoming a true Christian, I'm sure of it."

"You will marry her, then ?"

"She has hardly consented yet. She is so fearful of dragging me down, as she calls it."

"She *will* drag you down," said Greyburn, bluntly.

"How ?"

"Socially, for one thing. Your class of society won't receive her. Morally, for another. Mark me, Arthur, when the first flush of what you call her ' love ' is over, her real nature will re-appear and you will be the sufferer. Put a spoonful of ink into a pail of milk, and if the whole mass isn't darkened, never believe me."

"I shall marry her if she will have me," reiterated the clergyman, doggedly.

"See here !" cried Greyburn, stopping in the street,

"I am going to talk plainly to you. I've *got* to talk plainly. You *can't* marry that kind of a girl. How could you endure to walk or ride with her or take her to a public place where men you might meet could say, 'That's a former mistress of mine.' You would never want to meet me, nor Walter Campbell, nor Jacob Mendall, and God knows how many more, that you will never know about, and that she herself has forgotten. Think! It is of a *wife* that we are speaking—a *wife*, whose name, if not above reproach, is beyond all things the most hideous!"

Reycroft was very white. He leaned against a building for support.

"It is terrible," he said.

An hour later Greyburn rode toward the city, and that evening presented himself at the door of the residence of his former sweetheart. He was ushered into the parlor, and waited a quarter of an hour before she entered. When she came in he saw that she had been weeping violently; and this man, who had never seen aught but the sunniest smiles on her face, was shocked at her appearance.

She touched the hand which he extended and motioned him to be seated.

"I wish to speak of Arthur Reycroft," he said, thinking it wisest to reach the point at once.

"You see my condition," replied the girl. "This morning there were two persons in the world whom I loved with my whole soul. One of them has just left it—my—mother."

She sobbed aloud as she pronounced the words, and Greyburn rose, instinctively feeling that her grief was too sacred for his errand.

"I am very sorry indeed," he said. "If I had known, be sure I would not have intruded,"

She choked down her sobs and looked him full in the face.

"I had two friends," she said, hysterically. "One of them, the best, the dearest, has gone. I have only Arthur left, and you shall not take him from me. No, you *shall* not!"

He did not know what to answer her.

"His place is here," she continued. "He has vowed to love me as long as he lives. I need him now. Tell him that I have no other friend in the wide world and am alone with my dead mother. I will not hurt him. I will kneel at his side and pray if he asks me. Hector, will you tell him?"

"I will tell him," he answered, gravely, and left the house, very much troubled.

———•———

CHAPTER XXXIV.

THAT evening Greyburn packed up his movables, ordered a carriage, and drove to an obscure hotel in a remote corner of the city, where he took a room, stating to the clerk that he desired to see no callers. All the afternoon he sat silent in his chamber, but after dark he commenced writing. He made several copies, tore them up and made others, until at last he produced the following:

Last Will and Testament of Hector Greyburn.

This is my last and only will and testament. I bequeath all my property to John Bird, Esq., attorney, Astor House Buildings, unreservedly, to be applied by him to the purposes explained in a letter of even date herewith.   And I direct that no bonds be required of him on account of the said trust by the Probate Court.

John Bird, Esq.: When I am dead you will take all my property, convert it into money and after deducting the amount of your own charges, send the balance under seal to the Treasurer of the City of New York, endorsed " For the conscience fund."   Send the package secretly, but take pains to see that the amount is properly covered into the treasury of the city.

If my body comes to you, have it buried in some swamp where no human being can ever be contaminated by it.   Sink it in the mud with stones and make no mark to show what is there.   I am particular about this.

You are a lawyer and I feel sure that you will obey these requests without question.

HECTOR GREYBURN.

This was endorsed : " To be opened only after my death."

He slept soundly all night, ate a good breakfast in the morning, and at ten o'clock presented himself at the office of Bird & Bird.   The wil. was executed, and, with the accompanying letter, was placed in Mr. John's capacious safe.

Greyburn walked down toward the North River, gazing at the various signs on the pier-houses as he passed along.   He was so preoccupied that he almost fell over a man whom he encountered at one of the corners.   On recovering himself he saw that it was Walter Campbell, very dirty and rather drunk.

" Hullo, Hector !" said Walter, who was the first to recover from his surprise.   " D—d glad to see you, 'pon m' honor.   Couldn't lend me a V, could you, for a day or two ?"

Greyburn's face was a study. How many things crowded upon his mind at that instant.

"Come with me," he said.

They walked down one of the wharves, where a vessel was waiting which would sail that afternoon for a Southern port. Greyburn bought two tickets, and taking Walter aboard, went directly to his state-room and put him to bed, where he fell almost instantly into slumber. Then he went ashore again, but returned in a short time with his baggage. As he was going on board for the last time, a seedy-looking man touched his arm and beckoned him mysteriously aside.

"Are you going on that steamer, sir?"

"Yes; why?"

"You did me a favor once," said the man. "You see I know you, Mr. Greyburn. You've forgotten it, and it's no matter what it was, but I owe you good will. Now, that vessel isn't safe at this season of the year, and I know it. She just missed being condemned the last time she was inspected. She's insured way up, and her owners wouldn't care if she went down to-morrow. You'd better go by rail."

"You think the boat is very unsafe?" said Greyburn, absently.

"Yes, sir, I'm sure of it."

Greyburn walked up the plank and went aboard.

The vessel steamed out into the bay and took her course along the coast. She seemed safe enough and the passengers who gathered in the cabin after dinner evidently had no doubt that they were in a secure situation. Little card parties gathered around some of the tables. Several groups listened to amusing stories from fellow-travelers. A few persons wrote letter home, while others passed their time in reading. It was dark and cold on deck, but Greyburn went

there and walked up and down in his thick wrappings.

All at once there was a thrill of excitement in the
cabin. A young passenger, with dishevelled hair and
blood-shot eyes, reeled into the room and looked
vacanlly about him. As the steamer lurched a little
to one side, he caught at the nearest tablecloth and
pulled off with it, a set of dishes and glassware,
making a loud crash. He balanced himself for a
moment, gave another maudlin look around, made a
quick plunge toward the chair in which sat the prettiest girl on board and, before either she or any one
else dreamed what he was intending, had his arms
around her neck. She screamed with absolute fright,
and several of the stewards sprang to her assistance.
It was easy to see that he was irresponsible for his
acts. They tried to secure him without injury, but
he proved a hard subject to handle.

"Why, Gab'relle," he stammered, wrenching himself free from those who held him. "What's the
matter, girl? Ain't you got a kiss for me, to-night?"

As often as they grasped his arms, he threw them
away. The consternation in the cabin became frightful. Part of the women clustered in a group in one
corner, while the others cling to their male escorts,
begging them not to go near him for fear they would
get hurt.

"Hullo!" said the young man, fixing his vacant
gaze on another fair passenger. "Is that you,
Susanne? And Nettie, too, b'George! Old girl,
come to m'arms; I've got the whole house, now,
y'know."

Somebody brought the purser at last, whose presence restored, in a slight degree, the confidence of
the ladies.

"Who is he?" cried several voices at once.

"His name is Campbell. He's got a friend who's

up on the deck somewhere. Won't someboby go for him?"

Walter was doing no greater harm than staring at everybody in a maudlin way and talking nothing with rapidity when Greyburn arrived.

"Take him to his room," was his immediate decision.

But it was much easier to say this than to accomplish it. Walter had become possessed of the extra ordinary physical powers which so frequently accompany great mental activity, and pushed the men away easily. His eye lightened for a moment when he saw Greyburn's face.

"Hec," he said, with thicker utterance than before, "you've got y'money on th'girl and y'want to win it. Young, d'y' say? And beaut'ful, and 'n orphan? If you can't do that, never brag t'me ag'in."

Then he fell in a heap on the floor.

A medical gentleman, who had gone to bed, was roused by the purser and went to look at the body— for it was only a body—and said he could give no hope.

Greyburn did not say much when the stewards took the form and laid it out ready for burial. He did not *care* much. If he had any definite thought about it, it was that Walter had escaped from a life of suffering, while he had his own still to endure.

He went back to the deck and walked up and down again. Some of the passengers commented on his coldness of manner and lack of feeling on account of the death of his friend, as they talked over the sad event of the evening. He did not hear them, and would have paid no attention if he had.

A gale sprang up about midnight. The captain, who had turned in, was sent for to take his place on the bridge. He soon saw that he had a furious storm to encounter, and a very anxious look came over his weather-beaten features. A description of the scenes between that hour and sunrise was published in the New York papers two days after, and need not be repeated here at length. It is enough to say that the wintry storm was too much for the old vessel. At three o'clock the passengers were ordered to dress and to be in readiness to take the small boats if it should prove necessary. Before this hour most of them had become aware that they were in a certain danger, but this authentic announcement filled all hearts with dismay. At least, all hearts but one.

About five o'clock, when only the faintest glimmer of dawn was visible, it became evident that the steamer was sinking. The fury of the gale had somewhat abated and it was believed that the small boats might live in the sea long enough to reach land, which was supposed to be some miles away. The boats were lowered and manned. Cries and tears were heard on all sides and were not confined to the female passengers. It was a time when the stoutest heart might well quake. The sea rose and fell in huge waves and the cold was biting. Ice covered the masts and sheets and made the deck slippery.

The boats were lowered in very good order, but one of them, old like the ship itself, was dashed to pieces against the vessel's side, leaving the capacity of the others to be so severely tested. The sailors helped the ladies down the ladders. One, apparently about sixty years of age, seemed traveling alone. She shrank back when the man tried to help her in, crying out that the boats were not safe. Greyburn caught her slight form in his strong arms and carried her like a child to a seat with the others. She shivered and said it was freezing cold. He took off his heavy, fur-trimmed over coat and wrapped it about her. She tried to remonstrate but he was gone.

The boats were crowded. Only one man remained on the deck. He had assisted several to reach the boats, but always went back himself. All the boats had pushed off but one, and every moment which that one remained lashed to the vessel was fraught with danger. The captain called to the solitary passenger to hasten, but instead of doing so, he reached down and cut the painter.

"*Push off!*" he cried, above the noise of the wind and sea, "*I am not going.*"

A wave carried the frail craft a dozen yards the next instant, and the stout-hearted captain turned pale as he realized what had happened. But it was impossible to return for one man without imperilling all the others.

Greyburn's great coat was gone, but he felt no chill. He clung to a mast and unconsciously spoke his thoughts aloud :

"*Lena took her life rather than endure profanation. I take mine to save others from it. God must be merciful.*"

Then a great wave broke over the decks, and when it subsided the vessel had disappeared.

THE END.

HIS PRIVATE CHARACTER.

BY ALBERT ROSS.

A Novel Uniform with "Thou Shalt Not."

OPINIONS OF THE PRESS.

"There is a great difference between the productions of Albert Ross and those of some of the sensational writers of recent date. When he depicts vice he does it with an artistic touch, but he never makes it attractive. Mr. Ross' dramatic instincts are strong. His characters become in his hands living, moving creatures."—*Boston Globe.*

"The author is a genius. He has the great gifts of originality and ingenuity."—*Metropolis.*

"The conversation and experiences of the men and women in 'His Private Character' are remarkable and startling. The description of a stormy honeymoon at Montreal, a scandalous supper at a New York restaurant, and the resuscitation of one of the heroines in a Mississippi River cave, are realistic to a degree."—*Sun.*

"Lovers of the drama are talking a good deal just now of the 'Cleopatra' debut of 'Mrs. John Smith Johnson,' in Albert Ross' novel, 'His Private Character.' The actress, whose main attraction is her notoriety rather than her histrionic ability, receives a scathing rebuke."—*Herald.*

"Albert Ross, the now famous author of 'Thou Shalt Not,' has produced another entrancing piece of fiction under the title 'His Private Character.' Though told with less boldness than the former story, it is quite its equal in absorbing interest."—*Telegram.*

"Its interest never flags. The inevitable law that punishment follows sin, dragging down the innocent as well as the guilty, is set forth with a strong hand."—*Cambridge Tribune.*

"As a tale it is very original, one whose progress never flags, and very cleverly constructed as to plot. It is clever and original."
—*Sunday Times.*

"The characters are distinctly individualized, and the volume is absolutely devoid of dull pages."—*San Francisco Call.*

HER HUSBAND'S FRIEND

BY ALBERT ROSS.

A Novel Uniform with "Thou Shalt Not."

OPINIONS OF THE PRESS.

"Thoroughly original."—*St. Paul Dispatch.*

"A story well constructed."—*New Orleans States.*

"The situations are strong."—*Cleveland Plaindealer.*

"The author has decided talent."—*Cambridge Chronicle.*

"Many dramatic complications."—*Philadelphia Bulletin.*

"His large circle of interested readers."—*Boston Beacon.*

"Bright and interesting to the last chapter."—*Boston Courier.*

"A first edition of forty thousand is being issued."—*Nashville Herald.*

"Within the bounds of a healthy literary taste."—*New Orleans Picayune.*

"The heroine, Anna Darrell, is a very beautiful character."—*Boston Home Journal.*

"An interesting story. The threads of the novel are interwoven very neatly."—*N. Y. Telegram.*

"The book teaches the wholesome lesson of the folly of hasty and conventional marriages."—*Minneapolis Journal.*

"Mr. Ross has kept within bounds in this book, and given us a story that a person of sense can read with pleasure."—*Buffalo News.*

"This series has had a sale of 400,000 in two years, and yet there is no falling off in the demand."—*Publisher's Weekly.*

"This novel will be found entertaining from beginning to end. It is the best that this author has given to the public."—*Sunday Times.*

"It abounds in strong situations, thrilling passages, and that brightness of dialogue for which this author is famous."—*Charleston Budget.*

"The author has had a larger number of books sold in the first two years of his literary life than any other American, living or dead."—*Yankee Blade.*

MOULDING A MAIDEN.

BY ALBERT ROSS.

A Novel Uniform with "Her Husband's Friend"

OPINIONS OF THE PRESS.

"A very charming story."—*Inter-Ocean.*

"Albert Ross is never a dull writer."—*New York Journal.*

"It absorbs one's attention like a page of Collins."—*San Francisco Call.*

"He has struck one of the most popular veins of the day."—*Ohio State Journal.*

"The interest is unflagging, and the attention chained throughout."—*Kansas City Journal.*

"It is entitled to hold a better place in literature than any of his other works."—*Chicago Times.*

"A sensational story, with strong situations, making a vivid narrative to the end."—*Toledo Blade.*

"'Moulding a Maiden' is certain to add to the wide reputation of Mr. Ross."—*Norristown Register.*

"Original and ingenious. The best written story that this author has yet produced."—*Boston Home Journal.*

"Criticism is lost on a writer whose novels have sold to the extent of about half a million copies in thirty months."—*Louisville Times.*

"Nobody supposed that Albert Ross could be decorous, and it was not to be expected that he would be dull."—*Charleston News and Courier.*

"The growth of love and jealousy on the one hand and the development of noble traits on the other, are set forth as few authors have the power to do it."—*Nashville Herald.*

IN STELLA'S SHADOW.

BY ALBERT ROSS.

A Novel Uniform with "Her Husband's Friend."

OPINIONS OF THE PRESS.

Mr. Ross is one of the best novelists of the day, his popularity being attested by the sale of over three hundred thousand of his former productions. The story is as strong and full of interest as any he has written, and like the rest, it has an object or moral enveloped in its plot. The public taste demands a moral nowadays, provided it is not too conspicuous and is dressed in a fascinating garb.—*St. Louis Republic*

The ability of Albert Ross to entertain the largest of American literary constituencies has been abundantly shown. But in his latest work, "In Stella's Shadow," he has, in some respects, given us his strongest story "Stella" is said to be drawn from real life, and the story of her relations with General Vallalie will not perhaps be an entirely new one to many people in New York and Vermont.—*Chicago Herald.*

Into Stella's life has been woven those of a rich old gentleman and an impecunious young journalist. The connection leads to the practical ruin of both, and in the accomplishment of that result a strongly dramatic story has been built up.—*San Francisco Post.*

One may recognize the evident honesty of purpose of Mr. Albert Ross in the production of his novels, while deprecating the ultra-sensational methods whereby he seeks to give his convictions utterance. His study of Stella is, it cannot be denied, forcible and impressive.—*Boston Beacon.*

Albert Ross's new novel enters boldly into the secret life of New York and takes for delineation one of its exceptional characters. . . . The fascination of such a woman, when beautiful and cultivated and professing repentance, is shown with the power of "Thou Shalt Not," the wonderfully popular first novel of Mr. Ross. It is very interesting.—*Boston Sunday Globe.*

YOUNG MISS GIDDY.

BY ALBERT ROSS.

Uniform with other "Albatross" Novels

OPINIONS OF THE PRESS.

" Handled in a peerless manner."—*Grand Rapids Herald*

"An exceptionally fascinating story."—*Pittsburg Chronicle-Herald.*

" The story is well constructed and the pictures Southern life realistic."—*Louisville Times.* .

" 'Young Miss Giddy' introduces the reader to several interesting characters, and impresses some home lessons very practically."—*Inter-Ocean.*

" The Southern and Mexican scenes show Mr. Ross facility of description, and will undoubtedly assist greatly in increasing tropical travel."—*Buffalo Times.*

" It must be acknowledged that there is a great deal of mental acumen put into the book, some good character work and some excellent bits of development."—*Boston Ideas.*

" Daring as is this writer's treatment of themes usually considered forbidden or questionable, it is hardly to be pronounced either meretricious or coarse "—*New York Telegram*

" In this book, as in all the previous work of the author, there is to be detected the power of a close student of his kind ; one who not only lays bare but analyses in minutest detail the follies, vices and weaknesses of men and women. The moral is so plain that he who runs may read "—*Phila. City Item.*

' The fact is that Mr. Ross struck the public fancy with his first story and has held it. He has the art of exposing social errors without making them attractive; he knows how to treat a subject with boldness and yet with propriety ; he says what he has to say with no double meaning."—*Boston Globe*

THE GARSTON BIGAMY.

BY ALBERT ROSS

A Novel Uniform with all "Albatross Novels."

OPINIONS OF THE PRESS.

"As full of incident as its predecessors."—*Town Topics.*

"The most read man in America."—*New York Evening Post.*

"It has more strength and depth than his earlier efforts."
New York Recorder.

"The most widely read of modern novelists is Albert
Ross. His publishers report a sale in three years of
more than half-a-million of his works."—*N. Y. World.*

"Mr. Ross is a pleasing writer and a very popular one
His story is distinct, full of interest and plot, very pleas
antly narrated and developed."—*New Orleans Picayune.*

"The drawing of John Garston, Alvah Adams and
Colonel Staples is realistic, and the Iowa scenes have a
local color easily recognizable by any one who has lived
in that part of the West."—*Kansas City Journal.*

"Mr. Ross has a happy faculty of arranging his plots
in such a manner that the reader never loses interest or
the thread of the story. The purpose of the author is to
point a moral lesson of the strongest kind."—*San Francisco
Call.*

"There may be prudes who would find fault with the
occasional plainness of the dialogue, but they are of a
kind rapidly disappearing. If the reading masses are
not the true critics, we do not know where they are to be
found."—*American Bookseller.*

"That the author of 'Moulding a Maiden' and 'Thou
Shalt Not' is attaining loftier heights, the finished style
and marvellous drawing of peculiar human nature, as in
the case of John Garston, will prove. Mr. Ross has a
heart that feels. The dreamer and practical writer find
a pacific abode in his composition."—*Newsman.*

9 783337 818326